NHS BLACKPOOL HEALTH PROFESSIONALS' LIBRARY

MICROSOFT®
PUBLISHER 2000
FOR
DUMMIES®

Blackpool, Fylde and Wyre NHS Library

TV04975

MICROSOFT®
PUBLISHER 2000
FOR
DUMMIES®

by Jim McCarter

WILEY

Wiley Publishing, Inc.

Microsoft® Publisher 2000 For Dummies®

Published by
Wiley Publishing, Inc.
909 Third Avenue
New York, NY 10022
www.wiley.com

Copyright © 1999 Wiley Publishing, Inc., Indianapolis, Indiana
Published simultaneously in Canada

No part of this publication may be reproduced, stored in a retrieval system or transmitted in any form or by any means, electronic, mechanical, photocopying, recording, scanning or otherwise, except as permitted under Sections 107 or 108 of the 1976 United States Copyright Act, without either the prior written permission of the Publisher, or authorization through payment of the appropriate per-copy fee to the Copyright Clearance Center, 222 Rosewood Drive, Danvers, MA 01923, (978) 750-8400, fax (978) 646-8700. Requests to the Publisher for permission should be addressed to the Legal Department, Wiley Publishing, Inc., 10475 Crosspoint Blvd., Indianapolis, IN 46256, (317) 572-3447, fax (317) 572-4447, e-mail: permcoordinator@ wiley.com.

Trademarks: Wiley, the Wiley Publishing logo, For Dummies, the Dummies Man logo, A Reference for the Rest of Us!, The Dummies Way, Dummies Daily, The Fun and Easy way, Dummies.com and related trade dress are trademarks or registered trademarks of Wiley Publishing, Inc., in the United States and other countries, and may not be used without written permission. All other trademarks are the property of their respective owners. Wiley Publishing, Inc., is not associated with any product or vendor mentioned in this book.

LIMIT OF LIABILITY/DISCLAIMER OF WARRANTY: WHILE THE PUBLISHER AND AUTHOR HAVE USED THEIR BEST EFFORTS IN PREPARING THIS BOOK, THEY MAKE NO REPRESENTATIONS OR WARRANTIES WITH RESPECT TO THE ACCURACY OR COMPLETENESS OF THE CONTENTS OF THIS BOOK AND SPECIFICALLY DISCLAIM ANY IMPLIED WARRANTIES OF MERCHANTABILITY OR FITNESS FOR A PARTICULAR PURPOSE. NO WARRANTY MAY BE CREATED OR EXTENDED BY SALES REPRESENTATIVES OR WRITTEN SALES MATERIALS. THE ADVICE AND STRATEGIES CONTAINED HEREIN MAY NOT BE SUITABLE FOR YOUR SITUATION. YOU SHOULD CONSULT WITH A PROFESSIONAL WHERE APPROPRIATE. NEITHER THE PUBLISHER NOR AUTHOR SHALL BE LIABLE FOR ANY LOSS OF PROFIT OR ANY OTHER COMMERCIAL DAMAGES, INCLUDING BUT NOT LIMITED TO SPECIAL, INCIDENTAL, CONSEQUENTIAL, OR OTHER DAMAGES.

For general information on our other products and services or to obtain technical support, please contact our Customer Care Department within the U.S. at 800-762-2974, outside the U.S. at 317-572-3993, or fax 317-572-4002.

Wiley also publishes its books in a variety of electronic formats. Some content that appears in print may not be available in electronic books.

Library of Congress Cataloging-in-Publication Data:

Library of Congress Catalog Card No.: 99-61891
ISBN: 0-7645-0525-4

Manufactured in the United States of America
10 9 8 7 6 5 4

10/QV/QU/QT/IN

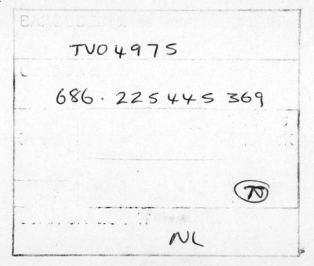

TV0 4975

686. 225445 369

NL

About the Author

Jim McCarter attended Webster University in Vienna, Austria, where he minored in foreign languages and graduated with a Bachelor's degree in computer studies. There he also launched his career as a computer consultant, which has now spanned 14 years and has included serving as technical reviewer for more than 55 books for IDG Books Worldwide, Inc. and other industry publishers. Jim divides his time between writing and editing computer-related books and freelance computer consulting. Jim lives in Greenfield, Indiana with his wife, Kathy, and two children, Rebecca and James.

Author's Acknowledgments

The author wishes to acknowledge the efforts of the many people who made this book possible. Kudos go first to our publisher, Dummies Press, and to Dan Gookin for creating a series of books that have captured the imagination of the entire computer world. These books have made many areas of technology palatable to a large number of readers, and many of the books in the series are the best books on that subject, bar none. To the many people at IDG Books Dummies Press, my publisher and editors, thanks. A particular thanks goes to Susan Christophersen for her tireless work as the project editor on this book, and to Kevin McCarter, my big brother, for ensuring the book's technical accuracy.

Publisher's Acknowledgments

We're proud of this book; please send us your comments through our online registration form located at www.dummies.com/register/.

Some of the people who helped bring this book to market include the following:

Acquisitions, Editorial, and Media Development

Project Editor: Susan Christophersen

Acquisitions Editor: Steve Hayes

Technical Editor: Kevin McCarter

Editorial Manager: Mary C. Corder

Editorial Assistant: Allison Walthall

Production

Project Coordinator: Regina Snyder

Layout and Graphics: Linda M. Boyer, Thomas R. Emrick, Angela F. Hunckler, Dave McKelvey, Brent Savage, Jacque Schneider, Janet Seib, Kate Snell, Michael Sullivan, Brian Torwelle

Proofreaders: Christine Pingleton, Nancy Price, Nancy L. Reinhardt, Marianne Santy, Rebecca Senninger, Ethel M. Winslow, Janet M. Withers

Indexer: Sharon Hilgenberg

Special Help
Suzanne Thomas

Publishing and Editorial for Technology Dummies
Richard Swadley, Vice President and Executive Group Publisher
Andy Cummings, Vice President and Publisher
Mary C. Corder, Editorial Director

Publishing for Consumer Dummies
Diane Graves Steele, Vice President and Publisher
Joyce Pepple, Acquisitions Director

Composition Services
Gerry Fahey, Vice President of Production Services
Debbie Stailey, Director of Composition Services

Contents at a Glance

Cartoons at a Glance

By Rich Tennant

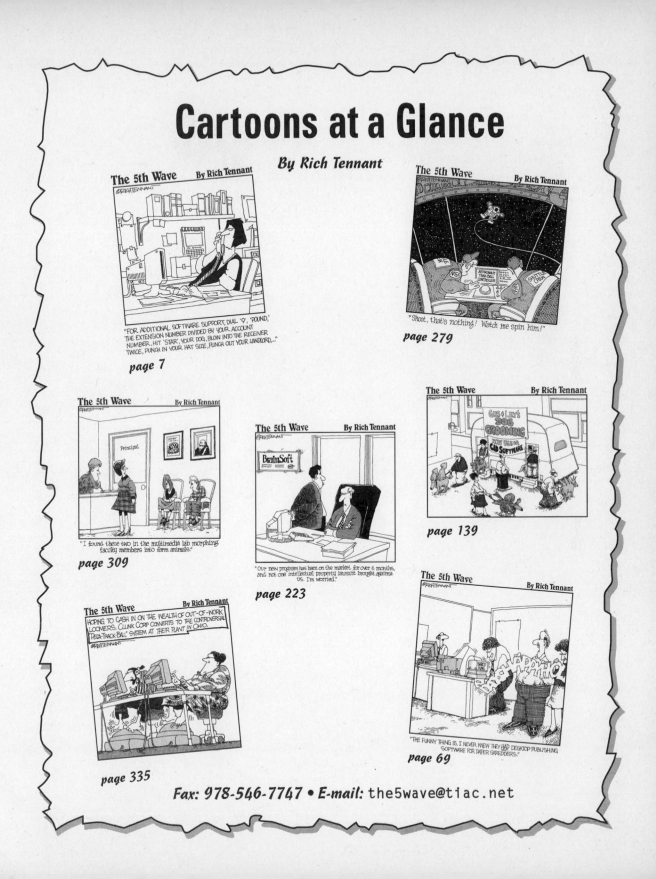

page 7

page 279

page 309

page 223

page 139

page 335

page 69

Fax: 978-546-7747 • E-mail: the5wave@tiac.net

Table of Contents

Introduction

· ·

*W*elcome to *Microsoft Publisher 2000 For Dummies*. If you have never used desktop publishing software and aren't really interested in becoming an expert at it, congratulations! This book that you hold in your hands is a great choice; it will help you complete your current project quickly — and with the least effort possible. I am pretty good at that least effort possible stuff. Just ask my editors.

Many computer users simply do not have the time or resources to become an expert on all the complicated software programs that they use. Oh, sure, some of you like to spend your spare time learning the most minute details about the software you use (I won't mention any names, Kevin). But most of us are content to learn just enough to get the job done in an efficient manner. We don't want to read page after page of esoteric information presented by some computer books that doesn't pertain to the job at hand. If you want to know a simple answer to a single question about desktop publishing with Microsoft Publisher 2000, then this book is for you.

Microsoft Publisher 2000, designed for Windows 95 and newer operating systems, is an inexpensive desktop publishing program. In fact, if you purchased any version of Microsoft Office 2000 other than the Standard version, you already own it. You use this program to create printed materials, such as brochures and flyers, and online documents known as Web pages. Even though Microsoft Publisher 2000 is low priced, it is definitely not underpowered. You can do things with Microsoft Publisher 2000 that a few years ago would have made the big boys (you know, those expensive desktop publishing programs) sit up and take notice. For example, you can create publications automatically through the wizards in Microsoft Publisher (something that you can't do with your Quirks and PageMonsters). I want to carry on with the *...For Dummies* tradition and help you have fun with Microsoft Publisher 2000 as you use this book. And remember, publish or perish!

About This Book

You can read this book from cover to cover, but you don't have to; you can use it as a reference book. When you need to know something about Microsoft Publisher 2000, just jump to the appropriate section and read about it. Most chapters are self contained. Typical sections that you may find include:

- ✔ You Want Fast? Well, Meet Mr. Wizard
- ✔ Things You Can Do with Files
- ✔ Keeping Good Margins
- ✔ Hide and Seek: Find and Replace
- ✔ Collecting and Using Type
- ✔ How Color Improves Your Page
- ✔ Printers and Output Quality

What you need to know is here in this book. Don't bother memorizing the contents, and don't even think about using this book to *learn* Microsoft Publisher 2000. What you find in this book is only the information that you need to get your work done. Because I tend to babble on, from time to time I post a Technical Stuff icon (which features the *...For Dummies* guy) to forewarn you in case you want to ignore my rantings.

Conventions Used in This Book

Because this book is a reference, you can look up a topic of interest in the Table of Contents or in the Index at the back of the book. These tools refer you to the sections that talk about that topic. If you need to know something specific in order to understand a section's content, I tell you so. I know that computer technology is loaded with confusing words and phrases and technobabble. (Sometimes I can't avoid slinging this stuff about like a short-order cook in a cheap diner.) But in some cases, I may send you off elsewhere to help you figure out the confusing terms.

I like to give you examples of how to do something. Because Microsoft Publisher 2000 is a Windows 95 program, most instructions tell you to *click here* or *click there,* to *choose File➪Print* from the menu, or to *press Alt+F,P* on the keyboard. Notice two things about these instructions: First, I underline the *hot keys* that you can use to select menu commands from the keyboard; and second, I show that you press and hold the *Alt* key while you press the *F* key by placing the + sign between them. Then you release both keys and press the *P* key. This keyboard combination produces the same action as using your mouse to choose the menu command. It's all standard Microsoft Windows fare.

If I want you to enter information from your keyboard, you may see a line that looks like the following (this comes up just a few times):

```
C:\>ENTER THIS STUFF
```

In the preceding example, you type the words **ENTER THIS STUFF** after the C:\> prompt and then press the Enter key. Notice that I don't use quotation marks around the text (that is, "ENTER THIS STUFF"), because I don't want you to enter quotation marks. I go on to explain why you do what I've told you to do and what happens after you do, so don't worry.

You've Been Warned

Desktop publishing can be a complicated endeavor, with many things that you may (or may not) want to know about. I include a few sections in the book on more advanced topics such as selecting paper, working with outside service bureaus, choosing color processes, and so on. Of course, if all you want to do is run the Birthday Card or Gift Certificates Wizard and print the results from your inkjet printer, then you might not need to look at these topics. I try to warn you when a section tends toward the technical or is limited to specific interests. But you may read these sections, and doing so will earn you a gold star in the Desktop Publishing Hall of Fame (but that's not what this book is meant to do).

Foolish Assumptions

I make only three assumptions about you in this book. The first we've already stated: You don't want to waste time studying useless trivia. You are in a hurry and you want to get your work done.

My second assumption is that you have an IBM personal computer or compatible computer (that is, a clone) that has Microsoft Windows 95 or later installed. Maybe you have set up your computer, or maybe someone else has. But it's working, and you can get the help you need to keep it working.

My third assumption is that you know your way around Windows well enough to perform simple operations in that environment. You already know how to move your mouse and stroke your keyboard. You should know how to select a menu command, know how to work with dialog boxes and windows, and be familiar with common Desktop items such as the Recycle Bin. I cover some of these topics (when the discussion is directly applicable to Microsoft Publisher 2000), but not in detail.

By the way, if finding your way around your new computer or Windows is still one of the mysteries of life for you, I want to direct you to the following books:

- ✔ *PCs For Dummies,* 6th Edition, by Dan Gookin and Andy Rathbone
- ✔ *Windows 95 For Dummies,* 2nd Edition, by Andy Rathbone
- ✔ *Windows 98 For Dummies,* by Andy Rathbone

All are from IDG Books Worldwide, Inc.

How This Book Is Organized

Topics in this book are generally arranged as if I were directing you through a desktop publishing project from start to finish. In the progression of topics, I try to address those issues that you commonly tackle first, first, and the issues that you tackle last, last. Clever, eh? The book has seven major parts; each part has two or more chapters. (My editors insist that each divided topic should have at least two subdivisions, and I slavishly follow their teachings.)

Aside from these considerations, you'll find that most chapters stand by themselves. You can start reading at any section. Great teachers tell us, "Tell them (the audience) what you are going to tell them." So, we've outlined the entire book as follows.

Part I: Getting Acquainted with Publisher 2000

When you create a project in Microsoft Publisher 2000 to print something, you are doing desktop publishing (DTP). When you create a project to place on the Internet, you are Web spinning. Desktop publishing replaces technology of past centuries and decades with something new and special. For many folks, desktop publishing is the reason they bought a computer. Part I tells you what desktop publishing is, how it came about, and where it's going. Also in Part I, I give you the skinny on design issues and provide the nickel tour on the basics that you need to know to run and use the program.

Part II: Mark This Page

Microsoft Publisher 2000, like most desktop publishing programs, uses the metaphor of a pasteboard. In this part, you work on creating a page, defining the layout, and then adding things to your page. You add objects to Microsoft Publisher 2000 pages inside frames, which I tell you how to work with in this part. "I'm innocent, I tell ya. I've been framed!"

Part III: 10,000 Words, One Maniac

An important part of desktop publishing is marrying text and figures on a page. In this part, you discover how to work with text on your page; not just how to enter text into a text frame, mind you, but also how to select and work with type. This part also guides you through importing text from Microsoft Word and including tables from Excel and Access in your Publisher 2000 publications.

Part IV: A Picture Is Worth $3.95

A picture is worth a thousand words. That works out to be about $3.95. Honest, I did the math myself! Microsoft Publisher 2000 lets you enhance your page with all kinds of pictures: drawings, images, and other forms of art, including PowerPoint slides and a chapter on using PhotoDraw. In this part, I tell you what you need to know to create and work with different kinds of pictures — and where to get help if you need it. I also use a chapter to talk about the related topic of using color in your publication.

Part V: Proof Positive

This part contains a cornucopia of important fruits of knowledge for you to nibble on. You see how to fine-tune your page: edit copy, hyphenate, add flourishes, and assemble your project. You also find a chapter in this part with a discussion on paper, printing, and working with commercial printing services.

Part VI: Publishing on the Internet

Publishing on the Internet is the latest rage. In this part, you learn how to create and edit a Web site, including adding graphics and hyperlinks, and adding color and texture to the background. You also find tips on previewing your Web site. Finally, I tell you how to publish your Web site.

Part VII: The Part of Tens

Other people have their lists and I have my lists. In this part, The Part of Tens, you get lists of ten things on topics that you should know about. I give you lists on design issues, text and type, colors, printing, commercial printing services, and other things. Have fun reading this part, and when you're done, we will part.

Icons Used in This Book

I don't use a lot of icons, but I do use a few. Here are my little nuggets of wisdom for you to savor:

Nerdy technical discussions that you can skip if you want.

Shortcuts and insights that can save you time, money, and trouble.

Our friendly Design icon points out principles that you want to employ.

A friendly reminder to do something.

Points out some of the little *gotchas* that life (or Microsoft Publisher 2000) has to offer. (**Hint**: Don't do this!)

Where to Go from Here

You're ready to use this book. Start by reviewing the Table of Contents to find a topic of current interest to you. Then, dive right in and read about it. Try some of my suggestions in your work and experiment. Microsoft Publisher 2000 is a very friendly and forgiving program. (If you save copies of your publication as you go, little can go wrong that you can't fix.)

When you find something that doesn't work quite the way you expect or something that you want to know more about, return to this book. Repeat the process. Finding out about Microsoft Publisher 2000 and Windows can and should be an exploration. Microsoft meant for these two programs to be a "discoverable environment" — that is, to be like a well-designed computer game that you can figure out as you play. I'm here to get you past any bumps or tilts that you might encounter.

Desktop publishing is fun. That's why so many people do it. And Microsoft Publisher 2000 makes it easier to do than any other program I know.

Part I
Getting Acquainted with Publisher 2000

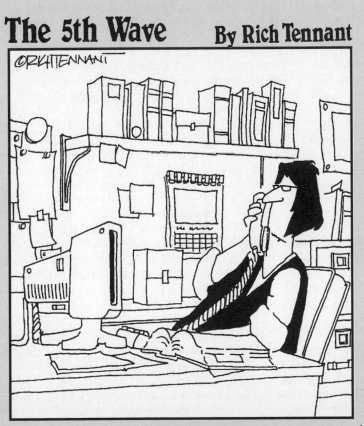

The 5th Wave   By Rich Tennant

"FOR ADDITIONAL SOFTWARE SUPPORT, DIAL '9', 'POUND,' THE EXTENSION NUMBER DIVIDED BY YOUR ACCOUNT NUMBER, HIT 'STAR', YOUR DOG, BLOW INTO THE RECEIVER TWICE, PUNCH IN YOUR HAT SIZE, PUNCH OUT YOUR LANDLORD,..."

In this part ...

*E*veryone wants to create publications that people will read. The quality of your printed work can directly influence your income, your career advancement, who shows up at your parties, and more. Attractive résumés get people interviews; attractive books get bought; attractive birthday cards get sent more often; attractive ads pull orders; and attractive people get more dates. (No, Microsoft Publisher 2000 won't make you more beautiful or handsome.) It is fair to say that the appearance of our designs affects what people think of us as a person.

Some of us are born designers; most of us are not. Microsoft Publisher 2000 lets you create professional-quality output easily, even if you are not artistically inclined. You do need to know something about what separates good design from poor design, and enough about the technology to create publications or page layout documents in Microsoft Publisher 2000. That is what Part I is all about. The chapters in this part provide an overview of desktop publishing, tell you what constitutes good design principles, and give you some basic information that you need to know in order to get started working in Microsoft Publisher 2000.

Chapter 1

Own the Printing Press

In This Chapter

▶ Deciding when to use Microsoft Publisher 2000

▶ Understanding desktop publishing

▶ Exploring the design process

▶ Using wizards

Desktop publishing uses page layout software and a personal computer to combine text, type, drawings, and images on a page to create books, newsletters, brochures, flyers, greeting cards, Web sites, and so on. Anything that you can print on a page can be put into a page layout program. Microsoft Publisher 2000 lets you place elements on a page, precisely position them, modify them, and specify a print job using techniques that commercial printers require. Whether you print to your inkjet or laser printer, run down the street to the Quick Copy Shop, or send your files to a commercial printer, Microsoft Publisher 2000 helps you prepare your work for that level of quality.

When Should You Use Microsoft Publisher 2000?

Many programs let you design and print pages to various levels of sophistication. These programs include word processors such as Microsoft Word, WordPerfect, and Ami Pro; graphics programs such as CorelDRAW! and Windows Draw; and even low-end integrated packages such as Microsoft Works or ClarisWorks. The program that I write in, Microsoft Word for Windows, enables me to type text, format the text, import pictures, create drawings, and even work with images.

If you can do all that in Word, why do you need a desktop publishing or page layout program like Microsoft Publisher 2000? The short answer is control. Microsoft Publisher 2000 lets you control these elements with finer precision and offers you many special tools besides.

How Microsoft Publisher 2000 measures up

Plenty of desktop publishing programs are out there, all claiming to be the best, most popular, friendliest, newest, or least likely to cause your computer to burst into flames. If you cut through all the marketing hype, though, these programs fall into just two categories:

- Programs that are inexpensive and easy to learn

- Programs that are expensive and difficult to learn

Programs such as PageMaker, QuarkXPress, FrameMaker, and Ventura Publisher are expensive — about five times the cost of Microsoft Publisher 2000 — and difficult to learn. These programs are designed for hard-core desktop publishers (usually in a commercial trade) for whom absolute precision is everything. These people are picky — *extremely* picky. Do you care whether you can nudge a graphic 1/1000th of an inch? Do you think that you'll need to change the size of an individual character by less than the width of a human hair?

Be prepared for weeks or months of dedicated study before you can master their intricacies. If you can use one of these programs to put together a decent publication within your first week of intensive learning, you'll be doing quite well.

Microsoft Publisher 2000 is about as powerful as these more capable programs were two years ago. That's a long time in the computer industry, but except for professional features, this category of software hasn't changed all that much. Microsoft Publisher 2000 gives you 80 percent of the capability of the more powerful programs by incorporating 20 percent of their features. That translates into projects that you can accomplish in Microsoft Publisher 2000 two or three times faster than in other programs. The bottom line is this: If you're not sure what Microsoft Publisher 2000 is missing that you need, it probably will be *plenty* good enough.

So, if you just want to stick your company's logo at the top of your letter and insert a copy of your scanned-in signature at the bottom, you don't need Microsoft Publisher 2000 to do that. If you want to create a company logo by combining a couple of graphics from different sources, some text, and some color, and then separate the output to give to a commercial printing service to print, Microsoft Publisher 2000 is a better choice. If you want to create a four-page newsletter, mix three and four columns of text on each page, and have the text wrap around some graphics, Microsoft Publisher 2000 is definitely the way to go. It does these things well.

How Desktop Publishing Works

Page layout software takes various parts and combines them into a single document, called a *publication*. The following list briefly covers the parts that you can meld together. In Figure 1-1, I labeled sample elements. Nearly all objects on a page are in frames or blocks that are created when you import or create the object:

- ✓ **Text:** Okay, I know that you know what text is. Text is the stuff that you type: all those individual characters that form words, sentences, paragraphs, and so on.

- ✓ **Type:** Man/Woman does not live by text alone. Type or typography are the various letter forms that you can use to make your text attractive. Microsoft Publisher 2000 lets you access WordArt, a text manipulation program that lets you add fancy effects to your text.

- ✓ **Pictures:** Computers make two kinds of pictures: drawn (vector, or object-oriented) and painted (raster, or bitmapped) images. You can import both types into a picture frame.

Microsoft Publisher 2000 ships with a Clip Gallery containing 225MB of clip art, including more than 10,000 clip art images, 1,500 photographs, 1,000 Web-related graphics, 340 animated GIFs (those cute pictures that seem to wiggle around on Web pages), and more!

Figure 1-1:
A sample publication with labeled objects.

✔ **Drawn objects:** Microsoft Publisher 2000 is not a drawing program, but some tools in its Objects toolbar enable you to create drawn images such as lines, ovals and circles, rectangles and squares, and a whole bunch of custom shapes.

✔ **Tables:** Although you can import tables from other programs as objects, either as drawings or as OLE (Object Linking and Embedding) objects managed by other applications, Microsoft Publisher 2000 has its own Table tool.

You can create these elements by using Microsoft Publisher 2000, or you can use other programs to create the objects and then use Microsoft Publisher 2000 to place them in your publication.

The Design Process

Page design is an iterative process. You can always find a better way to make a point with design, to use type and color, to refine a graphic, and so on. You can always return to a publication later and find something that you could have done better. Like all creative endeavors, a well-designed publication can be improved by planning before the fact, experimenting, and offering thoughtful criticism at all stages. The sections that follow describe some of the methods that designers use to make their pages stand out from the crowd.

Storyboarding

To get a good start on the process, you can block out the way that you want your publication to look. One block-out method is called *storyboarding*. Storyboards are like block diagrams. Cartoonists use storyboards to show a story's progression. Movie designers use storyboards to illustrate key frames in a movie, which enables them to present the movie in a preproduction form that others can view and understand. You can use this same technique.

Many people like to mock up their design projects with pencil and paper. They create a dummy of their publication, and when the publication spans several pages, they create storyboards. But this is all a matter of preference: The important thing is to plan your publication before you create it.

TECHNICAL STUFF

Shout OLE and watch the bull fly!

Microsoft Publisher 2000 is a heavy user of Object Linking and Embedding, or OLE (pronounced *o-lay*). This means that you can insert, or embed, data created in another application inside your publication and maintain a live link between the two. For example, you can insert an object created in a drawing program in your publication. You also can choose to link the publication to the object's source by placing a reference to that file in Microsoft Publisher 2000. This way, when the original object changes, you simply update the reference to have the changes reflected in your publication.

The advantage of embedding is that you have your object contained within your publication; the disadvantage is that your file size grows. The advantage of linking is that your publication's file size stays smaller; the disadvantage is that file management is required (Microsoft Publisher 2000 needs to know where to find the source documents).

One hand giveth, the other hand taketh away. I show you more about including content from other programs in Chapters 6 and 9.

I find Microsoft Publisher 2000 so easy to work with that I prefer to create my dummies inside the program. The tools for creating frames, lines, and boxes make these page elements easy to create and modify inside Microsoft Publisher 2000. I also find that working inside the program forces me to think, right from the start, about how I'll break apart a sample design and implement it.

Microsoft Publisher 2000 has a collection of wizards that build dummy publications for you based on the answers that you give in a series of dialog boxes. You see the wizards in the Catalog dialog box as the collection of sample documents that you can create. In effect, storyboarding is what the wizards do when they create a template for you. When you create a document by using the wizards, the result is a dummy of the document that you are creating. Figure 1-2 shows a four-panel brochure created with the Brochure Wizard. The wizard generates a sample document with a headline, graphics blocks, and text frames with sample text. Each element on the page can be modified, but the document's overall look is obvious from the result of the wizard. Your dummies or mock-ups should show similar use of text, graphics, and overall design.

Here's a trick that works well for many people. Try moving away from your design and looking at it from afar. Better yet, try zooming out so that you can see the overall layout, but cannot read the text. Select View⇨Zoom and choose 33% or 25% from the submenu that appears. Is its purpose obvious, or is clutter obscuring the purpose? If you have too many page elements, try eliminating some.

Assembling a page

After you have blocked out a page design, you can replace the dummy text, pictures, and other frames with the data that you want to include on the page. This is the assembly part of page composition. Depending on the type of object frame or tool selected, you can apply one of the Edit or Insert menu commands to bring the data into Microsoft Publisher 2000. The basics of importing text are covered in Chapter 6. You find the related topic of importing tabular data in Chapter 6 as well. For details on bringing graphics into your publication, see Chapter 10.

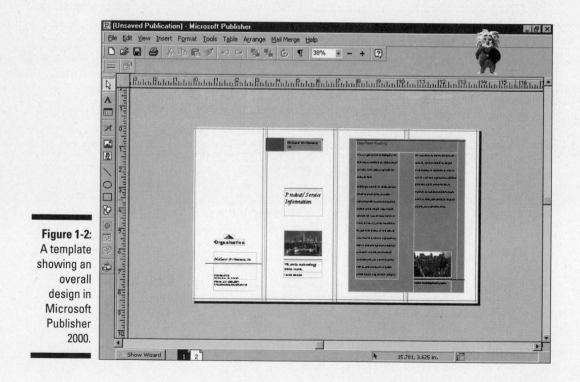

Figure 1-2:
A template showing an overall design in Microsoft Publisher 2000.

Chances are great that after you have all the frames composed and filled with real data, the page will require more tweaking. Microsoft Publisher 2000 contains a number of specialized tools for repositioning, resizing, and fitting objects on a page. Chapter 12 details the final steps in the assembly process. You also find information about preparing a publication for output to an outside printer in Chapter 13.

How it was done in the old days

When I was young (okay, younger — it doesn't seem that long ago to me), designers composed pages by printing the elements of a page, cutting and pasting them on a large board called, appropriately enough, a pasteboard, and photographing the result. If the page layout involved full color, the designers took three or four photographs with colored filters to create the colored printing plates needed to combine colored inks into full-color prints. That was how it was done in the *old days*, as late as the early 1980s. I have vivid memories of the difficulty and the time consumed by getting all elements to line up and work together properly.

Today, with Microsoft Publisher 2000, you have it easy. Microsoft Publisher 2000 takes the text that you type or import and lets you format it with type and spacing. You can place line art, scanned images, or any object that you can create in the computer on the page and make adjustments to have it all fit just so. You can change letter sizes and interletter spacing, word spacing, line spacing, and hyphenation to copy-fit your text onto a page. Similarly, you can easily make text flow around graphics just the way you want. You can resize your graphics as needed. You can do all this without resorting to sloppy cutting and pasting or trips back to a typographic print machine. That's why this software is called page layout or page composition software. Heaven.

When you're done, Microsoft Publisher 2000 replaces taking filtered photographs of your color pages with internal filters. The program includes an algorithm to *color separate* your pages. The effect is like looking at the world through a red, green, and blue plate of glass. What you see in each case is different. If you combine the three views, however, you see your color restored.

Print processes use three different colors to create colored pages. Each component of a color page comes out as a printed page. Typically, for a printer, these components are Cyan, Yellow, Magenta, and Black — or CYMK. I know, K for black seems a bit strange. I imagine someone thought that B might be mistaken for Blue or Brown. Now the color plates are still made by preparing film from printed output, but it is typically done on a high-resolution printer called an *imagesetter*.

You can output a publication in several ways:

- Black and White
- Grayscale — Shades of gray
- Spot Color — A single color appearing on the page in one or more places (not necessarily the color of your dog)
- Full Color

A single publication can use any or all of these output options.

You find related information on printing files in Chapter 13 and an explanation of how to work with color in Chapter 10.

Don't be surprised if the assembly process is largely comprised of the tweaking phase of the project. Leave enough time to get this tweaking done the way you want it. (Think of the builder who says that the house is 90 percent done when only 50 percent of the allotted time is spent.)

Outputting a page

After you have your page composed the way you want it, you are ready to print. You can choose to print files to local printers and select from any of the print drivers that came with Windows 95. Printing to a local printer is no different in Microsoft Publisher 2000 than it is in any other Windows application; you simply choose File➪Print. See Chapter 13 for detailed information about printing files.

Microsoft Publisher 2000 also allows you to set up a print job for a commercial printing service. The process is only slightly different than printing to a local printer. When you specify that your publication is meant to print to an imagesetter or color printer, Microsoft Publisher 2000 makes some selections for you that help your local print shop print your files correctly. Or you can use a disk file with your print shop's printer driver to compose your print job. See Chapter 13 for details on having close encounters with printers of the third kind (human ones, that is).

You Want Fast? Well, Meet Mr. Wizard

Using a wizard is the easiest way to create a publication in Microsoft Publisher 2000. A wizard is a set of dialog boxes that leads you through the creation of a project based on selections that you make. Starting and using wizards is pretty easy. Microsoft Publisher 2000 always opens the Catalog to the Publications by Wizard tab when you start the program. By the way, you can start Microsoft Publisher 2000 in the following ways:

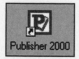

Publisher 2000

- ✔ Double-click the icon for the program on the Windows desktop.
- ✔ Choose the Start➪Programs➪Microsoft Publisher command, as shown in Figure 1-3. (Easy!)

If your computer is handy, you may want to try out the Origami Wizard that I describe in the following section.

If you already have Microsoft Publisher 2000 open on-screen, you can choose File➪New to see the Publications by Wizard tab, as shown in Figure 1-4. All the publication categories that you see on that tab open a wizard specific for that type of publication.

The Catalog is a modal dialog box, which means that you need to make a selection in it or dismiss it before you can go on. You can click and drag the Catalog window's title bar as you would any window's title bar.

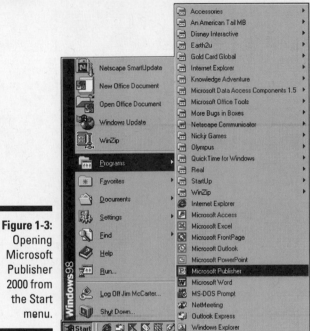

Figure 1-3:
Opening
Microsoft
Publisher
2000 from
the Start
menu.

Tableware made easy: The Origami Wizard

Microsoft Publisher 2000 has some really neat wizards; you can see their document types in Figure 1-4. But for now, I want to show you one of the more whimsical wizards. My two children, Rebecca and James, were more than a little skeptical when I told them that I could make a cup with my computer.

The Origami Wizard is dedicated to the prospect that if you put thousands and thousands of really bright people together in a place where the sun never shines and force-feed them Jolt Cola and high-octane candy, they produce genius for no apparent purpose. You rev up the Origami Wizard by selecting Origami in the Wizards pane of the Publications by Wizard dialog box, and then

- ✔ Double-click an origami in the Origami pane with the mouse pointer (try saying that fast ten times!).
- ✔ Highlight an origami and click the hot key Start Wizard button.
- ✔ Use the arrow keys to move about, and press the Enter key.

Figure 1-4:
The Catalog
with wizards
galore.

The preceding are all standard Windows dialog box selection techniques that work universally throughout Microsoft Publisher 2000. Generally, a wizard starts out with an introductory screen and runs you through several selections. Figure 1-5 shows the introductory screen. You can move to the next step in the wizard by clicking the Next button, or return to change a former selection by using the Back button. The Finish button actually creates the document on-screen. Figure 1-6 shows you the resulting origami inside a Microsoft Publisher 2000 window. Notice the warning labels that I placed on the sides of the cup. Wouldn't want anyone spilling hot liquids and suing me! I am sure you will agree that the hardest part of the Origami Wizard is folding the paper. Take a look at Page 2 of the publication for detailed folding instructions.

Facts about wizards

You need to know a couple important points about the wizards. Wizards are tools used to create new on-screen publications inside Microsoft Publisher 2000.

Figure 1-5:
Steps in the
Origami
Wizard.

Here's another fact for you to ponder. In Figure 1-6 (where you see the paper cup), the screen looks like the Print Preview window in other programs (such as word processors). Because Microsoft Publisher 2000 is designed to help you create printed output, it has only a single viewing mode for your publications, and it shows you what your printed document looks like. You never switch out of this view, although you can zoom in or out for a different perspective by using commands on the View menu or the Zoom control at the bottom-left corner of the window, next to the horizontal scroll bar.

Publications created with wizards are actually composed of many individual objects. If you click any part of a publication, selection handles (little squares on the edges; see Figure 1-7) appear around the selected part. You have fine control over the size, placement, color, and other properties of your publication's parts. If you use a wizard to create something in Microsoft Publisher 2000, however, you have only scratched the surface of what you can do with the program. I am happy to present what's under the surface as you read through the book.

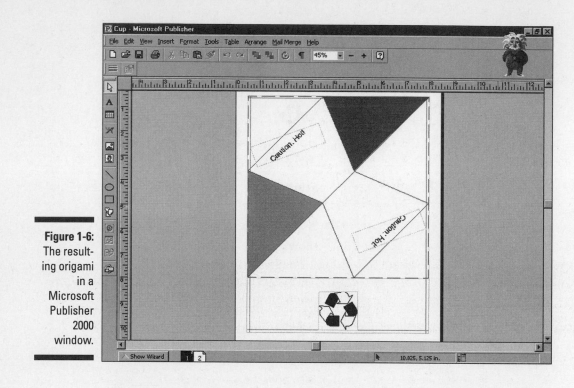

Figure 1-6:
The resulting origami in a Microsoft Publisher 2000 window.

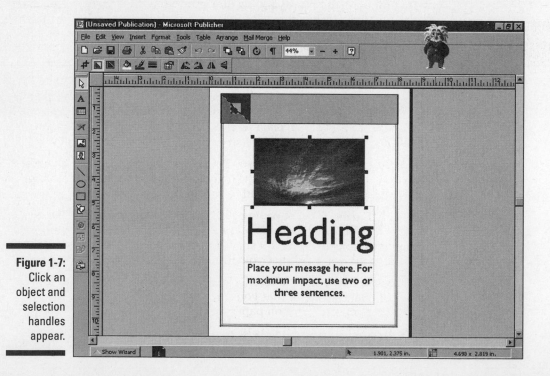

Figure 1-7:
Click an object and selection handles appear.

A page-layout program is really a specialized kind of draw program. If you are familiar with that kind of program, you find that many Microsoft Publisher 2000 operations also are familiar to you.

Okay, now meet Mr. Wizard's family

Each wizard can generate several kinds of publications of the same class, depending on the selections you make. Microsoft Publisher 2000 has 25 wizards:

- **Quick Publications:** Use this wizard when you want to create a single-page publication with a professional design and layout.

- **Newsletters:** Create multicolumn, multipage newsletters with ease.

- **Web Sites:** This wizard allows you to create multiple-page Web sites quickly and easily.

- **Brochures:** Six different styles of brochures are offered: Informational, Price List, Event, Fund-raiser, Special Paper Informational, and Special Paper Price List. These last two are intended to be printed on paper from PaperDirect. Phone: 800-A-PAPERS; or visit its Web site at www.paperdirect.com. Figure 1-8 shows previews of six of the twenty-five Informational brochures.

- **Catalogs:** Create catalogs to advertise your wares.

- **Flyers:** Includes styles for Informational, Special Offer, Sale, Event, Fund-raiser, Announcement, and Special Paper.

- **Signs:** The Signs Wizard creates 28 single-page signs — everything from Authorized Personnel Only to Lemonade for Sale to Wheelchair Access.

- **Postcards:** This wizard creates 15 categories of postcards: Informational, Special Offer, Sale, Event, Invitation, Holiday Party Invitation, Holiday Greeting, Holiday Thank You, Thank You, We've Moved, Announcement, Reminder, Tent Fold, Special Paper Informational, and Special Paper Invitation. Each category offers several types of postcards.

- **Invitation Cards:** Having a to-do? This wizard creates invitation cards for Party, Theme Party, Holiday Party, Birthday Party, Housewarming, Shower, Event, Celebration, and Fund-raiser.

- **Greeting Cards:** Tired of paying $3.50 for a greeting card? You'll love this wizard. It offers 14 categories of cards. Each of these categories offers you many choices. Figure 1-9 shows you an example of a professional-looking thank you card that you can create and send to your clients.

- **Business Cards:** The Business Cards Wizard lets you choose from twenty styles of business cards that you can print on plain paper and nine styles that you can print on paper from PaperDirect.

- **Letterheads:** The Letterheads Wizard offers you twenty styles of letterhead that you can print on plain paper and nine styles that you can print on paper from PaperDirect. Figure 1-10 shows an example of a letterhead using the Capsules style. After you create a letterhead for your business or personal use, Microsoft Publisher 2000 remembers the style that you used and asks whether you want to base your next letterhead on that style.

✔ **Envelopes:** The Envelopes Wizard creates 20 styles of plain paper envelopes and nine styles of PaperDirect envelopes that match the Letterheads and Business Cards styles. Microsoft Publisher 2000 remembers the style that you used and asks whether you want to base your next envelope on that style.

✔ **Business Forms:** This wizard offers you ten choices: Expense Report, Fax Cover, Inventory List, Invoice, Purchase Order, Quote, Refund, Statement, Time Billing, and Weekly Record. As you click each business form in the Wizards pane, a picture of the default form appears in the right pane of the Publications by Wizard tab. Figure 1-11 shows you an Invoice form that uses the Capsules style.

✔ **Banners:** The Banners Wizard offers nine types of banners: Informational, Sale, Event, Birthday, Welcome, Congratulations, Holiday, Romance, and Get Well. You can set a height and width, and you can choose to have graphics and borders on your banner.

✔ **Calendars:** You can choose between twenty-four Full Page and three Wallet Size calendars.

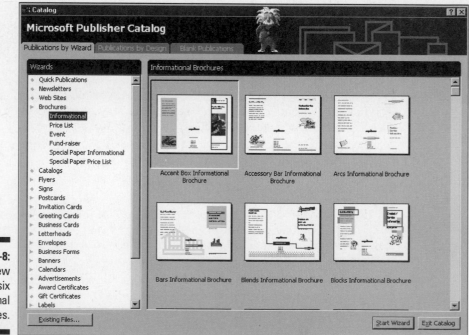

Figure 1-8:
Preview
of six
Informational
brochures.

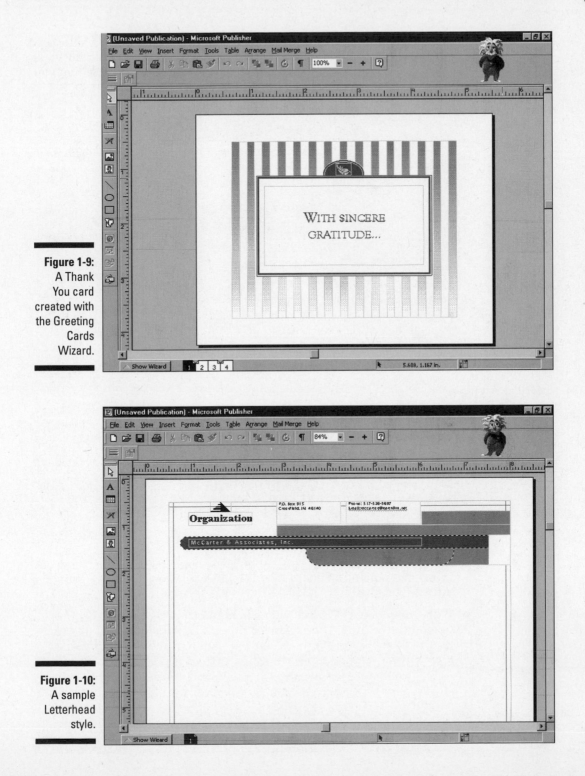

Figure 1-9:
A Thank
You card
created with
the Greeting
Cards
Wizard.

Figure 1-10:
A sample
Letterhead
style.

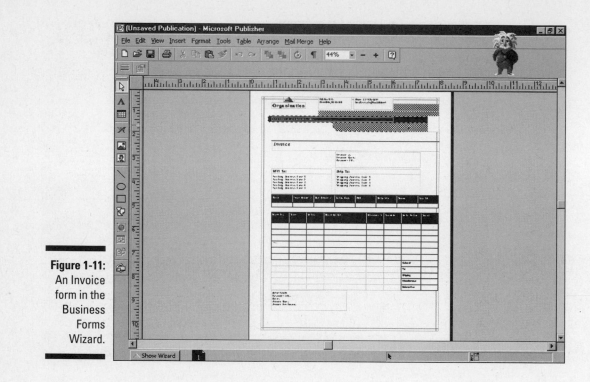

Figure 1-11:
An Invoice
form in the
Business
Forms
Wizard.

✔ **Advertisements:** This wizard lets you choose from six different styles of advertisement: Art Emphasis, Bring-In, Equal Emphasis, Mail-In, Text Emphasis, and The Works. Figure 1-12 shows you The Works style.

✔ **Award Certificates:** Choose among eight plain paper and six special paper award certificates.

✔ **Gift Certificates:** Forge, er, I mean create your own gift certificates! Choose from twenty gift certificate styles.

✔ **Labels:** You can create labels in any of the following 11 styles: Mailing Labels, Shipping, Return Address, Computer Disk, Cassette, Compact Disc, Video, Jar/Product, Binder, Bookplate, and Identification. Many of these labels match standard Avery labels. The Avery number is provided after the label name.

✔ **With Compliments Cards:** Choose from twenty styles of With Compliments cards. These come in handy when you have product samples and freebies to give away and you want to make sure that the recipient knows where they came from. Figure 1-13 shows a With Compliments card in the, you guessed it, Capsules style.

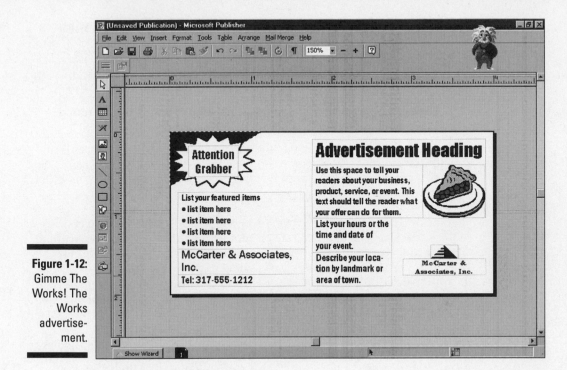

Figure 1-12: Gimme The Works! The Works advertisement.

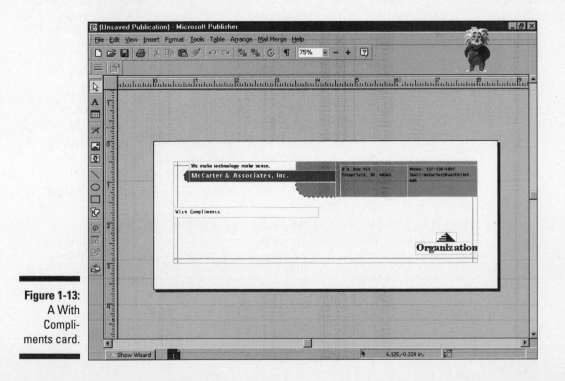

Figure 1-13: A With Compliments card.

- ✔ **Menus:** Have your own restaurant? The Menus Wizard lets you create Regular, Take-Out, Daily Special, and Wine/Dessert menus in a variety of styles.

- ✔ **Programs:** Create Music, Religious Service, and Theater programs with a few clicks of the mouse.

- ✔ **Airplanes:** This wizard creates four airplane types: Classic, Stubby, Whirlybird, and Wing Tip.

- ✔ **Origami:** This wizard creates the Japanese style of paper figures. The four types range from easy to create (the Boat) to hard (the Parrot). Still, they're fun to give, and pretty when printed on a color printer or with colored paper.

You aren't limited to accepting whatever the wizards give you. You can replace one font with another, one picture with another, one border with another, and so on. And you can always click the Show Wizard button to change any of the selections that you made in the Wizard dialog boxes. Knowing Microsoft Publisher 2000 well helps you quickly modify these wizards' output and makes the result something that you are proud to show to others.

Designer publication sets

Now that I have introduced you to all the wizards on the Publications by Wizard tab of the Catalog dialog box, it is time to meet the sets of publications on the Publications by Design tab. Those clever folks at Microsoft know that it is important for your business to have a consistent, identifiable image. Giving your various business publications a consistent look is a snap with the Publications by Design wizards:

- ✔ **Master Sets:** These sets include twenty different styles, each with twenty-eight different business publications.

- ✔ **Special Event Sets:** Three styles, each with five special event publications: Event Brochure, Event Flyer, Event Invitation, Event Postcard, and Event Web Site.

- ✔ **Fund-Raiser Sets:** Three styles, each with four Fund-Raiser publications: Fund-Raiser Brochure, Fund-Raiser Flyer, Fund-Raiser Invitation, and Fund-Raiser Web Site.

- ✔ **Holiday Sets:** Three styles, each with seven Holiday publications: Greetings Postcard, Party Invitation Postcard, Thank You Postcard, Newsletter, Web Site, Greeting Card, and Party Invitation.

- ✔ **We've Moved Sets:** Four styles, each with a Housewarming Invitation and two different We've Moved Announcements.

- ✔ **Restaurant Sets:** Two styles, each with a Web Site and four menus: Menu, Take-Out Menu, Wine/Dessert Menu, and Daily Special Menu.

- ✔ **Special Paper:** Nine Special Paper styles from Paper Direct, each with eight publications: Business Card, Envelope, Flyer, Informational Brochure, Informational Postcard, Invitation Postcard, Letterhead, and List brochure.

Chapter 2

Success by Design

*W*e live in a fast age. Before, you had time to read the occasional ad or brochure that appeared in your mailbox; now, you may receive 10 or 20 mailings every day. We are bombarded with so much stuff that we tend to ignore most of it.

So, here's the deal. Your publication has five seconds to get someone's attention. (Some design gurus claim that most pieces get about two seconds of review before being tossed.) If your published piece doesn't have something that interests your audience and makes people want to explore it further, *poof!* it's gone.

If you have only five seconds, you better make sure that your primary message is the first thing a reader sees. You have little room for error on this score. Consider any design device that you can use to repeat — and build on — the primary message.

This chapter shows you the design basics necessary to do your work in Microsoft Publisher 2000 quickly and well.

Know Your Audience

The first step to creating a successful project is figuring out who your audience is and how they will interact with your work. Knowing your audience helps you refine your publication's look and feel. In addition, it helps you determine your writing style, which is essential for good communication.

You can learn a lot about successful design by studying the work of marketing gurus, particularly those who do advertising. Advertising combines a creative art form with statistically measured results based on large populations of target markets. One of my favorite books on this topic is *Design for Response: Creative Direct Marketing That Works* by Leslie Sherr and David J. Katz (published by Rockport Publishers).

While you're designing your publication, show it to others so that you can figure out who your audience is and what they need.

When you know your audience, you can create a publication that has the correct "voice" or "tone" for that group. For example, a typeface that looks like lettering on a ransom note is inappropriate for business correspondence but may be perfect for birthday party invitations. Microsoft Publisher 2000 includes more than 1,600 professionally designed templates and more than 60 coordinated Color Schemes. Finding one that is appropriate to your audience shouldn't be too difficult.

Knowing your audience can help you decide which typeface to use on a page. If you don't like any of the 175 fonts that come with Microsoft Publisher 2000, you can always buy more. Some vendors sell type in packages designed for specific uses. Their catalogs (which are works of art in themselves) describe the best use for many typefaces and also suggest typefaces that work well together

The typeface that you use can flavor your publication for a particular audience.

Where Others Have Gone Before

When I first start the design phase of a publishing project, I try to collect the best examples of work in that area. I look at the overall design of a piece and look for style elements that I can use as a springboard to creating my own style. Keep file folders of ads that you like, marketing pieces that you get in the mail, and other publications. Then, when you're ready to create a piece, you can sit down and peruse your samples. Invariably, you'll find an idea or two to get you started. If you don't find anything that strikes your fancy, try one of the many templates that you can create with the Publisher 2000 wizards.

Make sure that you do not copy too much from anyone's design when making your own work.

Any artwork, images, templates, or designs that you find in Microsoft Publisher 2000 and its Design Gallery are there for your use. The Readme file states: "You are free to use Publisher clip art for any publication you print. You may not, however, sell or distribute Publisher clip art electronically as software, such as in a clip art library." Restrictions such as these are common for clip art. You should always check the license of any artwork that you use before incorporating it into commercial products.

When you use other people's work, you can adapt the designs that you collect, borrowing an idea here and an idea there. You cannot and should not copy an entire design or image from someone else, however. That's illegal. Most designs are copyrighted by the authors.

Sometimes a fine line exists between adapting an idea and copying one. You need to use good judgment. Note that the law in this area is volatile and subject to change. I recommend _The Desktop Publisher's Legal Handbook_ by Daniel Sitarz (published by Nova Press) as a good place to start learning about these issues.

Another resource to use when beginning the design phase is a study of before and after makeovers. You can find case studies in the design makeover columns in desktop publishing magazines and in some specialized books on desktop publishing. The following resources take this approach:

- _Desktop Publishing & Design For Dummies,_ by Roger C. Parker (published by IDG Books Worldwide, Inc.).

- _BEFORE & After: How to design cool stuff,_ 1830 Sierra Gardens Drive, Roseville, CA 95661; Phone: 916-784-3880 and Fax: 916-784-3995.

The Keys to Design Success

Most design gurus agree that you can apply certain principles to your designs to make them easier to understand and more attractive to the reader. The exact terminology for these principles may vary, but the set of principles is nearly always the same.

A list of these principles follows. When you begin to design a publication, you may not always analyze your work in terms of these principles, but you should at least keep them in mind:

- **Be consistent.** Elements on a page should be repeated in appropriate places. Consistency is particularly important in longer publications such as books. The more structured you make your design, the easier producing the piece will be.

The best way to enforce consistent design is to create a meaningful style sheet for your publication. Microsoft Publisher 2000 can help you apply styles or formats to text, objects, tables, and other page elements. Just as word processor documents can have style sheets, Microsoft Publisher 2000 can import or create text styles. You can put together your Microsoft Publisher 2000 project more quickly and more consistently if you use a well-developed style sheet and template rather than simply develop on the fly. Using one of 1,600 templates that Microsoft Publisher 2000 offers is a good way to ensure consistency. To ensure consistency across different document types, use the Publications by Design wizards.

✔ **Put things where people tend to see them.** People have a tendency to view a page in a diagonal from the top left to the bottom right. Elements in the center of the page get the most attention; elements at the bottom left and top right get the least attention.

Your design should treat a two-page spread as if it were a single page because the entire two-page spread is the unit of design that readers see.

✔ **Keep your message simple.** To make your reader focus on the content, consider the following:

- Use white space. Many well-designed pieces have a white space content of 50 percent.

- Limit yourself to no more than two fonts on a page.

- Be judicious with color — apply it as highlighting.

✔ **Keep related or similar information on a page.** Keep related information close together or aligned.

You can create a block of related elements by separating them from other elements on the page with rules (lines), frames (boxes), or white space. Likewise, if a graphic relates to a story, the graphic should appear close to the story. Any caption for the graphic should appear close to the graphic.

✔ **Align everything on a page with something.** Create a grid and place your page elements on that grid, as described in Chapter 4. Creating a *page grid* for a layout is akin to creating an outline for a written document.

The same page grid can produce order on pages *without* producing pages that look alike. For example, three- and four-column newspapers and newsletters are so common because you can produce many looks within those formats. You can have blocks in the grid that are not filled in, for example, and graphics that span multiple blocks. Figure 2-1 is a four-column grid with three rows. This layout generates 12 blocks and offers a lot of flexibility. Figures 2-2 through 2-4 show you three examples that use this grid layout.

✔ **Provide contrast to enliven your work.** Balance consistency by doing the unexpected.

✔ **Use a page hierarchy.** If you have a large headline, the reader will probably start reading the page there. You can use smaller headlines to divide a page into sections. You can also use vertical and horizontal rules to break your page into blocks and provide contrast. Emphasize what's important by making it look different, but don't emphasize parts of your page that have less importance.

Figure 2-1:
A 4-x-3
page grid.

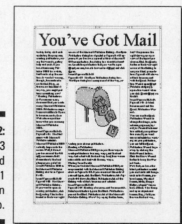

Figure 2-2:
The 4-x-3
page grid
with a 1:2:1
column
setup.

Figure 2-3:
The 4-x-3 page grid with a 2:1:1 column setup.

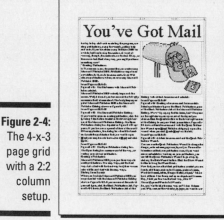

Figure 2-4:
The 4-x-3 page grid with a 2:2 column setup.

The columns in your page grid don't *have* to be the same width, and the pages in a two-page spread don't *have* to be balanced or symmetrical. I think that balanced pages are boring. I tend to vary the size and placement of graphics across columns. I also favor the use of sidebars, pull-quotes (short statements that summarize information on a page), large initial capitals, and column shadings to break up the page.

Desktop Style Resources

Desktop publishing has turned millions of people into typographers and typesetters. Using type and doing typography is not a skill that comes naturally to most people, however. The many rules and guidelines specific to page layout don't pertain to typewritten text or text prepared in word processors. The following resources can help you make the transition from text documents to desktop publications.

Two of the most accepted style guides for clear writing in the United States for the English language are the following:

- ✔ *The Elements of Style,* 3rd Edition, by William Strunk, Jr. and E. B. White (published by Macmillan)
- ✔ *The Chicago Manual of Style,* 14th Edition (published by The University of Chicago Press)

A number of texts specialize in the handling of type. In addition to *The Chicago Manual of Style,* the following books are worthy additions to your library:

- ✔ *Words into Type* (published by Prentice Hall)
- ✔ *Hart's Rules for Compositors and Readers* (published by University Press)
- ✔ *Pocket Pal,* 14th Edition (published by International Paper Company)

The following two small texts are noteworthy for beginning users because they deal with typographical issues in a friendly way:

- ✔ *The PC Is Not a Typewriter,* by Robin Williams (published by Peachpit Press)
- ✔ *The Desktop Style Guide,* by James Felici (published by Bantam Computer Books)

Desktop publishing has its own language. Each typography reference work mentioned in this section helps you keep your picas separate from your points, your en dashes from your em dashes, and your verso from your recto.

Everything Costs Money

Your budget can play a prominent role in the design of your publication. You don't want to merrily design something only to be shocked by the sticker price when you arrive at the printer. A good designer always asks the question, "How much were you intending to spend?" straight out because it helps to ground the project in reality. Perhaps good designers ask the question also because it helps them set their pay scale.

Just because a project has a limited budget doesn't mean that the publication has to be poorly designed. It simply means that you must rely on techniques that not only enhance your work but also are within your budget. I have seen creative, effective, and attractive pieces produced on a limited budget, and I have seen expensively designed pieces that belong in the Desktop Publishing Hall of Shame. It takes experience and good judgment to get the most out of what you have to spend.

Establish a good working relationship with the staff at your print shop. They can help you in the early design phase by suggesting paper and color selections. Inquire about their price breaks for quantity printing. They can also supply you with the correct printer driver to install so that your design both formats correctly on your screen and prints correctly to their printer.

Chapter 3

Basic Training

In This Chapter

▶ Launching Microsoft Publisher 2000

▶ Touring the Microsoft Publisher 2000 interface

▶ Customizing your options

▶ Creating, finding, opening, and saving files

1 call this chapter "Basic Training" because I discuss things that you need to know to get on with your work in Microsoft Publisher 2000. If you make a mess, this chapter tells you how to clean up after yourself.

If you know how to create, open, find, close, and save files, then you can probably get by without reading this chapter. Still, Windows 98 and Microsoft Publisher 2000 offer you new ways to perform these tasks. Chances are that you'll discover methods you didn't know about by reading this chapter. A few seconds saved here, a few seconds saved there, and before you know it, you have time to do all sorts of things. I think that this chapter will repay your reading time with improved productivity.

Launch Time

When you install Microsoft Publisher 2000 on your computer, the Installer creates an entry on the Programs submenu of the Start menu. Using the menus is probably the easiest way to launch, or start up, Microsoft Publisher 2000, but the following list contains other methods that you might want to know:

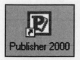

✔ Choose Start⇨Programs⇨Microsoft Publisher, as shown in Figure 3-1.

✔ Locate the program icon, shown in the margin, and double-click it.

The program itself was installed in the Microsoft Publisher 2000 folder that is located inside the Program Files folder, which you can navigate to by using Windows Desktop or Windows Explorer.

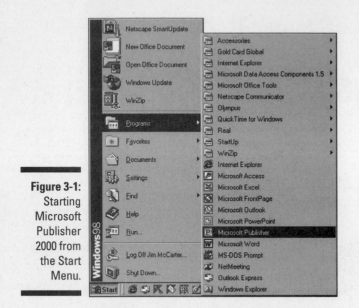

Figure 3-1:
Starting
Microsoft
Publisher
2000 from
the Start
Menu.

✔ Double-click the publication file icon that you want to open. Microsoft Publisher 2000 launches with the publication file you double-clicked open on the screen.

✔ Microsoft Publisher 2000 is a drag-and-drop–enabled program. You can navigate to and click the file icon for the publication that you want to open; then, you drag the file and drop it into Microsoft Publisher 2000. The program opens that publication on your screen.

What's All This on My Screen?

In this section, I show you the names and uses of all the buttons, bars, and bows within Microsoft Publisher 2000. I'm not going to give you fine details here about all the interface elements that are standard fare for Windows 98. I assume that you already know how to use the menu bar; title bar; scroll bars; Minimize, Maximize, and Restore buttons; and mouse pointer. If you are not familiar with standard Windows 98 features, please refer to a beginning text on Windows, such as *Windows 98 For Dummies,* by Andy Rathbone (published by IDG Books Worldwide, Inc.) or your Windows manual.

Microsoft Publisher 2000 uses the term *workspace* to refer to the Microsoft Publisher 2000 window and the customization options. Figure 3-2 shows a blank Microsoft Publisher 2000 publication in a window with labeled interface elements.

Microsoft Publisher 2000 places the following interface elements on your screen:

✔ **The Standard toolbar:** The toolbar contains icons that duplicate menu commands. When you move your pointer over each button, a ScreenTip appears to tell you what the button represents. Looking from left to right in Figure 3-3, you see the following buttons on the toolbar: New, Open, Save, Print, Cut, Copy, Paste, Format Painter, Undo, Redo, Bring to Front, Send to Back, Custom Rotate, Show Special Characters, Zoom, Zoom In, Zoom Out, and Microsoft Publisher Help. Depending on your program's current status, some buttons may be disabled.

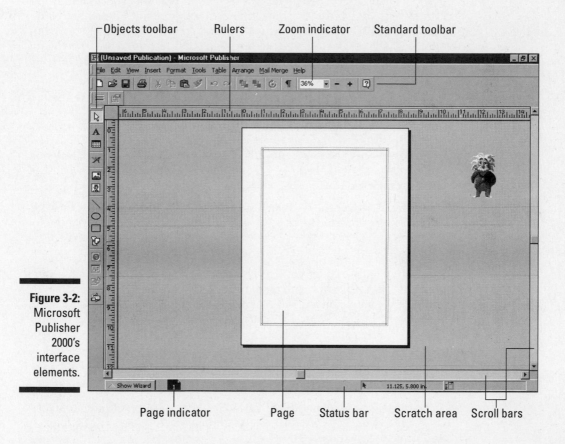

Figure 3-2: Microsoft Publisher 2000's interface elements.

Figure 3-3: The Standard toolbar with buttons labeled.

Save   Paste   Bring to Front   Zoom In
New   Cut   Undo   Custom Rotate   Zoom Out

Open   Copy   Redo   Zoom
Print   Format Painter   Microsoft Publisher Help
Send to Back   Show Special Characters

If you have an object selected on your layout, you may see an additional Formatting toolbar for that object below the Microsoft Publisher 2000 Standard toolbar (which is always on your screen). For example, when you have a line selected, you see a toolbar that lets you add arrowheads; flip and rotate the line; and change line weights, stroke (the outline), and fill colors.

TIP

If you find the ScreenTips distracting, or you just plain don't like them (I find them helpful) you can easily turn them off in the Toolbar Options dialog box. Select View➪Toolbars➪Options to open the Toolbar Options dialog box. Click to remove the check mark from the Show ScreenTips on toolbars checkbox. As you will notice when you open this dialog box, you can also show — or hide — ScreenTips for objects and show short-cut keys in ScreenTips.

You can customize the toolbars and rulers that you see by selecting the appropriate commands from the View menu. I talk about these in the following section.

✔ **The Objects toolbar:** The fourteen buttons in the Objects toolbar (on the left in Figure 3-2) let you create objects or insert objects from other sources. These buttons also display ScreenTips. The Pointer tool lets you select objects on a page. When you create an object on your layout, that object and the Pointer tool are automatically selected so that you can work with your new object.

TIP

Here's a good Objects toolbar trick. If you plan to use the same tool repeatedly, hold the Ctrl key and click the tool. That tool stays selected until you click another tool.

✔ **The rulers:** The horizontal and vertical rulers aid in positioning objects on your screen. You can move the zero point of the rulers by clicking and dragging the intersection button or the ruler.

A *guide* is a dotted line used to position objects on your page. If you want to create a guide, hold down the Shift key when you click and drag a ruler. You can set a feature called Snap to Guides by choosing Tools➪Snap to Guides (or Ctrl+W). Objects that you create close to the guide automatically move to align with the guide. You can also choose

Tools⇨Snap to Ruler <u>M</u>arks and <u>T</u>ools⇨Snap to Obje<u>c</u>ts for corresponding kinds of alignment. In the next chapter, I have much more to say about the rulers, guides, and methods that you can use for accurately positioning objects on a layout.

✔ **The Page Navigation Control:** To the right of the Show Wizard button — this may be labeled the Hide Wizard button if the Wizard window is open — on the Status Bar is the Page Navigation Control. The pages in your publication are represented by little page icons with numbers. The highlighted, or black, page shows your current page. To move to any given page in your publication, just click its icon. If you are viewing your publication in Two-Page Spread mode, two page icons will be highlighted.

✔ **The Zoom indicator:** If you have previously used Microsoft Publisher 98, you will notice that the Zoom indicator has been relocated to the Standard toolbar. Someone must have told those clever programmers at Microsoft that just about every other Microsoft program has the Zoom indicator located in the Standard toolbar. The indicator's text box shows your current magnification. You can click the down arrow to open a drop-down list that lets you change your magnification. You can also use the Zoom In (+) and Zoom Out (-) buttons next to the text box to change your view.

✔ **The scroll bars:** Click the arrows at the ends of the scroll bars to move incrementally; click the scroll bar itself to move a screenful; or click and drag the button (what some folks call the elevator) on the scroll bar to move your window view as much as you want.

✔ **The status bar:** Below the horizontal scroll bar is the status bar. It contains information that changes along with your changing activities on-screen. For example, if you have a layout object selected, the Current Position box shows the object's on-screen position; the Object Size box shows the object's dimensions. If you have not selected anything, the Current Position tracks your mouse pointer's position on-screen and the Object Size box indicates the size of any area that you've dragged around (a selection rectangle). Keep an eye on the status bar as you move about. It features other helpful messages and is a most useful positioning aid.

The dimensions that you see in the ruler and the status bar are in inches by default. You can set other units for dimensions and other program preferences by making selections from the Options dialog box. You open this dialog box by choosing <u>T</u>ools⇨<u>O</u>ptions.

✔ **The page:** The page is the white area where your page design appears, sometimes referred to as the *printable area*. Margins appear as blue dotted lines. The stuff that appears outside the margin box is the *nonprintable area*. Makes sense to me.

✓ **The work (or scratch) area:** Although the gray area surrounding your page looks dead and useless, it is not. The work area is a pasteboard that you can use to position objects that you want to use at a later date or to modify objects without having to disrupt your layout. You can think of the pasteboard as your scratch area, and you can use it for any purpose that comes to mind. Well, almost.

✓ **The Help system:** Microsoft has been hard at work updating Microsoft Publisher 2000 so that it looks and works more like the other programs in the Microsoft Office 2000 suite. One of the changes was the Help system. No more clunky Help windows trying to hog a third of your screen. Now you can get help from the same Office Assistants that the other Office 2000 programs use. Haven't met any of the Office Assistants? Let me introduce them:

- **Clippit:** Just a paperclip with eyes? Perhaps, but he knows all about Publisher 2000.

- **Dot:** A little red ball just bouncing off the walls to tell you about Publisher 2000.

- **F1:** A prototype 300/M series robot. Your question about Publisher 2000 is his command.

- **The Genius:** My personal favorite. He doesn't know any more about Publisher 2000 than the other Office Assistants, but he sure *looks* smarter.

- **Office Logo:** The least imaginative of the bunch, the Office Logo can help put the pieces of the Publisher 2000 puzzle together.

- **Mother Nature:** Watch as she transforms herself from a globe into a dove, a volcano, or a flower. A world of Publisher 2000 knowledge at your fingertips.

- **Links**: For the cat lover. Purrrfectly suited to helping you find the answers to your Publisher 2000 questions.

- **Rocky**: For the dog lover. Don't worry; he's Office-trained. Go fetch help, Rocky! Go on!

If your Office Assistant has wandered off, you can bring it back on the job by selecting the Office Assistant. The Office Assistant obligingly reappears, ready to answer your every Publisher 2000 question. Simply click the Office Assistant. A cartoon-like dialog box pops-up, asking what you would like to do. Type your question in plain English and click Search. The Office Assistant presents you with a list of topics that it thinks will best address your question. Click the topic you want help on, or click See more . . . for additional topics. When you click a topic, the Publisher Help window appears, as shown in Figure 3-4, and with luck it has the answer to your question.

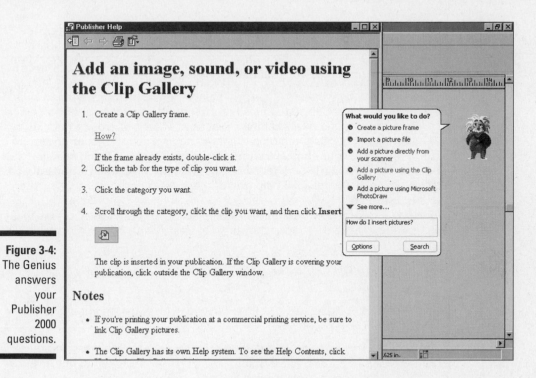

Figure 3-4:
The Genius
answers
your
Publisher
2000
questions.

If the topic you clicked brought you an answer to your question, great. Close the Publisher Help window by clicking the Close button. If the topic you clicked did not answer your question, you can click a different topic. No luck? Try rephrasing your question. Don't forget to click the Search button or else the Office Assistant stares at you as if you were a bug on a stick.

Microsoft Publisher 2000's excellent online documentation leads you to discussions on topics by using keywords. As you navigate tasks, you come to Help system screens called How Tos. They give you step-by-step directions on how to perform a task. Microsoft is now using this technique to "write down" its manuals and save trees.

The Help system has a number of features that you may want to check out, including Publisher Tutorials, keyboard shortcuts, technical support information, a connection to the Microsoft Publisher 2000 Web site, and even a Detect and Repair feature, which attempts to fix Publisher 2000 if it starts misbehaving.

For persons with a disability, Microsoft Publisher 2000 has alternate methods for using the interface. Open and read the PUBREAD.HLP file. Use Windows Explorer to open the file in \Program Files\Microsoft Office\Office.

Options and More Options. . .

I like to have things my way — just ask my wife — so I like to mess around with the way my programs work. I used to think that this was due to having too much time on my hands. But now I have no extra time on my hands, and I recognize that, although sometimes entertaining, spending a lot of time playing with a program's options can be a real time waster. Microsoft Publisher 2000 offers you options that you can set to change the way the program works. You make your choices in four tabs of the Options dialog box that you can view by choosing Tools⇨Options. The General tab of the Options dialog box, as shown in Figure 3-5, is the first of these tabs.

When you click the Edit tab and the User Assistance tabs of the Options dialog box, you view the dialog boxes shown in Figures 3-6 and 3-7, respectively.

Figure 3-5:
The General
tab of the
Options
dialog box.

Figure 3-6:
The Edit tab
of the
Options
dialog box.

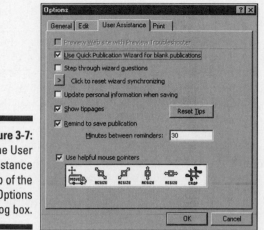

Figure 3-7:
The User
Assistance
tab of the
Options
dialog box.

Clicking the Print tab of the Options dialog box brings forth the dialog box shown in Figure 3-8.

Figure 3-8:
The Print
tab of the
Options
dialog box.

I refer to the selections in the Options dialog box throughout this book when the options that fit the features are being discussed. I want to draw your attention to the highlights. First, you can get a quick explanation of any option by right-clicking the option and selecting What's This? from the pop-up menu. Alternatively, if you click the Help button (?) at the right side of the dialog box title bar, you can left-click a feature to get the same explanation — standard Windows 98 behavior.

Some of the more useful options in Microsoft Publisher 2000's Options dialog box that you may want to reset are as follows:

✔ **Measurement units:** Found on the General tab. Select Inches (the default), Centimeters, Picas, or Points from this drop-down list box.

Inches and Centimeters are probably familiar to most people. If you haven't worked with type before, the Points and Picas options may be unfamiliar. A *point* is a unit of measure based upon the smallest feature that a designer was supposed to be able to make in lead type for move-able type. There are 72 points per inch; you can convince yourself of this fact by drawing a 1-inch line on-screen and changing the Measurement units to Points. Then you can read the object's new size in the status bar.

The use of points has a practical application in the design of computer monitors. Most computer monitors create pixels at approximately 72 dots per inch so that type is represented well on-screen.

Picas are a somewhat larger unit of measurement in the typographical world. A *pica* is equal to 12 points, or approximately ⅙ inch. Actually, a pica is 0.166 inch, making 30 picas equal to 4.98 inches. Most page-layout programs ignore this small differential, however, and set the pica to exactly ⅙ inch, as is the case with Microsoft Publisher 2000. (Be grateful that Microsoft Publisher 2000 doesn't trouble us with Ciceros, Didots, and other arcane typographical measurements.)

✔ **Use Catalog at startup:** Found on the General Tab. Turn this option off if you want Microsoft Publisher 2000 to start with a blank publication every time you launch the program.

✔ **Menus show recently used commands first:** Found on the General tab. One of the nifty new features of Publisher 2000 is its ability to remember which menu commands you use. By default, Publisher 2000 lists the menu choices you use first at the top of the drop-down menus. If you want to see all the menu items when you select a menu, click this check box to remove the check mark.

✔ **Use single-click object creation:** Found on the Edit tab. If you want to click an object and have it appear at a default size, leave this option checked. Otherwise, you must click and drag the object to create it. No matter which method you select, you can always resize any object later.

✔ **Use helpful mouse pointers:** Found on the User Assistance tab. Whether the iconic mouse pointers are useful and helpful is a matter of personal preference. If you want to have more standard Windows-type pointers, click this option off. The small window below the check box shows the style of mouse pointers that you have selected.

✔ **Show tippages:** Tippages? Well, that is a set of helpful hints and dialog boxes that pops up whenever you do something that Microsoft Publisher 2000 thinks you may be able to do better.

For example, if you draw a straight line manually, Microsoft Publisher 2000 pops up a dialog box telling you that you can constrain lines to the horizontal and vertical directions by holding down the Shift key. To reset tips so that they show up again when using a feature that you have used before, click the Reset Tips button.

✔ **Remind to save publication: Minutes between reminders:** This check box and its corresponding text box tell Microsoft Publisher 2000 to post a dialog box every so many minutes that you specify to remind you to save your work. I think that the default of 15 minutes is a reasonable one and recommend that you leave this feature set on. If you are more paranoid than I am — is that possible? — then set a lower number. Or live carefree and dangerously. It's your choice.

The only selection in the Print tab of the Options dialog box that you probably want to reset is the Automatically display Print Troubleshooter setting. (I cover printing in detail in Chapter 13.) The Print Troubleshooter can come in handy when your printed publication doesn't quite meet your expectations.

Microsoft has decided that Publisher 2000 should more closely resemble the programs in the Microsoft Office suite of applications. Changing the Toolbar options in Publisher 2000 (see the sidebar and Figure 3-9 that follow) will cause those same options to be changed in your other Microsoft Office 2000 applications such as Word, Excel, PowerPoint, Access, and Outlook.

Figure 3-9:
The Toolbar
Options
dialog box.

Help yourself

You don't like the Office Assistant? You can turn off the Office Assistant by removing the check mark from the Use the Office Assistant option on the Options tab of the Office Assistant dialog box. Access this dialog box by right-clicking the Office Assistant and selecting Options from the context menu. Click OK to close the Office Assistant dialog box.

TECHNICAL STUFF

Some sticky details about customizing Microsoft Publisher 2000

Microsoft Publisher 2000 customization is a fairly straightforward process. Most customization settings, such as Use helpful mouse pointers, are program-level settings. Program-level settings are in effect every time you use Microsoft Publisher 2000, or until you change them again. Other settings, such as Zoom, are session-level settings. Session-level settings remain in effect for as long as you remain in Microsoft Publisher 2000 without exiting. After you exit Microsoft Publisher 2000 and reload it, these settings return to their original states. Still other settings, such as Start publication with page, are publication-level settings. Publication-level settings are specific to individual publications; they have no effect on other publications.

How do you tell one type of setting from another? I favor a Ouija board. If you don't have a Ouija board (and the spirit moves you), by the time you finish this book, you should know. The best thing to do in the meantime is to check your settings anytime you begin working with a publication. And it's not really all that important that your copy of Microsoft Publisher 2000 works exactly as I describe — as long as you realize why it doesn't work that way and how you can fix it if you want to.

If you want to change your view of the interface elements that appear in Microsoft Publisher 2000, right-click a blank area of the workspace to view the context-sensitive menu and point to Toolbars. If a check mark appears next to an element's name in the menu, that interface element appears in your view of Microsoft Publisher 2000. To remove an element from view, click the interface element's name on the menu, thereby removing the check mark.

If you select the Options command from that menu, you view the Toolbar Options dialog box, as shown in Figure 3-9. (This command is available on the context menu that appears anywhere you right-click in Microsoft Publisher 2000. Just point to Toolbars and you will see it at the bottom of the submenu that pops up.) In addition to removing elements from view, you can choose to turn off Large icons (view small ones), remove or Show ScreenTips on toolbars and objects, and Show shortcut keys in ScreenTips. You can also elect to have menus display with a sliding or unfolding motion by selecting a Menu animations setting. I show you figures in this book with all these features turned on.

To show the Help system, do any of the following:

- ✔ Press F1.
- ✔ Click the Microsoft Publisher Help button at the extreme right of the Standard toolbar.
- ✔ Select Publisher Help from the menu.

The Help system window consists of two panes (see Figure 3-10). Use the pane on the left — the navigations pane — to ask your questions. Use the pane on the right — the topic pane — to read Publisher's answers to your questions. The Help system shows up in its own window. You can manipulate this window just like any other. You can resize or move the window to your heart's desire. After you have the information you are looking for displayed in the right pane, you may choose to hide the left pane by clicking the Hide button located on the left side of the button bar below the Title bar. Use the Back and Forward buttons — the left and right pointing arrows, respectively — to retrace the steps of your journey through Help land. The button that looks like a printer (I bet you knew this!) prints the contents of the right pane. The last button — the one that looks like a hand holding a piece of paper — is the Options button. Click the Options button to reveal a drop-down list that includes commands to hide the navigation pane, move back or forward through previously viewed topic panes, and print the current help topic.

To hide the navigation panel, click the Hide button.

The navigation pane of the Help window contains three tabs: Contents, Answer Wizard, and Index.

Figure 3-10: The Help system opens with both the navigation and topics panes showing.

The Contents tab lists a series of "books" containing information about various topics. Click a book to open it and reveal its contents. Books contain pages — no surprise there — and other books. Continue opening books until you see the page that describes the subject that you want help on. Click the page to have its contents displayed in the topics pane on the right.

The Answer Wizard tab works just like the Office Assistant. Simply type your question in the What would you like to do? text box and click Search. Click the topic that most closely describes what you need help with in the Select topic to display list box; your help information is then displayed in the topics pane on the right.

The Help system is not context sensitive. That is, you don't simply jump to a topic of interest based on your current condition or selected feature when the Index panel opens. You can tell Microsoft Publisher 2000 to jump to Help on a specific topic, however, by doing one of two things:

✔ Select a topic in the Index panel.

✔ Right-click an object in your window and select the Help command from the bottom of that context-sensitive menu.

Figure 3-11 shows you a sample context-sensitive menu for a table.

As you move from task to task in the Help panel, the Help system remembers your path through it.

Figure 3-11: A context-sensitive menu for a table.

✂	Cut
📋	Copy
📋	Paste
	Delete Text
	Delete Object
	Change Text ▶
	Change Table ▶
	Proofing Tools ▶
	Whole Page
	Page Width
	Actual Size
	Selected Objects
	Help on This Table

To return to a previous Help topic, click the Back button, which appears just above the Contents tab. By doing so, you retrace your steps in the reverse order.

Finding a topic

The Index tab works sort of like the Answer Wizard tab. Type a word in the Type keywords text box and click the Search button. Select a topic in the Choose a topic list box and read all about it in the topics pane on the right.

The manual contains a number of How To icons with keywords for you to search the Help system on. Enter those words into the "1 Type keywords" text box.

Try a synonym to find related instructions and explanations.

When you click the menu or anywhere else in the Microsoft Publisher 2000 window, the Help window disappears. Click the Publisher Help button on the taskbar to bring it back. When you are finished with the Help windows, click its Close button.

Inch-by-inch; step-by-step

When you click a topic in the navigation pane of the Help window, the topics pane will display either a list of related topics or, sometimes, a list of numbered steps to achieve your goal. Figure 3-12 shows an example of step-by-step instructions.

The topics pane may also contain blue, underlined text. Place the mouse pointer over the blue, underlined text and the pointer turns into a hand. The hand pointer indicates that you are pointing at a hyperlink. Click the hyperlink to view information that is relevant to the current help topic.

In How To help, colored text opens a pop-up window with an explanation, similar to the More Info topics.

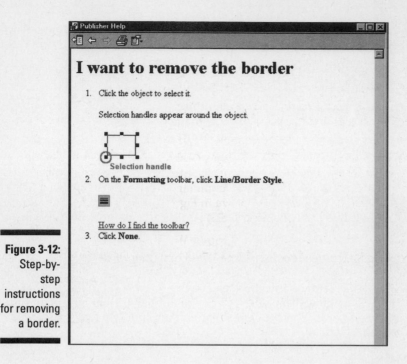

Figure 3-12:
Step-by-
step
instructions
for removing
a border.

Things You Can Do with Files

Files are what you use to store your work or your data in a computer. I like to look at my work, so I spend a lot of time staring at the Windows Explorer window. Microsoft Publisher 2000 files are called *publications* and have a PUB file extension. You can create files, open and close files, modify them, and save the changes that you make to your files. You need to do most file tasks that I've mentioned from within Microsoft Publisher 2000. You can apply what you know about files in general to Microsoft Publisher 2000 files, however.

Playing with files on the outside

Following is a short list of the tasks that you can do outside Microsoft Publisher 2000:

✔ **To select a file(s):** Click the file on Windows Desktop or Windows Explorer or click and drag a selection rectangle around a set of contiguous files. You can also hold down the Shift key and click additional files to extend or reduce your range of selected files.

✔ **To move a file:** On Windows Desktop or Windows Explorer, click and drag the file to a new location.

✔ **To copy a file:** On Windows Desktop or Windows Explorer, press Ctrl and click and drag the file to a new location.

Okay, I know that you can accomplish this same task inside Microsoft Publisher 2000 by using the Save As command to copy a file. But this is much, much faster to perform in the interface.

✔ **To create a shortcut file:** On Windows Desktop or Windows Explorer, click and drag the file to a new location with the right mouse button. Select the Create Shortcut(s) Here command from the context-sensitive menu, an example of which is shown in Figure 3-13. (This menu is also a shortcut to copying and moving files.)

✔ **To delete a file:** On Windows Desktop or Windows Explorer, click the file to select it and then press Delete. Or click and drag the file to the Recycle Bin.

Figure 3-13:
The context-
sensitive
menu for
dragging a
file in
Windows.

One of the things that I love about Windows 98 is that these actions are now recoverable. If you think that you've made a mistake, you can choose Edit⇨Undo or press Ctrl+Z in your current Desktop folder or Windows Explorer, and the action is reversed. Cool! If you make a mistake and delete a file that you didn't intend to delete, all is not lost. Open the Recycle Bin folder, select that file in the list, and choose File⇨Restore. Your file jumps back to its original location.

Your deleted file is not actually in jeopardy until you give the Empty Recycle Bin command or until the Recycle Bin fills up and needs the space. In that case, the first file in is the first one that is deleted (FIFO, or first in, first out). If the deletion was done through the menu command and not due to disk space requirements, you still may be able to recover your file. Restart your computer in MS-DOS mode and use the Recover command to try to get your file back. Or go out and get a file utility program such as Norton Utilities to provide you with the recovering function. The most important thing that you can do if you empty the Recycle Bin and need to recover a file is to perform no other file operations in the meantime. That way, the file system is less likely to overwrite the disk sectors that contain the information from the deleted file.

You should never need to recover a publication from the trash. Always keep adequate copies and save your files by using the Backup option described later in this chapter, and you'll be fine.

Now that I've briefly described the things that you can do with files outside Microsoft Publisher 2000 (that you don't want to or can't do inside Microsoft Publisher 2000), I turn my attention to the operations that you want to do inside Microsoft Publisher 2000.

Starting a publication

Microsoft Publisher 2000 prompts you to create a publication every time you start a session — that is, launch the program. You see the Microsoft Publisher Catalog dialog box first (if you haven't turned that option off). If you are already in a Microsoft Publisher 2000 session, you can get to the Microsoft Publisher Catalog dialog box (as shown in Figure 3-14) by choosing File⇨New.

In the Microsoft Publisher Catalog dialog box, Microsoft Publisher 2000 shows you three tabs that give you four ways to create a new publication:

- ✔ **Publications by Wizard:** Lets you create a new publication from a series of dialog boxes that builds your publication based upon selections that you make. Click the Publications by Wizard tab and select the wizard that you want to use. Then click a Preview in the right pane and click Start Wizard.

- ✔ **Publications by Design:** Lets you create sets of publications such as Business Cards, Envelopes, Fax Cover Sheets, and more, that have a consistent look and feel. Select a Design set in the Design Sets pane on the left, click a Preview in the right pane, and then click Start Wizard.

- ✔ **Blank Publications:** Lets you create a new publication from scratch with a generic or blank page format. On the Blank Publications tab, click the type of blank publication that you want to start with, click a Preview in the right pane, and then click Create. You can also click the buttons labeled Custom Page or Custom Web Page for advanced Page Setup options, which I discuss in detail in the next chapter.

- ✔ **Existing Publications:** The Existing Publications button, located in the lower-left corner of both the Publications by Wizard and the Publications by Design tabs, lets you open a publication that has been saved to disk. Click the Existing Publications button, select from the available publications, and click Open. You don't see the publication you want? You may have to navigate to a different folder.

Figure 3-14:
The Blank
Publications
tab of the
Microsoft
Publisher
Catalog
dialog box.

After you make your selections, Microsoft Publisher 2000 opens the new publication in the window on-screen with the title "(Unsaved Publication) - Microsoft Publisher" in the title bar.

You can also open any Microsoft Publisher 2000 publication and perform a Save As command (from the File menu) to create a new publication.

Don't forget to perform a Save or Save As command to save your new publication to disk; otherwise, it may exist only in your memory.

Opening remarks

Microsoft Publisher 2000's Open command now works just like any other Microsoft Office program's Open command. For those of you upgrading from Publisher 98, the Catalog dialog box no longer appears when you choose File➪Open. Publisher 2000 has finally been adopted as a full-fledged member of the Microsoft Office family.

When you open Microsoft Publisher 2000, the program opens the Microsoft Publisher Catalog dialog box to the Publications by Wizard tab. This is Microsoft Publisher 2000 prompting you to create a new file. If you really want an existing publication, though, follow these steps:

1. **Click the Existing Publications button in the lower-left corner of the Microsoft Publisher Catalog dialog box.**

   The Open Publication dialog box is shown in Figure 3-15.

2. **Select the publication of interest (click it).**

   You can look over the publication preview (that is, a thumbnail image of the first page of your publication) in the right pane of the Open dialog box by clicking the down arrow on the Views button and selecting Preview.

3. **Click Open to open the publication.**

After you are in a Microsoft Publisher 2000 session, you need to choose File⇨New to see the Microsoft Publisher Catalog dialog box again. Microsoft Publisher 2000 opens the Microsoft Publisher Catalog dialog box to the Publications by Wizard tab.

Are you smiling yet? What could be more friendly than this? The Open Publication dialog box is a standard Windows interface element, only slightly altered to account for the capabilities that Microsoft Publisher 2000 offers you. You locate files in the file hierarchy by clicking the Look in list box or by using the Up One Level button. The List button and Details button let you change the way that the list box displays the file contents for your current folder.

Figure 3-15:
The Open
Publication
dialog box.

You can filter your view of the File list box contents by selecting the appropriate filter from the Files of type list box. Click the Views button and select Preview if you want to preview the selected files. When you select a file, a preview shows up in the Preview section on the right of the Open Publication dialog box. Click the down arrow on the Open button and select Open Read-only to open the publication in read-only mode. The Open Read-only command lets you view a file without letting you make any changes.

To open two publications simultaneously, you need to launch Microsoft Publisher 2000 a *second* time. Then you can open one publication in each copy of Microsoft Publisher 2000. To move between running copies of Microsoft Publisher 2000, press Alt+Tab to move to the publication that you want to work in. You can also simply click the Taskbar buttons (at the bottom of the Windows 98 screen) to switch between your two running copies of Microsoft Publisher 2000. You can have as many copies of the program running in memory as you have memory to run copies in. I was able to open eleven copies before Windows gave me a low memory warning.

In some cases, having multiple publications open on your screen can actually be useful. Because Microsoft Publisher 2000 is drag-and-drop enabled, you can click an object or frame and drag it to another publication to create a copy of that object.

Finding files

Also tucked away in the Open Publication dialog box is a Find File utility. Select Tools⇨Find to see the Find dialog box shown in Figure 3-16. This dialog box lets you search for Publisher files on any drive that your computer can see. Select a drive to search by clicking the down arrow next to the Look in text box. Make sure the Search subfolders check box has a check, and click Find Now. You are returned to the Open Publication dialog box with all the Publisher files listed on the specified drive.

I want to tell you about a more advanced Find utility, though. To work with the Windows 98 Find utility, choose the Start⇨Find⇨Files or Folders command. The Windows Find dialog box lets you search for files by: name and location, date modified, and advanced searches. Advanced searches includes searching by file type, text contained within, and file size. In the Windows Help system, the "finding, files or folders" topic tells you how to perform searches.

Figure 3-16:
The Find: All
Files dialog
box.

Saving your files means never having to say you're sorry

Microsoft Publisher 2000 lets you save two kinds of files: Microsoft Publisher 2000 publication (PUB) files and various forms of text files. For the most part, when you do page layout in Microsoft Publisher 2000, you are interested in saving publications. Because you can create text in Microsoft Publisher 2000 in the form of stories or stand-alone text frames, Microsoft Publisher 2000 lets you save your text in a number of formats: plain text, interchange formats such as the rich text format (RTF), and any one of several word processor formats. This feature lets you move your text back and forth with agility between Microsoft Publisher 2000 and any standard word processor.

File-saving formats

A PUB file is Microsoft Publisher 2000's proprietary format for saving layout information. Many page layout programs save to a PUB file — but they are not Microsoft Publisher 2000's PUB files. To use a PUB file inside Microsoft Publisher 2000, you have to save a page layout file in another program as a Microsoft Publisher 2000 PUB file. To open a PUB file created in Microsoft Publisher 2000 in another program, you need a mechanism to convert the Microsoft Publisher 2000 PUB file format during the file opening process. Generally speaking, you will not be able to work with PUB files between Microsoft Publisher 2000 and other programs such as Quark XPress or PageMaker because page layout programs implement their page formatting in very different ways.

Windows 98 enables you to use long names with spaces and takes care of the translation to the previous convention (you know, eight-character names with a three-letter file type extension as a suffix, the dreaded *eight dot three*). Use this new capability and name your files something that you can recognize. Don't bother adding the PUB extension. Let Windows 98 handle that detail for you.

Start me up

Your computer has two chief places to keep information: memory (random-access memory or RAM) and storage. Memory exists within little chips buried deep inside your computer. Storage includes your hard disk, your floppy disks, and any CD-ROMs, tapes, or other such computer-information storage devices that you might have.

Memory is where all the work gets done. When Microsoft Publisher 2000 is running, it's running in memory. When you work on a publication, it's also in memory. Memory is very fast and capable, but there's a big problem with it: It's not very good at remembering things. When you shut off your computer or when the power goes off for a moment (someone kicks your power cord or randomly flips circuit breakers in the basement), everything in memory gets wiped out. Similarly, when you close a publication, you lose everything in memory that had to do with that publication. So you see, keeping things only in memory is a dangerous thing.

Storage to the rescue! Although storage is incapable and slow compared with memory, it's very good at remembering things. Even when your computer's power is off, storage can keep track of information. That way, your computer can remember important things from day to day, such as how to run your programs, what publications you created yesterday, and the phone number of that cute laptop computer it met the other day. When you load Microsoft Publisher 2000, your computer actually makes a copy of the program that's in storage, puts the copy in memory, and works with it there.

Saving is just the reverse process. When you save a publication, your computer takes a copy of what's in memory and places that copy in storage. That way, if memory gets wiped out for any reason, you still have a copy of your work. When you later want to look at your publication, you just ask your computer to reverse the process again, copying the publication back from storage into memory. This is called *opening*.

Publications — well, all computer files, actually — are quite unwilling to share their names with another file in the same folder. Multiple files with the same name can exist in different locations among your computer's disks, however. If you try to save a publication to a folder in which a publication of that same name already exists, Microsoft Publisher 2000 opens a dialog box to warn you of the impending duel to the death. Click the Yes button in this dialog box to overwrite the first file with your new one. Click the No button to return to your publication.

Working with text is an entirely different matter. There's a way of getting text into and out of just about any word processor that you want to work in. You can save text to any one of the following text formats:

- **Plain text:** This format saves text only as lower ASCII characters in a TXT file. Plain text includes alphanumeric characters and a few common symbols. All formatting and font information is lost. All word processors open TXT files. This is your lowest common denominator, but saving in this format does not preserve all your work.

- **Rich Text Format:** The RTF format is an *interchange* format developed by Microsoft to let programs exchange text files that contain formatting information. In the files, instructions on how to format specific characters and paragraphs are contained in directions given as plain text characters. Most word processors support opening and saving RTF files.

- **Word Processor Filters:** Microsoft Publisher 2000 contains some filters to save text to specific file formats. These formats include the following: Word 2.*x* for Windows; Works 3.0 for Windows; Works 4.0 for Windows; Windows Write; Word 6.0/95; WordPerfect 5.*x;* WordPerfect 5.1 for DOS; WordPerfect 5.*x* for Windows; WordPerfect 5.1 or 5.2 Secondary File; WordPerfect 5.0 Secondary File; Word 97 & 6.0/95 RTF.

Microsoft Publisher 2000 can open and import from most file formats to which it can save text; that is, it can bring text files from these other formats into your Microsoft Publisher 2000 layout. I say more about this aspect of Microsoft Publisher 2000 in Chapter 6. For the sake of completeness, though, here's the list of formats that Microsoft Publisher 2000 can use to import text files: Plain Text; Plain Text (DOS); Rich Text Format; Word 6.0/95 for Windows & Macintosh; Word (Asian versions) 6.0/95; Word 97; Recover Text from Any File; WordPerfect 5.*x;* WordPerfect 6.*x;* Microsoft Excel Worksheet; Windows Write; Word 2.*x* for Windows; Works 3.0 for Windows; Works 4.0 for Windows.

I must say that if you can't get your word processing files into and out of Microsoft Publisher 2000 by using this list of formats, it's time to replace your word processor. Every word processor I know of can convert at least one of these formats.

File-saving mechanics

Here's the deal about saving your files:

- Anything that you see on your screen belongs to your computer.

- Anything that you save to disk belongs to you.

  It's really that simple. If you forget to save your work, then anytime the power goes out, your work is lost. By default, Microsoft Publisher 2000 pops a dialog box on the screen, telling you that it is time to save your work. Get in the habit of clicking Yes.

Don't forget to save early and often. When you create a new publication, it doesn't really exist until you save it to disk.

To save your file, do one of the following:

- ✔ Choose the File➪Save (or Ctrl+S) or the File⌐Save As command.
- ✔ Click the Save button (shown in the margin) on the Standard toolbar.

For a new publication, the Save command is identical to the Save As command. If you choose either command, the standard Save As dialog box (shown in Figure 3-17) appears. The dialog box prompts you to choose a Save in location and to specify a File name. After you save the file once, any subsequent Save command saves your changes without posting the Save As dialog box again. The Save As command enables you to create a new file or overwrite your old one.

Figure 3-17:
The Save As dialog box in List view.

The Save As dialog box is a Windows 98 feature that is only slightly modified to account for features that Microsoft Publisher 2000 offers. If locating a file in the Windows 98 file system is new to you, you might want to read a basic Windows text such as Andy Rathbone's _Windows 98 For Dummies,_ from IDG Books Worldwide, Inc., or review the manual that came with Windows 98.

You can change how files look in the file list box by clicking the Views button just to the left of the Tools button below the title bar. Figure 3-18 shows you the Save As dialog box in Details view.

If you want to locate a file in the file system, you can use the Up One Level button to move up the hierarchy or click the Save in drop-down list box to move about any distance. If you want to create a new folder, go to the folder that will enclose it, click the New Folder button, and enter the name of the folder in place of the highlighted name of "New Folder" that you see in the text box.

Here's a good trick for you to remember. If you right-click an item in a standard file dialog box, you generally get help. When you right-click a file or folder in the file list box, you get a fairly substantial context-sensitive menu that gives you file-maintenance selections. Figure 3-19 shows you an example of this menu for a file in the Save As dialog box. The good thing about Save As dialog box tricks is that they work in Open dialog boxes as well.

Figure 3-18:
The Save As dialog box in Details view.

Figure 3-19:
A context-sensitive menu in the Save As dialog box.

As you create a publication, save multiple copies of it as you progress. Then, if you decide that you like the publication better in a previous state, you can return to it. You can never be too thin, have too much RAM, or have too many backups.

Insurance, please

I have figured out that I can't always count on a hard drive working, so I back up to another hard drive, tape, or floppy disks. And I assume that my first backup is going to fail, so I back up anything important once again. Have I told you that I am paranoid? Well, just because I'm paranoid doesn't mean that they are not out to get me.

If you click the down arrow on the Save button, you see a Save with Backup option. The Save with Backup option does two things for you. It allows you to return to your last previously saved state of the file — what other programs call a Revert — and it protects you from file corruption by giving you a backup to revert to. Publications can become large and complex, which makes them more susceptible to corruption than smaller files. (This is also true of files that are used frequently, such as font files.)

Backup files do not contain any changes that you made to your publication since you last saved the file. That is, if you save a publication three times during a session, the backup publication contains the file in the state that it was in after two saves.

You can recover from a computer disaster by saving a *backup* copy of a publication, one that contains the BAK extension. You don't see these files in the Existing Publications tab unless you have already opened them. You can search for backup files by using the phrase "backup of *" in the Find this file text box of the Find File dialog box (see discussion earlier in this chapter). Double-click the backup file of interest. It opens, and you can work in that copy and save it out to a new file with a name of your choosing. From then on, the backup file is one of your choices in the Existing Publications tab.

A backup file takes the same name as your original publication but uses the BAK extension. The only drawback to using the Backup option is that it doubles your disk space requirements.

Unless you are in a tight disk space situation, hedge your bet and always select the Backup option.

If you create backups, you can safely tell the dealer, "Hit me."

Canning templates

You can think of a template as a piece of stationery containing all the content and formatting that was in it when you saved the file as a template. Templates provide a convenient starting place for your work and capture details that you want to make sure that you don't change. Template files are stored as PUB files, commonly in the TEMPLATE folder at: <drive>/PROGRAM FILES/MICROSOFT OFFICE/TEMPLATES/PUBLICATIONS.

If you view a template's properties, you see that a template is a file with the Archive bit or file attribute set on. Different programs use this setting for different purposes. You are probably familiar with the use of the Archive bit to determine whether a file has been backed up. A backup program starts by turning off all the Archive settings and then turns them on individually as it performs a backup on that file. Microsoft Publisher 2000 uses the Archive bit to determine that the file is a template and that it cannot be overwritten (changed) by a Save command.

From a practical standpoint, a template lets you create a publication based on that template. That file opens as an *Unsaved Publication,* without any name. When you use a template, the program prompts you to perform a Save As operation. After you have done this and created a new file, this file behaves as any publication would. If you try to save the file to the same location with the same name, Microsoft Publisher 2000 posts a dialog box like the one shown in Figure 3-20. This dialog box warns that a publication already exists and you are going to overwrite the existing file. You can overwrite the file with another template or with a normal publication file.

Figure 3-20:
Overwrite
File alert
box.

Microsoft Publisher

The file M&A On-Site Network Support Brochure.pub already exists. Do you want to replace the existing file?

Yes   No

Nag me

Many programs *autosave* changes for you every so often. Page layout programs, being an artistic endeavor, do not, as a rule, do autosaves. You must manually save your file along with any changes that you make to it that you want to retain. Microsoft Publisher 2000 (being a good dobee, for those of you who remember *Romper Room*) does remind you, however, to save your work from time to time with a pop-up dialog box.

You can change this behavior by eliminating the prompt or changing the frequency of its appearance. Select the Tools⇨Options command and then click the User Assistance tab in the Options dialog box. At the bottom of this dialog box, click the Remind to save publication check box off or enter a new number in the Minutes between reminders text box. This sets the number of minutes that you work inside Microsoft Publisher 2000 before it reminds you to save your publication again.

Another behavior that you might want to set while you are in the User Assistance tab of the Options dialog box is the Show tippages check box. This option posts helpful dialog boxes the first time that you do a particular operation. It also posts dialog boxes when it detects an operation that is causing you difficulty.

Close calls

If you have no changes to save in a file, you can close your publication without further bother by choosing the File⇨Close command. If you made changes, Microsoft Publisher 2000 posts the Save Changes dialog box (shown in Figure 3-21) to ask you to save your changes first before closing the file. Click Yes to save your changes (the default), click No to discard them, or click Cancel to abort the Close operation and continue working in your publication.

Figure 3-21: The Save Changes dialog box.

I know of only four methods that let you close a publication:

- ✔ Choose the aforementioned File⇨Close command.
- ✔ Click the Close box of the Microsoft Publisher 2000 window, at the extreme right of the title bar.
- ✔ Open another publication.
- ✔ Select Exit from the File menu to leave the program.

Shut Down without Crash-Landing

You should close Microsoft Publisher 2000 whenever you are finished using the program or when you are through with your session and want to shut down your computer. You use the Exit command on the File menu to perform this task. If you try to exit Microsoft Publisher 2000 without saving changes made to a file, Microsoft Publisher 2000 posts a dialog box asking whether you want to save your changes. If you have no changes to save, the program closes directly and the memory (RAM) used to store the program is released for use by other programs.

To close Microsoft Publisher 2000, choose the File⇨Exit command or press Alt+F4. Also, you can automatically exit your various programs when you use the Shut Down command from the Windows Start menu.

So far, so good. You won't always be able to close Microsoft Publisher 2000 in the correct way. You may have a program freeze your computer (yes, it still happens in Windows 98, although not as often), or your power may go out. In either case, *all your changes are lost*. Your file saved to disk is unaffected by the power outage. (Oh, did I mention that you should save your work early and often?)

Microsoft Publisher 2000 writes temporary files to disk when it performs certain operations such as file or object insertions, saves, and spooling files to the printer. This protects you from file corruption but requires enough available disk space to complete the operation. The disk space required varies with the complexity of your file. If one of these operations fails, try deleting files and freeing up additional disk space before attempting it again.

TECHNICAL STUFF

Installation advice for the lovelorn

Microsoft Publisher 2000 is one resource-hungry critter. You can get by with running Microsoft Publisher 2000 on any machine on which you can run Microsoft Windows 98 — but you'll be sorry. Microsoft lists the system requirements as the following:

✔ An IBM PC computer or clone with a 486DX or higher processor; a Pentium is recommended. The faster, the better.

✔ Microsoft Windows 95 or the Microsoft Windows NT Workstation operating system version 4.0 or later; Microsoft Publisher 2000 does not run on Windows 3.1.

✔ 8MB of memory for Windows 95, with 16MB or more recommended.

✔ 12MB of memory for Windows NT Workstation, with 32MB recommended.

✔ 24MB disk space for a minimum install, running the program from files on the CD-ROM; 109MB for a typical installation. The CD includes an additional 225MB of clip art and images that you can install to your hard disk or access from the CD.

✔ VGA or higher resolution video adapter (Super VGA for 256-color support recommended).

✔ CD-ROM drive for the CD-ROM version; 2x or greater recommended.

✔ A mouse or other pointing device.

RAM and hard drives are pretty cheap. Consider upgrading if you are going to spend a significant amount of time using Publisher 2000.

Part II
Mark This Page

"THE FUNNY THING IS, I NEVER KNEW THEY _HAD_ DESKTOP PUBLISHING SOFTWARE FOR PAPER SHREDDERS."

In this part ...

This part shows you how to work with pages and objects in ways that make your page layout both faster and more precise. You also see how your selected printer affects your design.

Microsoft Publisher 2000 has many aids to help you design pages carefully, and many different page designs are already built into the program for you. This part also discusses *frames*, which are the containers for the various objects and elements that you place on a page.

Chapter 4

Working with Pages

*W*hen you start a publication, Microsoft Publisher 2000 sets up the basic features of the publication for you — the number of pages, the page size, some margin guides, and so on. This default feature is all well and good if you like the decisions Microsoft Publisher 2000 makes, but what if you want to change things? You may need to change the margins, for example, to accommodate your design and the capabilities of your printer.

This chapter describes your publication's basic element — the page — and how to change your publication's basic structure, from things as minor as adjusting margins to something as major as converting a three-fold brochure into a 15-foot banner.

In the Beginning: The Page

The most basic element of a Microsoft Publisher 2000 publication is the individual page. A page in the computer world is not that different from a page in the real world — it's just a chunk of words and pictures that, when printed, all fit on a single piece of paper.

Pages are designed singly or as part of a multipage spread. Microsoft Publisher 2000 makes it easy for you to move between pages, look at pages in different views and magnifications, and add or delete pages as needed to fit your goals.

Moving from page to page

The *current page* is the active page — that is, the page on which your cursor is currently located. At any time, only one page in your document is the current page, even when you're viewing more than one page at a time. The current page is indicated in the Page Navigation controls located in the lower-left corner of the Publisher window. The current page is the one represented by the black page. All the other pages are white. Figure 4-1 shows the Page Navigation controls.

Figure 4-1:
The Page
Navigation
controls
with page 3
as the cur-
rent page.

`[1 2 3 4 5 6]`

After you have more than one page in your publication, you can move to another page in several ways:

- ✔ Select View⇨Go To Page and then type the number of the page that you want to work on in the Go To Page dialog box, shown in Figure 4-2.

- ✔ Press F5 to open the Go To Page dialog box; Shift+F5 to move to the next page; and Ctrl+F5 to move to the previous page.

- ✔ Press Ctrl+G to display the Go To Page dialog box.

- ✔ Click the page that you want to go to in the Page Navigation controls.

Figure 4-2:
The Go To
Page dialog
box.

Go To Page	? X
Go to page	2
Your publication has 2 pages, numbered 1 through 2.	
OK	Cancel

Scrolling within a page

You use the scroll bars, arrows, and boxes along the right side of your screen to view different parts of the current page. Here's what you can do with the various scroll bar parts:

✔ **Scroll arrows:** Click a scroll arrow to slide your view a little bit in the direction of that arrow. If you press and hold the mouse button down, the publication continues to scroll.

✔ **Scroll boxes:** Drag the scroll box (it slides like an elevator in a shaft) to slide your view any amount in that same direction.

✔ **Scroll bar:** Click above or below the scroll box in the horizontal or vertical scroll bar (the elevator shaft) to slide your view up or down a screenful.

These techniques affect only your view of the current page and do not move you between pages. They are standard Windows interface techniques that work in any Windows window.

In addition to using the scroll bars to move your view of a page in the window, you can use the following keyboard shortcuts:

✔ Press PgDn (Page Down) to move your view a screenful down.

✔ Press PgUp (Page Up) to move your view a screenful up.

✔ Press Ctrl+PgDn to scroll to the right.

✔ Press Ctrl+PgUp to scroll to the left.

With the last two shortcuts, you scroll an amount that varies, depending upon your current magnification and view.

If all this makes Microsoft Publisher 2000 seem like a game of MotoCross Madness or Microsoft Combat Flight Simulator, that's all for the good. These keystrokes save you a lot of time.

Changing What You See On-Screen

In precise page layout work, you want to move quickly between different views and magnifications. You can work with a detail on your layout and then jump to a view that lets you get an overview of your document to see how the change looks in context.

If you are familiar with all the different views that you find in a word processor — for example, the Normal, Outline, and Page Layout views available in Microsoft Word — you may be surprised to find that Microsoft Publisher 2000 offers only one kind of view: a *live* or editable page preview. Why does it offer just this one mode? Because the purpose of a page layout program is to create and display a page the way it will look when you print it.

Even so, Microsoft Publisher 2000 does give you ways to change how your page looks on-screen. Most of these ways reside within the View menu. You can choose to see a single page or a two-page spread, and you can change the magnification of the page or pages that you're viewing.

Two-page spreads

Many publications, including this very book, are designed with pairs of pages that form *facing pages*. Facing pages, also known as a *two-page spread,* are what your reader actually sees — and what you, as a designer, design for.

If you are looking at a single page and want to see your layout as a two-page spread — that is, to see two facing pages side by side — choose the Two-Page Spread command from the View menu. Odd-numbered pages (1, 3, and so on) display on the right side of the Microsoft Publisher 2000 screen, whereas even-numbered pages (2, 4, and so on) display on the left side (unless you've changed the Start publication with page option in the Options dialog box).

The standard setup for professional publications, such as this book, has the text beginning on a right-hand page. Therefore, if your publication has an even number of pages, the first page of the publication displays by itself on the right side of the screen and the last page displays by itself on the left side of the screen. If your publication has only one page, that one page displays by itself on the right side of the Microsoft Publisher 2000 screen.

After you choose the Two-Page Spread command, a check mark appears next to the command on the View menu. Clicking the Two-Page Spread command a second time returns you to the Single page view at your current magnification.

Your publication doesn't *have* to be a facing-page publication to take advantage of the Two-Page Spread view. Use this view at your convenience.

Whole Page and Page Width views

In addition to switching between one- and two-page views, you can view whole pages at one time, or view the pages in the largest magnification that still shows the entire width of the page or two-page spread:

> ✔ Choose View➪Zoom➪Whole Page or press Ctrl+Shift+L to resize your current page or two-page spread so that it appears at the largest possible magnification to fill your screen. This view gives you an overview of your layout.

✔ Choose View⇨Zoom⇨Page Width to switch to a view of your document
that fills the screen horizontally, whether you are in Single page view or
Two-Page Spread view. In this view, you will probably have to scroll vertically to see the entire document, but you won't have to scroll
horizontally.

If you select one or more objects before selecting the command, you will see
a new item on the Zoom submenu: Selected Objects. Selecting this command
will cause Publisher 2000 to resize your page to the largest magnification that
still shows the selected objects.

Figure 4-3 shows a single-page document in Whole Page view. Figure 4-4
shows the same document in Page Width view.

Zoom Indicator Box

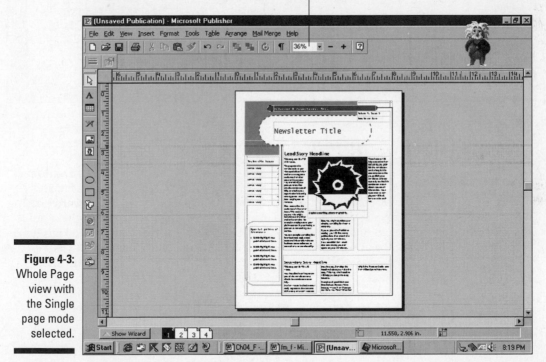

Figure 4-3:
Whole Page
view with
the Single
page mode
selected.

Figure 4-4:
Page Width
view with
the Single
page mode
selected.

Zooming around

The Zoom box (located on the Standard toolbar) tells you your current magnification in a percentage, with 100% being the actual size. To enlarge and reduce the on-screen size of your publications — much as if you were holding a magnifying glass to the screen and then removing that glass — click the down arrow in the Zoom box to reveal the drop-down list, shown in Figure 4-5. The Zoom drop-down list offers the following magnifications: 400%, 200%, 150%, 100%, 75%, 66%, 50%, 33% 25%, 10%, Whole Page, Page Width, and Selected Objects. If you have used the Zoom feature in other Microsoft Office programs, you should feel very comfortable with this feature in Publisher 2000. It works the same way in Publisher 2000 as it does in the other Microsoft Office programs.

This drop-down list is the same menu that you see when you select View⇨Zoom from the menu bar. You see the Selected Objects command on the Zoom drop-down list only when you have an object selected on the layout. This command magnifies the layout to the largest view that still contains the object, and centers the object on your screen. If you right-click anywhere on the layout, you will see the Whole Page, Page Width, and Selected Objects commands. You will also see the Actual Size command. Choosing the Actual Size command has the same effect as selecting 100% from the Zoom menu.

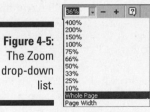

Figure 4-5:
The Zoom
drop-down
list.

Lining Things Up

No matter how comfortable you are with your mouse, aligning things free-hand is tough work. I know because I've been working with a mouse almost daily for many years now, and I *still* have trouble getting things to line up without some help. Fortunately, the Microsoft Publisher 2000 electronic guidance devices can help to steady your trembling hands so that objects fall into perfect place with ease. (Don't confuse the Publisher 2000 electronic guidance devices with those used in so-called "smart bombs" developed for the military.) This section looks at layout guides and ruler guides and then shows you how to activate the powerful Snap-to commands to get everything to line up neatly.

Margin and grid guides

Layout guides are an excellent way to determine where to place various objects on each page. Layout guides don't appear on your printout. On-screen, however, these blue or pink lines provide visual references on every page. Using the Microsoft Publisher 2000 Snap To feature, you can almost magically align objects with these blue or pink lines.

Microsoft Publisher 2000 provides two types of layout guides:

- *Margin guides* define the boundary of your printable area.
- *Grid guides* let you set up a grid to make it easier to design your publication.

Margin guides appear automatically in every publication. Margin guides generally indicate where you should and shouldn't plop objects and help you align objects along the perimeter of each page. You're free to put objects anywhere you want, regardless of the margins, however. (Whether those objects look good there and whether they actually print are other matters altogether.)

Grid guides, like the lines on graph paper, are excellent tools for aligning any and all objects that you don't want to align to the margin guides. For example, you may want to set a graphic in the direct center of the page. Grid guides can help you do this.

Professional designers — whether they work on a computer or on paper — generally lay out pages according to grids. For example, when creating a three-fold brochure, they use a three-part grid to visually separate the three panels of each page where that brochure eventually will be folded. Or they may divide nonfolding pages into a grid of rows and columns to see how different parts of the page visually relate to each other and to the page as a whole. In this way, designers can ensure that their pages are readable, uncrowded, and visually appealing with appropriate spacing and correct alignment.

When you use certain wizards or templates to begin a publication, Microsoft Publisher 2000 sets up grid guides automatically to save you the trouble of doing it yourself. Of course, you can always change them if you like. To set up or change layout guides, select Arrange⇨Layout Guides. The Layout Guides dialog box shown in Figure 4-6 appears.

You set the margins for your printed page in the Margin Guides section of the Layout Guides dialog box. Different printers require different margin settings. If you set margins narrower than your printer will print, your page won't print properly. Text and/or figures will be cut off at the margins. (We discuss printing in depth in Chapter 13.)

Figure 4-6:
The Layout Guides dialog box for a three-column brochure.

In the gutter

If you want different margin guides for your left-facing pages than for your right-facing pages, be sure to select the Create Two Backgrounds With Mirrored Guides check box in the Preview section of the Layout Guides dialog box. This option is important for facing-page publications that will be bound, such as books. When you check this option, the Left and Right text boxes under Margin Guides change to Inside and Outside text boxes. Any change that you make to the Inside setting affects the right (inside) margin of left-facing pages. The Inside setting also affects the left (inside) margin of right-facing pages. The Outside setting does just the reverse.

It's typical for facing pages to have different *gutters* (internal margins) to accommodate the binding. If you're preparing facing pages that will be bound, be sure to set different numbers in the Inside and Outside text boxes. In general, the inside margins should be larger than the outside margins by the amount that the binding will consume. (Ask the person who will be doing the binding to provide this measurement.)

With this setup, you can easily create the extra room necessary on each page to accommodate the room lost due to the binding. Without this extra room, your pages can look lopsided and objects on those pages can get buried in the gutter.

When your gutters are properly set, you can spread objects across facing pages. Depending on your target printer's capabilities (its margins, for example), the object may not print completely. But for objects for which the cut-off doesn't matter — patterns, spot color, and fills — this is a valuable technique.

In the Grid Guides section of the Layout Guides dialog box, enter the number of Columns and Rows that you want. Grid guides evenly divide the space contained by the margin guides.

If you can't see your layout guides after setting them, check the View menu to see whether the Hide Boundaries and Guides command is hiding your guides. If the Show Boundaries and Guides command appears on the menu, select that command or press Ctrl+Shift+O. To hide the guides again, reapply the Hide Boundaries and Guides command or press Ctrl+Shift+O once again. If you still can't see your guides, they may be covered by other objects, such as lines or a frame boundary.

Ruler guides

In addition to layout guides, you can also set *ruler guides* anywhere on your page. Ruler guides let you arrange elements on your page at any horizontal or vertical position that you want. You can create as many ruler guides as you need. Here's how ruler guides work:

- ✔ To create a vertical guide, press and hold the Shift key and click and drag from the vertical ruler right to the desired position on your layout. Your cursor changes to include the word *adjust,* and a green dotted line appears when you release your mouse button.

- ✔ To create a horizontal guide, hold the Shift key down and click and drag from the horizontal ruler down to the desired position on your layout.

- ✔ To place a vertical guide in the exact center of your view, choose Arrange⇨Ruler Guides⇨Add Vertical Rule Guide.

- ✔ To place a horizontal guide in the exact center of your view, choose Arrange⇨Ruler Guides⇨Add Horizontal Rule Guide.

- ✔ To move a ruler guide, just click and drag it while holding the Shift key.

- ✔ To remove a ruler guide, hold the Shift key and drag the ruler off the page.

- ✔ You can remove all ruler guides by choosing the Arrange⇨Ruler Guides⇨Clear All Ruler Guides command.

Snap to it!

Guides would be interesting visual aids but not generally worth the bother if you couldn't automatically align objects to them. Microsoft Publisher 2000 (like most layout and drawing programs) has a feature called Snap to Guides, which directly aligns objects that you place close to a guide.

The Snap to commands make it appear as if the guides magnetically tug at your objects as those objects draw near, just as Batman might use a powerful electromagnet to suck the gun out of The Joker's hand. With these "magnetic" forces in place, you can be sure that any objects you draw or drag near a guide automatically align both with that guide and with each other. You can also make objects snap to the nearest ruler mark (increment) if you like. You can even make objects snap to other objects.

Here's how you toggle the Snap to commands on and off:

- ✔ Choose Tools⇨Snap to Guides (or press Ctrl+W) to align with your layout guides.

- ✔ Choose Tools⇨Snap to Ruler Marks to align with your ruler marks.

- ✔ Choose Tools⇨Snap to Objects to align with selected objects on-screen. See Chapter 5 for more about objects.

A check mark next to the command name means that the option is turned on; click it to turn it off. The absence of a check mark means that the option is turned off; click it to turn it on.

In my experience, the Snap to Guides command is ever so much more useful than snapping to ruler marks. That's why it gets the special Ctrl+W shortcut. I find this command more helpful, in part because you can set up your own guides (whereas you can't control the ruler marks) and in part because those rulers have so many darn marks.

Microsoft Publisher 2000 offers other commands that aid you in precise placement of objects on your layout. (We discuss these in Chapter 5.) In particular, you may want to explore the use of the Align Objects command to precisely align objects to your page. Microsoft Publisher 2000 also has a Nudge command that lets you move your objects a very small amount at a time in any direction. Select Arrange➪Nudge to open the Nudge dialog box, and then type the amount to nudge the selected object by in the Nudge by box. The minimum and maximum amounts that you can nudge an object are:

- ✔ **Centimeters:** Type any number between 0.03 and 5.08 followed by the letters *cm*.

- ✔ **Inches:** Type any number between 0.01 and 2 followed by " or the letters *in*.

- ✔ **Picas:** Type any number between 0.06 and 12 followed by the letters *pi*.

- ✔ **Points:** Type any number between 0.72 and 144 followed by the letters *pt*.

Using Virtual Rulers

You can use the status bar to determine an object's position and size, or you can use the on-screen rulers, located along the top and left edges of the scratch area. The current position of your cursor is indicated by a sliding dashed line that appears in each of your rulers. To do fine measuring with the rulers, you can enlarge them simply by zooming in on the page. As you magnify a page, the rulers also grow larger.

The unit of measurement on each ruler is determined by the Measurement units setting in the Options dialog box, opened by choosing Tools➪Options. See the preceding chapter for option details.

If your rulers aren't showing, you can display them by selecting View➪ Rulers. An even more convenient approach is to right-click and select Rulers from the context-sensitive menu.

To move a ruler, simply click and drag it to a new location. When you place your mouse pointer over a ruler, the cursor changes to a two-headed arrow that points up and down if you're pointing at the horizontal ruler, or left and right if you're pointing at the vertical ruler. As you drag, an outline of the ruler accompanies your pointer. When you release the mouse button, the ruler appears in its new location. To return a ruler to its original location, just drag it back in place.

You can move both rulers simultaneously by clicking and dragging the Move Both Rulers box at the intersection of the two rulers.

By default, the zero mark on each ruler is set to the upper-left corner of the page or two-page spread. You may find it convenient to *rezero* a ruler — that is, to change the position of its zero mark, as if you were sliding the ruler end-to-end over a page.

For example, if one object's right edge ends at the 2 ¼ mark on the horizontal ruler, and another object's left edge begins at the 5 ⁵⁄₁₆ mark, how much space is between those objects? Is this math class? Who knows, and who really cares? Wouldn't it be easier to measure this if the horizontal ruler's zero mark aligned with one of those edges?

To move a ruler's zero mark, simply point to a ruler, press and hold the Shift key, and click the *right* mouse button to drag the zero mark to a new location. As it does when you move a ruler, your mouse pointer changes to a two-headed arrow, pointing up and down if you're pointing at the horizontal ruler, or right and left if you're pointing at the vertical ruler. As you drag, the ruler stays in place but a solid line follows your pointer. When you release the right mouse button, the ruler rezeroes at that line.

To reset a ruler's zero mark, double-click it. To rezero both rulers to the upper-left corner of the page or two-page spread, double-click your left mouse button in that blank box at the intersection of the two rulers.

When you're working inside a text or table frame, a subsection of the horizontal ruler automatically provides a special zero mark just for that frame or current table column. (We discuss text and table frames in Chapter 5.)

Creating Background Pages

When you create a multiple-page publication, you may want certain objects to appear on all or most of the pages. These objects could include the publication's title, your name, page numbers, a company logo or some other graphic, a plea to send money — whatever. Microsoft Publisher 2000 lets you create a *background* that appears on each page of your publication.

The benefits of using backgrounds are as follows:

✔ They eliminate the boring, repetitive work of placing and managing objects that appear on every page.

✔ They eliminate a source of bloated file sizes because information that needs to be repeated is entered only once.

✔ They enforce design consistency.

To understand Microsoft Publisher 2000 backgrounds, imagine each regular publication *(foreground)* page as a piece of see-through tracing paper laid over a cardboard backing. You can see all the objects on the backing, along with the layer of objects on the tracing paper. As you move from page to page, the tracing paper changes but the backing remains the same. If you change something on the tracing paper, only the tracing paper changes. If you change something on the backing, however, that change affects the appearance of any tracing paper laid over that backing. The Microsoft Publisher 2000 backgrounds work just like that cardboard backing; the foreground pages work like the pieces of tracing paper.

Any objects on a background repeat on foreground pages throughout the publication. Those *background objects* that are not obscured by objects above them in the foreground print together with any *foreground objects* present on each foreground page. To work with the background or any object on it, you must first move the foreground pages out of the way, just as you would lift tracing paper from a cardboard backing.

Back to the foreground

To move to the background, select <u>V</u>iew⇨<u>G</u>o to Background or press Ctrl+M.

The Ctrl+M shortcut derives from the word *Master.* Most page layout programs let you create master pages, which work like the Microsoft Publisher 2000 backgrounds.

Rarely does anything radical happen when you move to the background. Any on-screen changes usually are very subtle, and the background may look like just another blank publication page, sporting the same layout guides as your publication's foreground pages. One way to tell whether you've moved to the background is to look at the Page Navigation controls at the bottom-left of your screen. If the Page Navigation controls are still there, you're in the foreground. If the Page Navigation controls have been replaced with one or two *background buttons,* as shown in Figure 4-7, you've successfully moved to the background.

Figure 4-7:
The L and R
replace the
page num-
bers when
you are
working in
the back-
ground.

To return to the foreground pages, select <u>V</u>iew➪<u>G</u>o to Foreground or press
Ctrl+M. (This command is a toggle with the Go to Background command.)
You return to the last foreground page that you were in, and the normal page
controls return in triumph.

Working with multiple backgrounds

When you start a publication, Microsoft Publisher 2000 sometimes creates
just one background for you and other times creates two, based on the type
of publication you create. To determine whether you have one or two backgrounds, move to the background and then observe the area usually
occupied by the Page Navigation controls. If you see only one background
button, your publication has only one background. If you see two background
buttons, your publication has two backgrounds.

One major difference between Microsoft Publisher 2000 and more complicated layout programs is that the other programs let you create any number
of *master pages* (backgrounds) and put them at any position in your publication. That flexibility adds additional complexity, but I think that not having
the feature is a significant design loss.

To create a second background if you have only one, open the Layout Guides
dialog box from the Arrange menu and click the Create Two Backgrounds
With Mirrored Guides check box, as previously shown in Figure 4-6. When
you create separate, mirrored layout guides for left- and right-facing pages,
you automatically create a second background.

When you create a second background, three things happen:

  ✔ The original background becomes the right background.
  ✔ The new background becomes the left background.
  ✔ Microsoft Publisher 2000 copies everything on the original (right) back-
    ground — guides and objects — and places it in mirrored positions on
    the new (left) background.

If you have two backgrounds and delete one (by unchecking the Create Two Backgrounds With Mirrored Guides check box), Microsoft Publisher 2000 permanently deletes all left-background objects. (Fortunately, Microsoft Publisher 2000 warns you of this before actually deleting the background.) Either way, every page in your document now uses the remaining (what was the right) background.

If you later return to using two background pages, Microsoft Publisher 2000 copies everything from the single (right) background to mirrored positions on the new (left) background.

To move between background pages (if you have two of them):

✔ In Single Page view, click the background buttons to move back and forth from the right to the left background page.

✔ In Two-Page Spread view, you can see the two buttons, but they are not active. Just click directly on the page and element or object that you want to work on.

Two backgrounds are great for creating facing-page publications. Unfortunately, having twice as many backgrounds means twice as much work setting them up, so use only one background if that's all you need. You can return to a single background by unchecking the Create Two Backgrounds With Mirrored Guides check box in the Layout Guides dialog box. The left background page is eliminated. If any objects are on your left background, Microsoft Publisher 2000 opens a dialog box to warn you that those objects will be deleted.

In addition to providing separate areas for different sets of layout guides, having two backgrounds enables you to set up separate sets of background objects — one set that repeats on left-hand foreground pages, and another set that repeats on right-hand foreground pages. Separate left- and right-hand repeating objects are quite common in facing-page publications. For example, look at the header text along the top of these two pages. On the left-facing page is a page number followed by the name of the current book part; this information is aligned along the page's left (outside) margin. On the right-facing page is the name of the current chapter followed by the page number; this information is aligned along the page's right (outside) margin.

Adding background objects

Adding objects to backgrounds is just like adding objects to foreground pages, which we describe in Chapter 5. Because background and foreground objects must share the final, printed page, however, you should consider a couple of things before you add a background object.

If you have only one background, any object that you put on that background repeats on every foreground page. If you have two backgrounds, any object that you put on the left background repeats on every left-hand foreground page, any object that you put on the right background repeats on every right-hand foreground page, and any object that you put on both backgrounds repeats on every left- *and* right-hand foreground page. You can eliminate any and all background objects from specific foreground pages, however, as we explain later in this chapter.

You should place your background objects where they won't interfere with foreground objects. The easiest solution is to keep background objects near the margins. If you choose to put an object in the middle of a background instead, it might get covered up by a foreground object. Try to add all your background objects before you begin adding foreground objects. Otherwise, you may need to rearrange your foreground objects to make room for your background objects.

Creating headers and footers

To Microsoft Publisher 2000, a *header* is stuff — text, graphics, or both — that repeats along the top of pages, whereas a *footer* is stuff that repeats along the bottom of pages. (You're probably already familiar with this concept from your word processor, and it's the same in Microsoft Publisher 2000.) Headers and footers usually contain such boring and traditional information as the publication title, current chapter or other division title, author's name, company or publication-specific logo, and/or page number. Because headers and footers are supposed to repeat on most or all pages, the background is the perfect place to put them.

To create headers and footers, follow these steps:

1. **Select View⇨Go to Background or press Ctrl+M to go to the background.**

2. **Add an object(s) where you want your header or footer to appear.**

   The objects that you add could be frames or drawn objects such as lines or circles. Chapter 5 describes how to work with frames and drawn objects.

3. **If appropriate, fill and format the object and then format its contents.**

Headers and footers should line up with the top or bottom margin. Otherwise, they wouldn't really be headers and footers — they'd be "middlers"! To help your headers and footers line up perfectly, set a ruler guide for the bottom of the header and the top of the footer. Also, make sure that the Snap to Guides command is turned on before you add your object(s) to the header and footer. See the discussion earlier in this chapter on lining things up for more information on the Snap To feature.

If you're working on a facing-page publication, it's also a good idea to have the headers and footers align to the outside margins, as the headers in this book do. This design makes seeing those headers and footers easier for readers when flipping through your printed publication.

If your object is a text frame, you may want to type the text, add a fancy border around the frame, make the text larger and bolder, and right-align the text within the frame. To really make the header or footer stand out, you can add a drawn object, such as a rectangle that's filled with a color and has a thick border. You can even use WordArt (see Chapter 9) to create special text effects that you can place in your headers and footers.

Here's a way to save some work if you need two backgrounds with similar headers and footers. Set up the headers and footers on one background, make sure that you're in Two-Page Spread view, and then create the second background. Microsoft Publisher 2000 automatically copies your headers and footers to mirrored positions on the new background.

Inserting page numbers

One of the most common uses for headers and footers is to hold page numbers. Microsoft Publisher 2000 is more than happy to number your pages for you. Nice program. Good program. Sit. Stay. Have a bone.

To number pages, all you need to do is add a semi-secret page-numbering code called a *page-number mark* to a header or footer text frame in the background. If your publication has two backgrounds and you want page numbers to appear on both left- and right-hand pages, you need to insert a page-number mark on *both* backgrounds.

Follow these steps to add page numbers to a header or footer:

1. **Choose <u>V</u>iew⇨<u>G</u>o to Background or press Ctrl+M.**

   Switch to the Background so that your page numbers show up on every page. If you want to put a page number on just one page, skip this step.

2. **Click the text frame to which you want to add the page-number mark and position the insertion (I-beam) cursor in it.**

   A selected frame displays eight little black boxes, or *reshape handles,* along its perimeter.

   To create a text frame, click the Text Frame Tool in the toolbox and drag your frame on the layout.

3. **Type some identifying text, such as the word Page (optional).**

4. **Choose the <u>I</u>nsert⇨Page N<u>u</u>mbers command from the menu bar.**

   The page-number mark appears. Although this mark appears to be just a pound sign (#), it changes to the appropriate page number on each foreground page. Honestly!

5. Format the page-number mark as you would any text (optional).

Formatting text is covered in Chapter 8.

Don't try to be sneaky and just type a pound sign from your keyboard to indicate where you want page numbers to appear. Although it looks just like a page-number mark, it produces only pound signs on your foreground pages.

In the foreground, each page proudly displays its own page number. Microsoft Publisher 2000 uses only Arabic numerals (1, 2, 3, and so on) for page numbering. If you want to number your pages some other way, perhaps with small Roman numerals (i, ii, iii, and so on) for the introductory pages of a book, you have to number each page manually. Sorry.

Make sure that you leave enough room in your text frame to fit the longest page number in your publication. Otherwise, longer page numbers may get cut off. If you have this problem with an existing text frame, see Chapter 5 to find out how to resize a frame.

If you're desktop-publishing something that requires separate series of page numbers, such as several report sections that will be printed with other report sections, create each section of your publication in a separate file to accommodate those separate series. You can then set your page numbers in each publication to start at something other than 1. Choose Tools➪Options and use the Start publication with page text box in the Options dialog box for this purpose. Microsoft Publisher 2000 lets you use any number up to an amazing 16,766. This affects the page numbering only for the current publication.

Getting a date

Placing dates and times in your headers and footers isn't much different than putting page numbers there. Follow the procedure described in the preceding section, but substitute the Insert➪Date and Time command from the menu bar in place of the Insert➪Page Numbers command. Microsoft Publisher 2000 opens up the Date and Time dialog box, as shown in Figure 4-8. Click the format of choice and then click the Update automatically check box if you want to create a placeholder that updates the date whenever you open or print your publication. The program cleverly uses the dates and times set in your Windows Date/Time control panel. If you leave the Update automatically check box empty, Microsoft Publisher 2000 simply inserts the current date or time and doesn't update it.

Figure 4-8:
The Date
and Time
dialog box.

Suppressing background objects

Traditionally, headers and footers are left off a publication's first page. In larger publications, headers and footers are also usually left off the first page of each chapter or other major division. The headers in this book are a prime example. Go ahead: Flip through this book and you'll see.

To hide *all* background objects, move to the foreground page for which you want to hide background objects, and select the Ignore Background command from the View menu.

No ambiguity here. If you're viewing a single page, the background disappears. When you apply this command to a two-page spread, Microsoft Publisher 2000 opens up the Ignore Background dialog box, shown in Figure 4-9, to ask you to select which page you want to ignore — the Left Page, Right Page, or both.

TIP

Electronic masking tape

Sometimes, you may want to hide some, but not all, background objects. Perhaps you have a nice company logo that you want on every page, but you want to leave the page number off the first page. To do this, you can employ a trick that we like to call *electronic masking tape.* The secret of electronic masking tape lies in the fact that any opaque (not see-through) foreground object can cover up any background object.

Because text frames are one of the few Microsoft Publisher 2000 objects that are opaque by default, they make a convenient choice for electronic masking tape. Simply move to the foreground page and draw a text frame (as explained in Chapter 5) over the background object that you want to hide. Or you can use just about any other object that you want. If the object is transparent, you can make it opaque by selecting it and then pressing Ctrl+T. Pressing Ctrl+T a second time will make the object transparent again.

Figure 4-9:
The Ignore
Background
dialog box.

The Ignore Background command is one of those toggle commands: Issue it once to turn it on, issue it again to turn it off. If you're viewing two pages, the Ignore Background dialog box appears again. Just uncheck one or both boxes and then click OK.

Adding and Deleting Pages

Microsoft Publisher 2000 offers you several ways to add pages — perhaps more ways than you'll ever need. And if you end up with *too* many pages, you can, of course, delete them.

Adding pages

When you create a blank publication, Microsoft Publisher 2000 generally gives you only one page to begin with. The wizards give you a number of pages depending upon the document type. Regardless of how many pages Microsoft Publisher 2000 creates by default, you can always add more blank pages if you need them.

Your new pages may not appear entirely blank. They may display the margin and other layout guides that you've set up to appear on every page of your publication. They may also display some background objects. We discuss background pages and objects in Chapter 5.

Microsoft Publisher 2000 provides an easy way to insert a blank page (or two) at the end of your document. Just click the Page Navigation control to advance to the last page in your document, and press Ctrl+Shift+N.

If you're in Single page view, Microsoft Publisher 2000 inserts one new blank page and moves you to that page. If you're in Two-Page Spread view, Microsoft Publisher 2000 inserts two new blank pages and moves your view to those pages.

Oops. If you insert a page by accident, you can choose Edit➪Undo Insert Page, press Ctrl+Z, or click the Undo button on the Standard toolbar to remove it.

You aren't limited to adding pages to the end of your publication. If you select the Page command on the Insert menu, you can insert any number of pages before the current page, after the current page, or, if you are in a two-page spread, between the current pages. You can add blank pages, add pages with a single text frame, or even duplicate the contents of a single page.

Follow these steps to insert a new page or pages into your publication:

1. **Move to the page or spread that you want to immediately precede, follow, or flank your new pages.**

2. **Choose Insert➪Page.**

   The Insert Page dialog box appears, as shown in Figure 4-10. This dialog box is one of the most useful ones you'll encounter, and its options for page creation can save you a lot of time.

Figure 4-10: The Insert Page dialog box for a two-page spread.

Although Ctrl+Shift+N is listed on the Insert menu as a shortcut for the Insert➪Page command, Ctrl+Shift+N does *not* open the Insert Page dialog box. Instead, it immediately adds one blank page (if you're in Single page view) or two blank pages (if you're in Two-Page Spread view) after the current page or spread. No questions asked. I object to listing keystrokes that don't exactly call up a menu command, and I think it should be a bug (it quacks like a bug!), but the same behavior existed in the previous versions of Microsoft Publisher.

3. **In the Number of new pages text box, type the number of pages that you want to insert.**

   The default is 1 for Single page view and 2 for Two-Page Spread view.

Inserting pages in even numbers is a good idea so that your left-hand pages don't become right-hand pages and vice versa. This rule of thumb isn't as important at the very beginning stages of a publication, but inserting pages in odd numbers can really wreak havoc if you insert them after having laid down some objects.

4. **Click the radio button that indicates where you want your new page(s) to be inserted.**

   Your choices are Before left page, After right page, and Between pages.

5. **Under Options, click to indicate what kind of pages you want to insert:**

   - **Insert blank pages:** Inserts pages that have no objects of their own, just like those pages that are added when you insert pages using page controls.

   - **Create one text frame on each page:** Places a blank text frame on each new page that you create. Each text frame matches your publication's margin guides. This option is an excellent choice for publications such as books, which have page after page of primarily text.

   - **Duplicate all objects on page**: Makes a copy of whatever objects already exist on the page number you specify in the option box and places those objects on each of the new pages.

6. **Click OK.**

If you accidentally insert pages, you can remove those pages by immediately choosing the Edit⇨Undo Insert Page command from the menu bar.

You have to place the objects on the source page *before* you issue the Insert⇨Page command.

You may be tempted to use the Duplicate option to copy objects that you want on every publication page, such as headers, footers, and page numbers. Don't. Doing so creates larger file sizes. Use *backgrounds* instead. With a background, a single instance of an object serves all your printed pages. See the discussion of backgrounds earlier in this chapter for more details.

If you're importing a great deal of text and you don't know how many pages you need to fit that text, you can have Microsoft Publisher 2000 automatically add the necessary number of pages for you, create text frames on those pages, and then fill those frames with the text. Chapter 6 tells you more about this labor-saving feature.

Deleting pages

Deleting a page, especially from Single page view, can be frighteningly easy — and shouldn't be taken lightly. When you delete a page, it's as if the page you deleted never existed. No mourning. No nothing. No kidding. (Have we mentioned backup recently? Like in the last page or two?)

When you delete a page, all the objects on that page are also deleted. Only objects off the page, on the scratch area, remain untouched. Microsoft Publisher 2000 then automatically renumbers the remaining pages so that you don't end up with a wacky page sequence.

Follow these steps to delete a page:

1. **Move to the page you want to delete.**

2. **Choose Edit⇨Delete Page.**

   Note that this command is not available if you are currently viewing the background of your publication.

   If you are in the Single page view when you select the Edit⇨Delete Page command, Microsoft Publisher 2000 displays a confirmation box asking whether you really want to delete the page. Click OK to delete the page. Click Cancel if you are having second thoughts. Use this command with caution. Press Ctrl+Z if you accidentally delete a page.

   If you are in the Two-Page Spread view, Microsoft Publisher 2000 opens the Delete Page dialog box, as shown in Figure 4-11.

3. **Click the radio button for the option you want: Both pages, Left page only, or Right page only.**

4. **Click OK.**

Figure 4-11:
The Delete Page dialog box for a two-page spread.

If you accidentally delete pages, you can restore them and their contents by immediately choosing Edit⇨Undo Delete Page or by pressing Ctrl+Z.

Deleting pages, even with an alert box, is dangerous. Pay particular attention to page deletions, as they are an excellent method for losing work.

As with inserting pages, it's a good idea to delete pages in even numbers so that your left- and right-hand pages don't get fouled up. If you delete just a left- or right-hand page in the Two-Page Spread view, Microsoft Publisher 2000 opens a dialog box asking you to consider deleting pages in even numbers instead.

Try as you might, and as much fun as it might be to do it, you cannot delete the only page in a single-page publication. If you try, Microsoft Publisher 2000 simply deletes any objects on that page but leaves the page itself in place. The background is not affected when you try to delete the only page in a single-page publication.

Modifying the Page Layout

Every publication you create, no matter how basic, already has a specific page layout that determines each page's physical size, orientation, and whether the paper requires special folding to create the individual publication pages. But just because the page layout is determined the moment you start a publication, that doesn't mean that you can't change it later through the Page Setup command on the File menu.

Do you get the feeling that there isn't *anything* that you can't change later on in a publication? We don't think that there is, but changing things — including page layouts — exacts a heavier and heavier toll as you go along. For example, if you lay down all the text and graphics in a 16-page pamphlet and then change the size of the pages, you may find yourself with plenty of work to do just to get your text and graphics to fit properly again. Making the correct choices early in your project saves you considerable time later on. The time that you spend fixing up your publication is time that you don't spend doing the creative work that makes desktop publishing fun.

Always select your target printer, as discussed in Chapter 12, before you spend any time adjusting the page setup.

To change the page setup of a document, Select File⇨Page Setup. The Page Setup dialog box, shown in Figure 4-12, appears.

Microsoft Publisher 2000 provides five major page-layout categories:

Figure 4-12:
The Page
Setup dialog
box for a
Normal
setup.

- ✔ **Normal:** Creates newsletters, brochures, flyers, and many other layouts
- ✔ **Special Fold:** Creates greeting cards, tent cards, and book folds
- ✔ **Special Size:** Creates posters, banners, business cards, and index cards
- ✔ **Labels:** Creates mailing labels and full-page labels
- ✔ **Envelopes:** Creates #10, #6, or custom-sized envelopes

The sections that follow describe these categories and their myriad options.
Regardless of what page-layout category you choose, however, you can also
set an orientation for your paper:

- ✔ **Portrait:** The most common orientation, this prints your publication
  pages from top to bottom along the length of the paper — as you normally would if you were using a typewriter or word-processing program.
  In full-page publications, this option creates pages that are taller than
  they are wide.

- ✔ **Landscape:** This orientation turns the paper sideways so that your
  pages print from side to side along the width of the paper. In full-page
  publications, this option creates pages that are wider than they are tall.
  Spreadsheets, reports, and many graphs are often printed using this
  orientation.

Some printers, particularly the more ancient ones, don't enable you to
change the paper orientation. If this is the case with your printer, the orientation options are dimmed. It might be time to consider buying a new printer.

By combining various layout categories, options within those categories, various custom settings, and paper orientation, you can get Microsoft Publisher 2000 to print just about any publication conceivable, no matter how large or small.

The Normal layout

The Normal layout option consists of *full pages* — pages that match the size of the paper they're printed on — and requires little or no special handling.

Notice that the Paper Size area of the Page Setup dialog box displays the size of the paper that your target printer is currently set up to print on. To change the paper size and the source of the paper, you need to make selections from the Print Setup dialog box. You can access this dialog box by selecting File⇨Print Setup. What's "normal" in terms of your printer's capabilities is determined by the print engine and the printer driver software that you have.

The Special Fold layout

The Special Fold layout option is for publications that require you to fold a single sheet of paper once or twice to create the individual publication pages. That is, one sheet prints with two or four publication pages on one side, and folding the sheet separates those pages. The advantage of special folds is that you end up with print on multiple sides of the publication while actually printing on only one side of the sheet of paper. Take a look at double-folded commercial greeting cards sometime to see what we mean.

When you select the Special Fold option, the Page Setup dialog box changes and appears as it does in Figure 4-13. Notice the new options in the Choose a Special Fold list box. It now offers you the following setups:

- ✔ **Book Fold:** Use this layout to create single-fold books and booklets. You fold the printed sheet in half with the two long edges touching to create two pages.

- ✔ **Tent Card:** Use this layout to create single-fold tent cards. You fold the printed sheet in half with the two short edges touching to get a free-standing tabletop card.

- ✔ **Side-Fold Card:** Use this layout to create double-fold greeting cards. You first fold the printed sheet in half with the two short edges touching and then fold the sheet in half in the opposite direction to produce a card that opens along the side.

Figure 4-13:
The Page
Setup dialog
box for a
Special Fold
setup.

✔ **Top-Fold Card:** This layout also creates double-fold greeting cards. In this case, though, you first fold the printed sheet in half with the two *long* edges touching and then fold the sheet in the opposite direction to produce a card that opens along the bottom.

By default, pages in a special-fold publication are exactly one-half or one-quarter of the paper size. You can manually adjust the Width and Height settings in the Page Setup dialog box to have each page take up less (but not more) than that amount of space. If you do change these settings, keep in mind that you then have to trim the extra paper off the sheet *and* fold it to produce the final publication. What a pain! A better solution is to set up your target printer to use a different paper size (assuming that you can get that size paper and that your printer supports that size). This strategy saves you both the trouble of changing the settings and manually trimming the paper.

By their very nature, special-fold publications contain either two or four pages. If you have something other than the appropriate number of pages in your publication, Microsoft Publisher 2000 opens a dialog box after you click the OK button and offers to add or delete pages as necessary to give your publication the correct number of pages. Click Yes to let Microsoft Publisher 2000 adjust your pages for you, or click No if you're feeling especially obstinate.

Not all folding publications (brochures, for example) require special-fold layouts. They may, however, benefit from appropriately set grid guides, as explained earlier in this chapter.

The Special Size layout

The Special Size layout option is for publications whose pages are either larger or smaller than the paper they are printed on. Publications that may be larger than the paper they're printed on include banners and posters; to create the final publication, you have to tape several sheets of paper together. Publications that may be smaller than the paper they're printed on include business and index cards; to create the final publication, you trim off the parts of the paper that you don't need.

When you select the Special Size option, the Page Setup dialog box looks as it does in Figure 4-14. Among the size options that you are offered in the Choose a Publication Size list box are the following:

Figure 4-14:
The Page Setup dialog box for a Special Size setup.

✔ **Printer Sheet Size:** This selection is redundant. It's the same as choosing the Normal layout option in the box above, so ignore this option.

✔ **Index Card (5 × 3 in.):** This selection creates index cards, with one card per sheet.

✔ **Business Card (3.5 × 2 in.):** This option creates business cards, with one card per sheet.

✔ **Poster (18 × 24 in.)** and **Poster (24 × 36 in.):** These two options create posters by printing out several sheets that you tape together.

✔ **Custom:** This is a catch-all option. It creates publications in any size you want, just in case none of the other options does the trick for you.

- ✔ **Banner (5 ft.), Banner (10 ft.),** and **Banner (15 ft.):** These options create banners by printing the publication over several sheets of 8 ½ × 11-inch paper that you tape together later.

- ✔ **Custom Banner:** This option is the catch-all option for banners. It enables you to set height and width to create banners in any size you want.

- ✔ **Postcard (5.5 × 4.25 in.), Postcard (5.85 × 4.13 in.),** and **Postcard (3.94 × 55.83 in.):** These options create postcards in U.S., European, and Japanese standard sizes, respectively.

As you select these different options, watch the Preview box to get an idea of how your publication will print.

The whole point of a Special Size layout is that it can create a special size. Therefore, you will undoubtedly want to enter new settings in the Width, Height, Banner Width, and/or Banner Height text boxes, depending upon the layout you choose. If you do change any of these settings, Microsoft Publisher 2000 changes your special-size option to Custom or Custom Banner accordingly.

Notice that, when you change the orientation for a Special Size layout, you are not changing the orientation of your publication, but rather the orientation of the sheet(s) of paper you're printing it on. If you'd rather change the orientation of the publication (for publications other than banners), instead use the Width and Height text boxes above the orientation section.

The Labels layout

The Labels layout option is for creating mailing labels or full-page labels. When you select the Labels option, the Page Setup dialog box looks as it does in Figure 4-15. You can choose from 80 Avery label sizes.

As you select these different label types, a description of the label appears at the bottom of the dialog box showing the label name, the number of columns, and the number of labels per column.

You can use the Labels layout options to create a mail merge using the commands on the Mail Merge menu, or to create labels manually.

Figure 4-15:
The Page
Setup dialog
box for a
Labels
setup.

The Envelopes layout

You can use the Envelopes layout options to create either standard #10 or #6
envelopes. You also have the option to create custom-sized envelopes. When
you select the Envelopes option, the Page Setup dialog box looks as it does in
Figure 4-16.

As you select these different envelope types, the Width and Height of the
envelope appears at the bottom of the dialog box.

You can use the Envelopes layout options to create a mail merge using the
commands on the Mail Merge menu, or to create envelopes manually.

Figure 4-16:
The Page
Setup dialog
box for a #10
Envelope
setup.

Getting Your Pages Set to Print

Perhaps the most common design mistake that starting desktop publishers make is doing their page layout with the wrong printer driver. The mistake is easy enough to make, even for experienced desktop publishers who are aware of the problem. A change in printers, the service that you are using, or the specifications for the publication itself can result in changing printer drivers. And you may not have control over those situations.

If you lay out your pages using the wrong printer driver, many of the page setup options that you take for granted may not exist when you send your file out to be printed. After all your hard work of carefully nudging objects around the page, you may find that objects are cut off, blurry, or otherwise poorly printed. If you are having your publication printed through a printer service, talking about the printer driver before you initiate a design project can really help you out and save you time. See Chapter 13 for more detailed information about printing your publication.

Make sure that you are designing your page for the correct printer as early in the project as possible.

Chapter 5

Objects and Frames

● ●

In This Chapter

▶ Understanding frames (what they are and why you need them)

▶ Working with frames

▶ Creating and working with drawn objects

▶ Creating special effects with layers

▶ Using groups to speed up your work

● ●

The preceding chapter discusses the basic elements of your publication's pages. It's now time to add structure to your pages with frames and drawn objects. In this chapter, I focus on how you use frames and drawn objects to create a design framework into which you can add the content that makes each publication unique.

In Microsoft Publisher 2000 language, an *object* represents any publication design element: a text or graphic frame, a line, a circle, or other item on a page. Objects fall into different categories, and each category has a set of properties. After you know how one object in a category works, you can understand the behaviors and properties of related objects in that same category. With a good set of objects, you can conquer the world.

This chapter focuses on two types of objects: those that are contained in frames and those that aren't. *Frames* are container objects into which you place the content of your publication. Text and graphics are two common examples of publication elements that require frames. You can also use frames to create tables and special text effects.

Not all objects on a layout use frames, however. Some objects — such as lines, circles, rectangles, ovals, and other shapes that you draw using the tools in the Microsoft Publisher 2000 toolbox — are complete, in, of, and by themselves. You find out how to create these types of objects in this chapter as well.

Working with Frames

As I mentioned, frames are *container objects* that hold your publication's content. Frames have properties that you can change. Frames have a size and shape, and they can be resized and moved. They can be transparent or opaque, have color or patterns applied to them, and have other properties common to *drawn objects*. Frames exist as separate objects, but you can associate frames together as a group by using the equivalent of electronic glue.

Frames also have special properties that are not common to objects in general. Frames can be linked so that the contents of one frame flow into the next frame. This is particularly valuable for text in a long document, when you may want an article to begin on one page and continue on another.

Microsoft Publisher 2000 provides four frame types:

- ✓ **Text frames:** These frames are containers for text. Text frames can be linked to create what Microsoft Publisher 2000 calls *stories.* Some text frames are part of a Personal Information Set. A Personal Information Set contains information about you or your organization. See the section "Personal info" later in this chapter for details.

- ✓ **Table frames:** These frames are containers for (surprise!) tables. They help you arrange text in tidy rows and columns. Table frames are useful for creating graphic arrays or matrixes, providing a dense representation of data, or creating things such as a table of contents in a publication.

- ✓ **Picture frames:** Microsoft Publisher 2000 requires that you put pictures and other graphics inside picture frames. Picture frames have special properties that let you modify the way graphics look in them.

- ✓ **WordArt frames:** WordArt, a separate OLE server program, creates graphic objects based on type (you know, the characters and symbols that you make with your keyboard). By using WordArt, you can create many special text effects that are useful in headlines and other places.

Each of the program's four frame types behaves a little differently. In addition to holding different sorts of objects, each type varies in how you create, delete, and otherwise manipulate it.

Creating frames

To create a frame, you select the appropriate tool in the Objects toolbar and click and drag with the tool on your layout. Figure 5-1 shows you where each tool is located in the Object toolbar. The tool that you select determines the frame's type, whereas your drawing action determines the frame's size and position in the publication.

TIP

OLE! OLE!

A WordArt frame would be better termed an *OLE frame*, after the kind of object that fills that frame. Microsoft Publisher 2000 makes good use of OLE (Object Linking and Embedding), a technology that enables you to incorporate into your layout many kinds of data that the program doesn't directly support or can't directly create. Although Microsoft Publisher 2000 incorporates WordArt directly in its package, you can create frames by using any OLE server.

OLE is a special form of cut-and-paste and is implemented by using the Edit⇨Paste Special command on the menu bar. You can create either *embedded* OLE objects or *linked* OLE objects. When you create an embedded object, the object is placed and stored — that is, embedded — right in your publication file, as is the information that enables Microsoft Publisher 2000 to link back to the program used to create the object. With a linked object, the only thing that's stored in your publication file is the data needed to link back to the original OLE server program.

Whether you create linked or embedded OLE objects, you make any changes to them in the OLE server program rather than in Microsoft Publisher 2000. You can specify that you want the changed objects to be updated automatically in your layout or that you want to update objects manually, on a case-by-case basis. Also, you can choose to apply changes made to embedded data to the copy of the object that exists in your publication only.

The Insert⇨Object command enables you to select an OLE server program and create an OLE frame. Microsoft Publisher 2000 ships with two other server programs, Microsoft Draw 2000 and a picture browser for the Microsoft Clip Gallery. Select the OLE server (such as Microsoft Excel Chart or Microsoft Word Document) from the Object Type box to choose from any OLE server registered with Windows.

Although OLE is nice to use in other kinds of programs, it's an essential part of working in a page layout program such as Microsoft Publisher 2000. If you understand this feature, it can save you time, disk space, maintenance, and grief. I revisit OLE throughout this book.

As soon as you click a tool, a Formatting toolbar appears underneath the Microsoft Publisher 2000 Standard toolbar with buttons that let you change the format of your frame or the objects that you put in it. For the most part, these formatting buttons are duplicates of menu commands. Plenty of formatting tools are available for text and table frames, but just a few tools apply to WordArt and picture frames.

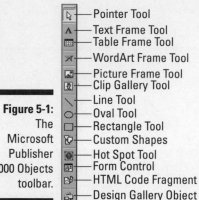

—Pointer Tool
—Text Frame Tool
—Table Frame Tool
—WordArt Frame Tool
—Picture Frame Tool
—Clip Gallery Tool
—Line Tool
—Oval Tool
—Rectangle Tool
—Custom Shapes
—Hot Spot Tool
—Form Control
—HTML Code Fragment
—Design Gallery Object

Figure 5-1:
The
Microsoft
Publisher
2000 Objects
toolbar.

Follow these steps to draw a text or picture frame:

1. **Click the Text Frame Tool or Picture Frame Tool in the Objects toolbar.**

   Your cursor changes to a crosshair.

2. **Move the crosshair over the publication page or scratch area.**

   The sliding ruler lines and the status bar's position box show your exact position.

3. **Click and drag to create the outline of your frame.**

   As you drag, the program draws a sample to show you the size and shape of your new frame. The status bar's size box indicates the frame's size.

   To draw a frame from the center out, hold the Ctrl key as you draw. To draw a perfectly square frame, hold the Shift key. To do both, hold down the Ctrl+Shift keys together as you drag.

4. **Release the mouse button to create the frame.**

   Microsoft Publisher 2000 creates your text or picture frame and selects it (makes it active) so that you can work with it further.

Figure 5-2 shows you a selected text frame. Picture frames and text frames look the same except that text frames can have buttons used to link frames together for automatic content flow control.

To draw a table, the steps are the same as for creating a text or picture frame. But after you release the mouse button to create the frame, Microsoft Publisher 2000 opens the Create Table dialog box, shown in Figure 5-3.

Figure 5-2:
A newly created and selected text frame.

Figure 5-3:
The Create Table dialog box.

You then need to take the following additional steps:

1. **Select the number of rows and columns that you want in your table.**

2. **Choose a format for your table (optional).**

3. **Click the OK button.**

   Your table frame is now complete. A sample table frame is shown in Figure 5-4.

So far, so good. All three frames that we've just discussed behave similarly. The WordArt frame is somewhat different, though. WordArt is an OLE server, so when you draw a frame for that object type, the WordArt program opens, as shown in Figure 5-5.

Figure 5-4:
A sample table frame.

Figure 5-5:
A WordArt
frame being
edited in
place.

You then have two choices: You can create your WordArt graphic or you can press the Esc key twice to close WordArt and complete the frame. You can always return to work with your WordArt object by double-clicking the frame. When you do, WordArt opens up on your screen and you can make any changes without leaving Microsoft Publisher 2000 (this process is called *editing in place,* in OLE lingo). You find out more about WordArt in Chapter 9.

After you draw a frame, Microsoft Publisher 2000 automatically deselects the frame tool and activates the Pointer Tool so that you can manipulate your object. This feature is a pain if you want to draw several frames of the same type one right after the other. To get a frame tool to stay selected, press the Ctrl key and click the tool icon. When you're done drawing frames with that tool, deselect the tool by clicking any other tool in the toolbox. Or click outside your frames to deselect them. These techniques work for any tool in the toolbox (for example, the Line, Box, and Circle Tools), not just for frame tools.

Selecting things

In Microsoft Publisher 2000, before you can change a frame or object, you have to select it. After you select an element, you can fill it, resize it, move it, delete it, or do whatever your heart desires. You can also select multiple frames or any set of objects on a page, thus enabling you to perform the same operation on a set of frames or objects simultaneously — provided that the operation is legal for the selected elements.

For example, if you have two text frames selected, Microsoft Publisher 2000 lets you add borders to both of them at the same time. If you try to paste text from the Clipboard into two selected text frames simultaneously, however, the program gets confused and creates a third text frame with your text.

A frame is automatically selected after you finish drawing it, as shown back in Figure 5-2. You can tell that a frame is selected because it displays eight little black boxes, called *selection handles,* around its perimeter. Some selected frames display more than just selection handles. A text frame may display a Go to Previous Frame button or a Go to Next Frame button, and a table frame displays two selection bars (Select Cells) along its top and left edges. (A table frame looks and acts like a miniature spreadsheet, which is what it is.) You find out how to connect text frames and work with tables in Chapter 6.

Use the Pointer Tool to select frames and objects in Microsoft Publisher 2000. The following are selection techniques that you can use:

✔ **To select a single frame, just click it.**

✔ **To select additional frames, hold down the Shift or Ctrl key and click the frames.**

✔ **To deselect one frame from a range of selected objects, hold down the Shift or Ctrl key and click the frame.**

✔ **To select multiple frames that are close to one another, click and drag around the frames.** As you drag, Microsoft Publisher 2000 shows you a *selection box* — a dotted line that indicates the area you're encompassing. When the selection box surrounds all the frames (or objects) that you want to select, release the mouse button.

✔ **To select everything on the current publication page(s) and the scratch area, choose the Edit⇨Select All command.** (You don't need the Pointer Tool selected to perform this task.)

These same selection techniques work for all types of objects, not just frames.

Figure 5-6 shows you several frames and objects selected on a layout. The selected objects are, clockwise from top left, a shape, two text frames, and a table frame. Notice that you find a single *bounding box* (the rectangle that encompasses the selected items) around them, but each object still has its own set of selection handles. (The rounded-arrow shape is not selected with this range of objects.)

Figure 5-6:
A multiple
selection of
objects and
frames
(ungrouped).

You can tell that this multiple selection is *ungrouped* because the picture on the Group Object button so indicates (it looks like two unjoined puzzle pieces) and because each object retains its own selection handles. In the ungrouped condition, the objects and frames retain their individual identities. (Microsoft Publisher 2000 handles the objects as independent entities unless they are *grouped;* you find out about grouping later in this chapter.) Because a multiple selection is not a single object, you cannot resize the selection or any individual component, but you can move the selection about and apply other commands, such as formatting. For example, if you apply a border to the multiple selection, each component of the selection takes on that border format.

Sometimes when you click a frame (or object), you can't select or modify it. If this happens, check out the following possibilities:

✔ **The frame or object may be a background object.** To select a background object, move to the background by choosing <u>V</u>iew⇨<u>G</u>o to Background or pressing Ctrl+M.

✔ **The frame or object is grouped.** Figure 5-7 shows you the same set of objects shown in Figure 5-6, but this time they are grouped together. You can click the Group button to ungroup a group; look for more about groups later in this chapter.

After you're done working with a particular frame or set of frames, deselect them so that you don't accidentally delete or change them in some way. Selected frames can be frighteningly easy to delete. Many programs offer a Lock command to freeze objects to prevent you from accidentally moving or deleting them. But Microsoft Publisher 2000 does not have this handy feature, so you must be especially careful.

Figure 5-7:
A selected,
grouped set
of objects.

To deselect frames, click in a blank area of the publication page or scratch area. Or click a single frame or object to deselect every other frame and select just that one.

Editing frames

Because frames are container objects, you can make two types of deletions:

- ✔ You can delete the entire frame itself, which also deletes all its contents.
- ✔ You can delete the contents of the frame and leave the frame intact.

To delete a frame, you select the frame and choose Delete Object from the Edit menu. If the frame that you want to delete is empty, simply select the frame and press Delete. In the case of a table frame, you have a container with many "drawers"; you can delete the contents of each cell in the table by selecting the contents of that cell and pressing Delete. When you have selected text in a text frame or an insertion point in a cell of a table frame, you must select the frame and press Ctrl+Shift+X to delete the frame. Using only the Delete key in those cases deletes the selected text or the contents of the current cell in the table.

In the case of text or table frames, you may notice that the commands Delete Text and Delete Object appear on the Edit menu. These Delete commands bypass the Windows Clipboard and simply remove the object from your layout. If you want to make use of the Windows Clipboard, you need to use the Cut, Copy, and Paste commands, which you also find on the Edit menu.

The Windows Clipboard is a piece of computer memory (RAM) that can store text, formatted text, graphics, and other objects. It's sort of like a temporary holding tank where you can keep data that you want to use again. You can use the Windows Clipboard to work with frames and the contents of frames within Microsoft Publisher 2000. The operations that I outline in the following bulleted list work with frames and, generally, with objects of other types. When you use the Clipboard between Windows programs, you can transfer only the contents of the Clipboard that the receiving program understands. For example, you can't paste a Microsoft Publisher 2000 frame into WordPad, but you can move formatted text between the two programs.

The Edit menu's Cut, Copy, and Paste commands work as follows:

- ✔ **Cut:** Choose Edit➪Cut or press Ctrl+X to place the current selection onto the Windows Clipboard and remove it from your layout. The previous contents of the Clipboard are lost.

- ✔ **Copy:** Choose Edit➪Copy or press Ctrl+C to make a copy of your selected element and place it onto the Windows Clipboard. The selection remains intact on your layout. The previous contents of the Clipboard are lost.

   Copying is a great timesaver and an ideal way to make exact duplicates of frames that you've already drawn. Here's a great shortcut: To quickly copy a selected frame or object, press Ctrl and drag it to a new location.

- ✔ **Paste:** Choose Edit➪Paste or press Ctrl+V to place the contents of the Windows Clipboard on your layout at your current position. The previous contents of the Clipboard remain intact. You can apply the Paste command any number of times you want.

   Pasted text is placed at the insertion point. If it finds no insertion point, Microsoft Publisher 2000 creates a text frame in the center of your screen and places the text in it. If a cut or copied text frame is on the Clipboard, the Paste command puts the frame back on the page at the position from which it came.

   If an object such as a line is on the Clipboard, Microsoft Publisher 2000 pastes that object at a position that's offset slightly from the original selected object. If you move to a new page after you place an object on the Clipboard, the object, when pasted, is placed on the new page at the same position that it appeared on the original page.

   When you flush the contents of the Clipboard, either by replacing them (with another Cut or Copy command) or by restarting your computer, the contents are gone and cannot be restored.

The Cut, Copy, and Paste commands also show up on the context-sensitive (or *shortcut*) menu that appears when you right-click a frame or object. Figure 5-8 shows you this menu for a text frame. You can select the entire contents of a page or publication and cut and paste it to another page or publication. You can also drag and drop text, frames, and other objects between publications if you have two copies of Microsoft Publisher 2000 open on your screen.

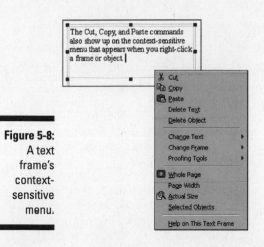

The Cut, Copy, and Paste commands also show up on the context-sensitive menu that appears when you right-click a frame or object.

Figure 5-8:
A text frame's context-sensitive menu.

TIP

You should definitely explore the right-click menus for every frame and object that Microsoft Publisher 2000 creates. They offer many editing and modification commands that provide useful shortcuts.

The Edit menu also offers another Paste command: Paste Special. Paste Special calls up objects that must be managed by outside programs through object linking and embedding, or OLE. Earlier in this chapter, in the section on creating WordArt frames, I discuss one example of OLE. Microsoft Publisher 2000 can be an OLE client and use the services of any OLE server program that is recognized by Windows for a particular object's file type.

Filling frames

Frames are so important to creating publications that I devote some entire chapters in this book to them. Mourn the trees! Chapters 6 and 8 offer more information about text frames, and Chapter 6 discusses table frames as well. Because WordArt frames create special text objects that are really graphics, I save the discussion of them for the chapter on type, where the lingo flies fast and thick — that is, Chapter 8. Chapter 9 covers picture frames.

Moving and resizing frames

For one reason or another, frames don't always end up the right size or shape or at the place where you want them to be. Nobody's perfect.

To move a frame or object, move your pointer over the border or the shape itself until the pointer turns into a truck with the word *Move* on it. Then, click and drag the frame or object to a new location.

You can constrain a move to either the vertical or horizontal direction by holding down the Shift key.

As you drag, a dotted outline of the frame follows your pointer. When the outline is where you want your frame, release your mouse button.

If you want to move a frame or set of frames to a different page within your publication, drag the frame or set completely off the publication page and onto the scratch area. Then move to the destination page and drag the frame or set from the scratch area to that page.

Perhaps you need to make a graphic bigger or create more room for your text. Rather than delete the frame and any work you've done on it, use the frame's selection handles to resize the existing frame. As you move the cursor over the selection handles, the mouse pointer becomes a resize pointer and you should see the word *Resize*. After the resize pointer appears, you can do any of the following:

- Click and drag a selection handle to resize a frame horizontally or vertically.

- Hold the Ctrl key and drag a selection handle to resize both horizontal or both vertical edges at the same time.

- Click and drag a corner selection handle to resize a frame both horizontally and vertically at the same time.

- Hold the Shift key down and drag a corner selection handle to resize a frame along its diagonal and retain the relative proportions of its height versus its width.

- Hold the Ctrl key down and drag a corner selection handle to have the frame's center retain its position on the page.

- Hold down the Shift and Ctrl keys together as you drag a corner selection handle to maintain a frame's proportion and resize it around its center.

You resize and move objects in the same manner as you do frames, using the selection handles that you find on each object's bounding box.

Many page layout programs offer features that enable you to resize a frame to a specific dimension or to reduce or enlarge a frame by a percentage. Microsoft Publisher 2000 is no exception. Select the frame and then choose Size and Position from the Format menu. The Size and Position dialog box appears, as shown in Figure 5-9. Enter the height and width of the object in the Size area. Enter the exact position in the Position area. The Horizontal setting specifies the horizontal distance from the upper-left corner of the page to the upper-left corner of the object that you are positioning. The Vertical setting specifies the vertical distance from the upper-left corner of the page to the upper-left corner of the object that you are positioning.

Figure 5-9:
The Size
and Position
dialog box.

Entering a negative number in either the Horizontal or Vertical Position boxes places the object in the scratch area.

How resizing a frame affects the contents depends on the frame's type. Resizing a picture or WordArt frame changes the size of the picture or WordArt object within that frame. Resizing a text or table frame, however, merely changes the amount of area available for the text within the frame; the text itself doesn't change size but rearranges itself to fit the new shape of its home.

If this doesn't give you enough control, just click the Show Toolbar button in the bottom-left corner of the Size and Position dialog box. The Size and Position dialog box goes away and the Measurements toolbar appears. Figure 5-9 shows the Size and Position dialog box and the Measurements toolbar. This is the same toolbar that appears when you select View⇨Toolbars⇨ Measurements. It's not a particularly user-friendly toolbar, as you can plainly see. The first column of text boxes control the horizontal and vertical position of the object. The second column controls the width and height. The text box in the third column controls the rotation. The fourth column controls text scaling (horizontally) and tracking. *Tracking* is the general spacing between characters. The fifth and final column controls kerning and line spacing. Kerning is the amount of space between pairs of characters. In addition to resizing frames, you can move a frame about as easily as you can slide a brand-new playing card across a freshly waxed table. Swoosh!

In the spirit of giving you more options than you could possibly use, Microsoft Publisher 2000 provides four ways to move frames and objects: dragging, nudging, lining up, and the ubiquitous cutting-and-pasting (discussed in a prior section of this chapter). I cover the first three options in more detail in later sections of this chapter (after I dispose of the details of working with drawn objects). Each method for moving frames and objects has its own advantages, depending on where you want to move a frame and how adept you are with the mouse.

Personal info

To relieve you from the tedium of entering information about yourself, your business, or your organization every time that you create a publication, Microsoft Publisher 2000 provides four Personal Information Sets. Every publication that you create has a Personal Information Set associated with it, although you won't see the information unless you, or a wizard, inserts it into the publication. Personal Information Sets contain information about you or your organization. The four Personal Information Sets are as follows:

- ✔ Primary Business
- ✔ Secondary Business
- ✔ Other Organization
- ✔ Home/Family

By default, every new publication has the Primary Business Personal Information Set selected. Each Personal Information Set contains eight components:

- ✔ Name
- ✔ Job or Position Title
- ✔ Organization Name
- ✔ Address
- ✔ Tag Line or Motto
- ✔ Phone/Fax/E-mail
- ✔ Logo
- ✔ Color Scheme

Switching Personal Information Sets

To switch to another Personal Information Set, select Edit➪Personal Information. The Personal Information dialog box, shown in Figure 5-10, leaps to the screen. Click one of the four available Personal Information Sets to select it. If you have not previously done so, you may now enter the information into the selected Personal Information Set. You may also change any existing information. Click the Update button to apply your changes and close the Personal Information dialog box.

Figure 5-10:
The
Personal
Information
dialog box.

Have you made any changes to the components in the currently selected Personal Information Set? Be sure to save your publication before switching to a different Personal Information Set or you will lose your changes.

Inserting Personal Information Set components

With the exception of the Color Scheme component, each component can be inserted into a publication. Select Personal Information from the Insert menu and then click the name of the component that you would like to insert. The Personal Information Set component is inserted into the publication with eight little black boxes, called *selection handles,* around its perimeter. With the exception of the Logo component, Personal Information Set components look and behave just like text frames.

You can tell a plain old text frame from a Personal Information Set component by pointing at the box (with the mouse — your finger just leaves smudges on the screen). When the ScreenTip appears, it will either say "Text Frame," for a plain old text frame, or something akin to "Personal Name Text Frame," which means that it is the Name component of the currently selected Personal Information Set.

Changing Personal Information Set components

In Publisher 98, the only way to change Personal Information was directly in the publication. You had to insert a Personal Information component, modify the component, and then save the publication. Publisher 2000 makes life much easier for you. Open the Personal Information dialog box by selecting Information from the menu. Make the desired changes to any or all Personal Information sets and click Update. That's all there is to it!

Don't like to take the easy way out? Or are you comfortable with the old method of changing Personal Information Sets? The friendly programmers at Microsoft the Magnanimous accommodate you. Sort of. You first have to tell Publisher 2000 that you want to be able to change Personal Information Set components directly in a publication. Here's how:

1. **Select from the menu.**

2. **Click the User Assistance Tab.**

3. **Click to place a check mark in the Update personal information when saving check box.**

4. **Click OK.**

Now you're ready to modify Personal Information Set components directly in the publication. Make sure that the Personal Information Set you want to change is selected. See the previous section on switching Personal Information Sets. Click the component that you want to change. Selection handles appear around the component to let you know that it is selected. Highlight the information that you want to change and type your changes. Have I mentioned saving lately? Save your publication to save the changes to the Personal Information Set.

If the Personal Information Set component that you want to change is not in the publication, you will have to insert it before you can change it.

Removing personal information

There are three ways to remove personal information. The first method simply deletes a Personal Information Set component from the current publication but leaves the Personal Information Set unchanged. Click the component that you want to remove and press Ctrl+Shift+X. Poof! The component is gone. If you change your mind, just press Ctrl+Z to undo the deletion, or select Insert⇨Personal Information and click the component name to re-insert it into the publication.

The second method clears the information from the Personal Information Set. This method works only if you clicked to put a check mark in the Update personal information when saving check box on the User Assistance tab of the Options dialog box. Click the component and highlight the information that you want to clear. Press Delete. The information is deleted from all instances of the component in the current publication. If you clear all the information in a component, that component will be blank when inserted into all future publications.

The third method also clears information from the Personal Information Set. Select Information from the menu. The Personal Information dialog box appears. Make the desired changes to the components and click the Update button. The information is changed in all instances of the components in the current publication. If you clear all the information in a component, that component will be blank when inserted into all future publications.

Changing the Color Scheme component

A color scheme is a set of colors associated with a publication. Microsoft Publisher 2000 comes with more than 60 color-coordinated color schemes. The easiest way to change the Color Scheme component is from the Personal Information dialog box. Open the Personal Information dialog box by selecting Information from the menu (refer to Figure 5-10). Make sure that the Include color scheme in this set check box in the Color Scheme area is checked. Click the down arrow in the For print publications text box to select a color scheme for print publications. Click the down arrow in the For web publications text box to select a color scheme for Web pages that you create. Click the Update button to apply your changes and close the Personal Information dialog box.

If you checked the Update personal information when saving check box on the User Assistance tab of the Options dialog, you can change a Personal Information Set's color scheme from the Color Scheme dialog box:

1. **Select Scheme from the menu to open the Color Scheme dialog box, shown in Figure 5-11.**

2. **Select a color scheme in the Available schemes box.**

   Take a peek at the Preview box to see a sample of how the new color scheme will look in your document.

3. **Click OK and then click Save to save the publication.**

   The color scheme for the current Personal Information Set is updated.

Figure 5-11:
The Color
Scheme
dialog box.

Working with Drawn Objects

If you read the first part of this chapter, you already know an awful lot about working with drawn objects. And if you've ever used a drawing program, these objects are more familiar still. Microsoft Publisher 2000 is nothing more than a fancy drawing program.

Earlier sections in this chapter explain how to create objects, resize them, move them, and delete them. But the program offers eight additional toolbox buttons for creating objects that I haven't discussed yet. Later, I move on to some of the general properties of objects; the various kinds of formatting commands that you can apply to them; and how you align, layer, and group objects. The following list describes the five drawing tools that are pertinent to this topic in the toolbox; you find all the tools labeled in Figure 5-12:

Figure 5-12: The drawing tools.

— Line Tool
— Oval Tool
— Rectangle Tool
— Custom Shapes
— Hot Spot Tool
— Form Control
— HTML Code Fragment
— Design Gallery Object

✔ **Line Tool:** Used to create lines on your layout. Click and drag a line from a starting point (where you click and begin dragging) to an ending point (where you release the mouse button).

✔ **Oval Tool:** Used to create an oval. If you want to create a perfect circle, press the Shift key while you click and drag.

✔ **Rectangle Tool:** Used to create a rectangle. Press the Shift key while you click and drag to create a square.

Use the Shift key to constrain your shapes to the horizontal, vertical, or diagonal direction (45-degree angles). When you use the Shift key with the Oval and Rectangle Tools, you create perfect circles and squares — by necessity. Use the Ctrl key to draw shapes from their center point out and use the Ctrl+Shift keys together to combine these constraints.

In the language of *object-oriented* or *vector* programs — which is what techies like to call drawing programs when they don't want normal people to understand what they are saying — a basic shape is called a *primitive*. Lines, circles, and squares are primitives. More complex shapes (such as the custom shapes) that can be broken apart into unrelated line segments or that are a grouped set of shapes (such as those you see in the Design Gallery) are shapes that you can create for yourself in Microsoft Publisher 2000. The Custom Shapes and Design Gallery libraries exist to make your task in Microsoft Publisher 2000 easier.

✔ **Custom Shapes Tool:** Used to create more complex shapes. I'm fond of this special tool because it lets you easily create interesting shapes that you can use for captions, callouts, product bursts, and many other purposes. Figure 5-13 shows you the pop-up menu for the Custom Shapes Tool. Click to select the shape that you want from the menu and then drag to create your object on the layout.

✔ **Design Gallery Object Tool:** Lets you select from a library of objects. Click the Design Gallery Object Tool to open up a browser, shown in Figure 5-14, that lets you select from a number of objects in a library and inserts your selection into your publication.

Figure 5-13:
The Custom Shapes pop-up menu.

The Objects by Category tab allows you to view the Design Gallery objects grouped by category. Click Mastheads to see all the styles of mastheads that are available. Click Tables of Contents to see all the available styles of tables of contents. Click Reply Forms to, well, you get the idea.

Figure 5-14:
The Design Gallery.

The Objects by Design tab allows you to view the Design Gallery objects grouped by style. Click a Design Set to see all the Design Gallery objects that are available in that style.

You can add your very own objects to the Design Gallery. Select the object that you want to add. Click the Design Gallery Object Tool to open the Design Gallery, and then click the Your Objects tab. Click the Options button and select Add Selection To Design Gallery. The Add Object dialog box appears. Enter an Object name and Category for your object and click OK.

You can think of the Design Gallery as a clip art collection of useful objects. Use them as special elements in your publication for pull quotes, captions, and so on. Most Design Gallery objects are groups of other objects that you can modify for your own use. See Chapter 9 for more detail on this tool.

Microsoft included these drawing tools in the program specifically for their importance in page composition. In the desktop publishing game, lines are called *rules* and they are often used to separate headlines from body copy, one column from another, and so on. Boxes are important because they let you frame areas of the page, shade them, or apply spot color. Similarly, ovals can be used to frame pictures. Other shapes that you may see in general drawing programs are less useful to page layout and, therefore, aren't incorporated directly in the toolbox. You can use an OLE server program such as Microsoft Draw to access these other tools.

Understanding object properties

Objects have some basic properties that you probably already know about. This is head-banging stuff, but it lets me introduce some terms that are useful in discussions to come. If the italicized words in this section are familiar to you, you are not a pilgrim, and you should mosey on.

Size and shape

The first thing that you notice about an object is that it has a *shape*. (Strange, most people tend to notice that!) A shape is the actual defined area of the object and is indicated in Microsoft Publisher 2000 by its border. When you select a shape, the shape is surrounded by the smallest rectangle that will encompass that object — called a *bounding box*. Figure 5-15 shows you a shape with its bounding box. The bounding box has the properties of a frame, and when the encompassed shape has right angles (like a rectangle), the shape's bounding box and border coincide.

Figure 5-15:
An object
and its
bounding
box.

Use the selection handles on the bounding box to resize a shape or object. When a shape is irregular, you can see the bounding box and the border separately. If you look closely at Figure 5-15, you notice that the lower-left vertex of the trapezoid (the shape) displays a light-gray, diamond-shaped handle. That handle lets you reshape the trapezoid by changing its defining angle.

Borders, colors, and fills

Even if no border is applied to a shape, Microsoft Publisher 2000 draws a dotted line so that you can see the shape and work with it. If you don't like this dotted line, you can apply a border — technically called a *stroke* — to the shape. Publisher 2000 lets you define a border thickness of between 0 and 1.76 inches. Only the author likes to work with invisible shapes and writes and talks to invisible people.

To apply a border to a shape, start by choosing Format⇨Line/Border Style⇨ More Styles from the menu or by clicking the Line/Border Style button on the Formatting toolbar and selecting More Styles from its pop-up menu. The pop-up menu is shown in Figure 5-16. In either case, you get to the Border dialog box, as shown in Figure 5-17.

Figure 5-16:
The
Line/Border
Style button
and menu
from the
Formatting
toolbar.

You can apply a weight to a shape's line or stroke. *Weight* is a term used by typographical folk to describe the thickness of the line. Microsoft Publisher 2000 keeps things simple by using the term *thickness* in the Border dialog box. Usually, line weight is measured in *points,* which is a common unit of measurement used in publishing. Publisher 2000 gives you the option of defining the thickness of a border in inches, centimeters, picas, or points.

Figure 5-17:
The Border
dialog box.

You can also apply a color and even a pattern to a border stroke. Or, described another way, a stroke can have a *fill* and a *fill effect.* Using the term *fill* in this way can be confusing, though, because it's more commonly used to refer to the interior of a shape — the part surrounded by the stroke. Like a stroke, the interior of an object can have a color and pattern applied to it.

Microsoft Publisher 2000 lets you apply BorderArt (with patterns and colors) to frames and boxes. I tell you more about BorderArt in Chapter 10. Other, more capable programs give you finer control and let you apply any attribute to a stroke that you can apply to an object's fill.

In addition to having fills and fill effects, lines can have arrowheads. You open the Line dialog box by choosing Format⇨Line/Border Styles or by clicking the Line/Border Style button on the Formatting toolbar and selecting More Styles from the pop-up menu. This dialog box lets you assign arrowheads, line color, and line widths to a selected line. Figure 5-18 shows the Line dialog box.

Figure 5-18:
The Line
dialog box.

Color is a big subject and a very technical one for desktop publishers. I tackle it in detail in Chapter 10. For now, remember it as one of an object's basic properties. To apply a color to the fill of a selected shape, you need to access the Colors dialog box. You can do this in two ways:

✔ Click the Fill Color button on the Formatting toolbar to reveal the pop-up selection menu, as shown in Figure 5-19. From this pop-up menu, access the Colors dialog box by clicking the More Colors button.

✔ Choose Format➪Fill Color➪More Colors from the menu. The much larger and more capable Colors dialog box, shown in Figure 5-20, appears.

Figure 5-19:
The Fill Color button and menu on the Formatting toolbar.

To apply a pattern, shading, or gradient to the selected object's fill, first access the Fill Effects dialog box as follows:

✔ Click the Fill Color button on the Formatting toolbar to reveal the pop-up selection menu, as shown previously in Figure 5-19. From this pop-up menu, access the Fill Effects dialog box by clicking the Fill Effects button.

✔ Choose Format➪Fill Color➪Fill Effects from the menu.

Figure 5-20:
The Colors dialog box.

In the Fill Effects dialog box, click the radio button for the Style of fill that you want to use. Figure 5-21 shows the options available when you select the Patterns radio button.

Figure 5-21:
The Fill Effects dialog box.

In the vocabulary of color, a *Tint/Shade* is a mix of a color with white. Patterns use a base color for the lines or dots and a background color — normally black and white, respectively. *Gradients* are effects in which the color is varied in some manner and in a specific direction (for example, from dark to light and outward from the center of the object). I think that the effects you can get with gradients are so cool!

Cool-looking gradients can take up a lot of memory and create challenges for your printer. Make sure that the printer you select can handle these large files. See Chapter 13 for more about printing.

Seeing through an object

Objects also have the property of being *transparent* (see-through) or *opaque* (not see-through). Many fancy drawing and page layout programs let you control the degree of transparency of an object and even the type of color that shows through. Microsoft Publisher 2000 lets you assign a property of only *clear* or *transparent* to an object. A clear object lets other objects beneath it show through; for most desktop publishing purposes, this option is sufficient. Don't blink, though, or you'll miss the setting for clear. To locate it, click the Patterns radio button in the Fill Effects dialog box. The pattern all the way on the left — the one with a circle and a slash through it — is the clear setting.

To make an opaque object or frame transparent, press Ctrl+T. Press the keystroke again to make a transparent object or frame opaque — a technique that works less often because not all object types support it.

Relative positions

Another property that objects have in a layout is their position with respect to one another. When you create an object, it goes on top of all the other objects created before it. There is a strict order from back to front. You can change this automatic order — often referred to as the *layering order* or *stacking order* — by using a set of commands that I cover later in this chapter. Use these commands to send objects backward or forward in the stacking order. You can also align objects with each other and create groups of objects that behave like a single object. I talk about alignment and grouping later in the chapter, too.

Even this very basic set of properties allows you to create many special effects. For example, you can't apply BorderArt to a box, but you can create a text frame, apply BorderArt to that frame, and then place it behind the box to create the illusion of a box that has BorderArt applied.

Using the Format Painter

When you get an object's properties just so, you'd like to lock the object and prevent it from being changed. This very important command is unfortunately missing in Microsoft Publisher 2000, which makes it imperative that you take care when you delete objects. The program does offer the Format Painter, however — a "just so" command that lets you apply the same set of formatting from one object to another object. The two objects don't even have to be the same kind of object.

You can copy an object's format in the following two ways:

✔ Select the object whose format you want to copy. Then click the Format Painter button on the Standard toolbar; it's the button that looks like a paintbrush. Finally, click the object that you want to format.

✔ Select the object whose format you want to copy and choose Format⇨Pick Up Formatting. This command "fills" the Format Painter's brush. To paint another object with the formatting, select the object and then choose Format⇨Apply Formatting.

If you want the Format Painter's brush to stay "loaded" with your format until you change it, double-click the button. Now you can click as many objects as you want and the same formatting will be applied to all of them. You can also use the menu to apply a format to multiple objects at one time. Select the objects to be formatted and then choose Format⇨Apply Formatting.

Aligning and positioning objects

The most natural method for moving an object or frame is to drag it. Dragging an object is the electronic equivalent of using your finger to slide a playing card across a table. In Chapter 4, I explain some of the tools used for precise positioning of objects and frames on a layout when you are dragging them into position: position measurements in the status bar, ruler marks, layout and grid guides, and ruler guides.

Ruler marks and guides work with Snap To commands, also covered in Chapter 4, to help you position objects precisely. When you get an object's border or center axis (either horizontal or vertical) close to a ruler mark or guide, it snaps into alignment with the mark or guide.

Three additional sets of commands, found on the Arrange menu, are also used for precise positioning or alignment:

✔ **Align Objects:** This command opens the Align Objects dialog box, shown in Figure 5-22. Selected objects are aligned using the Left to Right and Top to Bottom options that you choose. You can set either or both of these alignment options. The Sample section shows you an example of your choices.

You can also align objects to the page margin — one object must already be aligned to the page margin before you check the Align along margins check box for this option to take effect. I think that the Align Objects dialog box is clear cut and well implemented, and I doubt that it will give you any trouble. Use the dialog box's Apply button to see your changes before you dismiss the dialog box, and use the Cancel button to undo those changes. I just wish there were a keystroke that called this dialog box up quickly, because it is so useful.

Figure 5-22:
The Align
Objects
dialog box.

✔ **Nudge:** The Nudge command opens the Nudge dialog box, shown in Figure 5-23. *Nudges,* for those of you not in the know (nudge, nudge, wink, wink), are small movements of an object in one direction.

Most programs give you a nudge. Some programs give you a swift kick in the pants. Microsoft Publisher 2000 gives you a dialog box. The traditional way of implementing nudges is to select an object and press the arrow keys. Each time that you press an arrow key, your object moves one pixel in that direction. Microsoft Publisher 2000 requires that you hold the Alt key down and press the arrows keys to perform this action. You can also click the arrows in the Nudge dialog box to perform this simple function — a technique that makes me, how shall I say this — nudgey.

Were it not for the ability to set the nudge distance in the Nudge dialog box's Nudge by text box, I'd think that the Nudge dialog box was totally useless. Leave this box blank if you want each press of an arrow key to move your object one pixel. Or, enter a value of up to 2 inches. When entering your measurement, use the abbreviation *in* for inches. You can also use *cm* for centimeters, *pi* for picas, and *pt* for points.

✔ **Rotate or Flip:** Microsoft Publisher 2000 offers five commands to rotate and flip selected objects: Custom Rotate, Rotate Left, Rotate Right, Flip Horizontal, and Flip Vertical.

The second and third commands rotate your object(s) 90 degrees counterclockwise and clockwise with each application; the last two commands reflect your selection through a horizontal and vertical mirror plane. The four Formatting toolbar buttons, shown in Figure 5-24, duplicate these four flip and rotate commands.

The Custom Rotate command is more interesting. You can also use the Custom Rotate button (shown in the margin) at the right of the Standard toolbar to invoke the command. Either way, you open the Custom Rotate dialog box, as shown in Figure 5-25. In this dialog box, you can set an angle and rotate a selection in either direction.

Figure 5-23:
The Nudge
dialog box.

Figure 5-24:
The Flip
and Rotate
buttons
on the
Formatting
toolbar.

Figure 5-25:
The Custom
Rotate
dialog box.

To perform a free rotation, hold the Alt key and use the Pointer Tool to click and drag on the object's selection handles.

Working with layers

The position that an object has on a page is uniquely defined by its layer. In the natural creation order, the first object created is at the back and the last object created is at the front. It's like football players diving for a fumbled ball: Whoever gets there first ends up on the bottom. Fortunately for your publication, frames don't suffer from broken bones and torn ligaments. Both the background and foreground have separate layer orders, and they can't be mixed.

Grouped objects are considered to be in the same layer — that is, until they are ungrouped. Then they return to their natural relative order, one ungrouped object to another. You can defeat the natural layering by using a set of commands on the Arrange menu. Layers have some important implications. Opaque objects obscure the object(s) behind them. Text and table frames are opaque by default; picture and WordArt frames are transparent by default.

No matter what order you use to originally layer frames, however, you can rearrange these layers any way you want using the four layering commands on the Arrange menu:

✔ **Bring to Front:** Choose Arrange⇨Bring to Front, click the Bring to Front button on the Standard toolbar (shown in margin), or press F6 to bring the selected object(s) to the top layer.

✔ **Send to Back:** Choose Arrange⇨Send to Back, click the Send to Back button on the Standard toolbar (shown in margin), or press Shift+F6 to send the selected frame(s) to the bottom layer.

✔ **Bring Forward:** Choose Arrange⇨Bring Forward to bring the selected frame(s) up one layer.

✔ **Send Backward:** Choose Arrange⇨Send Backward to send the selected frame(s) down one layer.

No matter how far down you send a frame or other object on a foreground page, it always remains on top of any background object. And no matter how far up you bring a frame or other object on a background, it always remains below any foreground object.

Adjusting the layers and transparency of objects so that other objects either show through or are hidden is called *layering* by Microsoft Publisher 2000. It is one of the most important design techniques you can apply to your publications. By using this technique, you can place text in front of a picture so that it appears to be part of the picture, apply fills and patterns that the object doesn't support by itself, wrap text around a graphic (another layering technique discussed later), and more. Figure 5-26 shows you an example of a labeled starburst with a transparent text frame on top.

Figure 5-26:
An example
of layering.

Wrapping Text around Objects

Take a look at Figure 5-27, which shows you one of the most important types of layering — text wrapping. This is a special layer effect created with intelligent frame margins. Notice how the text makes room for the graphic, neatly wrapping around it? Is the text just being well-behaved or did the graphic forget to put on its deodorant this morning?

Figure 5-27:
Text
wrapped
around a
picture
frame.

Creating regular text wraps

Back in the bad old days of traditional publishing, wrapping text like this required painstaking hours of cutting, pasting, and rearranging individual lines of text. And pity the poor fool who suggested making a change to the text after the wrapping was complete!

In Microsoft Publisher 2000, though, wrapping text is amazingly easy. Just place any type of frame — even another text frame — on top of a text frame, and the text underneath automatically wraps around the frame above.

Text doesn't wrap if one frame is on a foreground page and the other is on the background page; both frames have to be on the same page, so to speak.

Although the program tries its best, it can sometimes wrap text too closely or too loosely around a frame. My wife has had occasion to declare that I am not wrapped too tight. Closely wrapped text can be difficult to read, whereas loosely wrapped text can waste space and create big gaps on the page. With all frames except table frames, you can easily change the amount of space between the wrapping text and the frame it wraps around by changing the margins of the wrapped-around frame.

To increase the margins of a text frame, click the text frame and then choose Format⇨Text Frame Properties from the menu. Make your selections from the Text Frame Properties dialog box, shown in Figure 5-28. Turn text wrap on and off by checking or unchecking the Wrap text around objects check box. The Margins section changes the amount of space between the text in a frame and the border of the frame.

Figure 5-28:
The Text
Frame
Properties
dialog box.

To increase the margins of a picture or WordArt frame and change the text wrap properties, do the following:

✔ Select a picture or WordArt frame and then choose Format⇨Object Frame Properties from the menu. Make your selections from the Object Frame Properties dialog box, shown in Figure 5-29, which is the object frame's equivalent of the Text Frame Properties dialog box.

✔ Just as you can adjust the margins in a text frame, you can change the margins that a picture has inside the picture frame. More important, you can adjust the way text wraps around a graphic so that it wraps around the entire picture frame or just the graphic contained therein — as shown by the example in the Wrap text around section of the Object Frame Properties dialog box.

Figure 5-29:
The Object
Frame
Properties
dialog box.

Depending on the option set under Wrap text around, either one or four margin settings are available. Changing a frame's margins doesn't change the frame's overall size. Rather, it increases or decreases the amount of available space *within* the frame. When you change a picture or WordArt frame's margins, the graphic inside the frame grows accordingly smaller or larger. When you change a text frame's margins, however, the text in that frame stays the same size but rearranges itself according to the new space available.

Don't confuse *frame margins* with *margin guides*. Frame margins control the amount of space between a frame's perimeter and its contents. Margin guides mark the margins of an entire publication page. (We discuss margin guides in Chapter 4.)

If you set the margins of a picture or WordArt frame unequally, the graphic within that frame loses its original proportions, becoming squished in one direction or another. To return your graphic to its original proportions, either set the frame margins equally or resize the frame in the opposite direction of the squeeze.

Although you can set margins for individual cells within a table frame, you can't set margins for an entire table frame. If text wraps too tightly around one of your table frames, place an empty picture frame behind that table frame; the text now wraps around the picture frame. If you need to adjust the text wrap, just resize the picture frame accordingly.

By default, Microsoft Publisher 2000 wraps text in a rectangular pattern around the perimeter of a frame, as shown earlier in Figure 5-27. If you're working with a picture or WordArt frame, however, you can have your text wrap to the actual shape of the graphic within that frame by selecting the Wrap Text to Picture button on the Formatting toolbar or by selecting the Picture only radio button in the Object Frame Properties dialog box. Figure 5-30 shows you an example of this. Very cool!

Figure 5-30:
Text
wrapped
around a
picture.

information to a targeted audience. Newsletters can be a great way to market your product or service, and also create credibility and build your organization's identity among peers, members, employees, or vendors.

First, determine the audience of the newsletter. This could be anyone who might benefit from the information it contains, for example, employees or people interested in purchasing a product or requesting your service.

You can compile a mailing list from business reply cards, customer information sheets, business cards collected at trade shows, or membership lists. You might consider purchasing a mailing list from a company.

If you explore the Publisher catalog, you will find many publications that match the style of your newsletter.

Fine-tuning your text wraps

Picky, picky, picky. Some folks like their text wrapped around their graphics just so. It is very important to them. Depending upon the justification that you use in your text, Microsoft Publisher 2000 can do a poor job of wrapping text around a graphic to match its shape. This is particularly true when you use justified text. The program wraps text around most of its own clip art because the text boundaries are built in already. But Microsoft Publisher 2000 can get mighty confused about the shapes of "foreign" graphics and can be especially pitiful when it comes to creating text boundaries for WordArt objects.

A couple of tools offer some help in this area. The first tool lets you create and adjust an irregular boundary on your graphic to control how text wraps around it. To create this kind of effect, select the graphic and make sure that the Wrap Text to Picture button on the Formatting toolbar is selected. Then click the Edit Irregular Wrap button, which is also on the Formatting toolbar. Both buttons have equivalent commands on the Format menu.

Notice that each graphic has reshape handles for text wrap. Click and drag these handles where you want them. You can also add a handle by holding the Ctrl key and clicking the outline of the graphic. To remove a reshape handle, press Ctrl+Shift and click it. Figure 5-31 shows you an example of this kind of text wrap. The topic "Irregular Text Wrap" in the Microsoft Publisher 2000 online Help system gives you more information.

You can help the program out by manually adjusting the text boundary your-self for a graphic where the text is *wrapped around the frame.* To do this, first select the frame that contains the graphic and make sure that the Wrap Text to Frame button is selected on the Formatting toolbar. In that case, Microsoft

Figure 5-31: Editing a figure with an irregular text wrap effect.

information to a targeted audience. Newsletters can be a great way to market your product or service, and also create credibility and build your organization's identity among peers, members, employees, or vendors.

First, determine the audi- ence of the newsletter. This could be anyone who might benefit from the information it contains, for example, employees or people interested in purchasing a product or requesting your ser- vice.

You can compile a mailing list from business reply cards, customer information sheets, business cards collected at trade shows, or membership lists. You might consider purchasing a mailing list from a company.

If you explore the Pub- lisher catalog, you will find many publications that match the style of your newsletter.

Publisher 2000 places a Crop Picture button on the Formatting toolbar in place of the Edit Irregular Wrap button. Cropping lets you shave off part of your frame, just as if you were cutting paper with a pair of scissors. The command to do this is the Format⇨Crop Picture command on the menu bar.

Your graphic once again has just eight selection handles. Point to one of the selection handles until the mouse pointer becomes a Crop pointer. This pointer has two scissors and the word *Crop* in it. Then drag to change the text boundary's shape. Repeat this as necessary with the other handles. Just be careful not to drag any handles too far inward, or you may block out portions of your graphic.

When you crop a graphic, you don't remove part of the figure. You only hide some of the figure from view. If you make a mistake, you can crop your figure again to enlarge it and return the missing piece. You can find out more about working with graphics in Chapter 9.

Grouping Objects

Some things in "the real world" just seem to go together: peanut butter and jelly, macaroni and cheese, death and taxes. In your publications, too, some things might belong together: several drawn objects that comprise a logo; a graphic and its caption; a table frame and the picture frame that you stuck behind it to make text wrap the way you want; the assorted text and graphics that might comprise a company logo.

When you want different objects on your layout to stay together and behave like a unit, you can apply some electronic glue to stick them together in a *group*. There, they can share their most personal problems: "Hi, my name is Igor. I'm a picture frame trapped in a table frame's body."

Actually, grouping tells Microsoft Publisher 2000 to treat the collection of objects as a single object. Thus, you can easily move or copy a group while keeping the objects in the same positions relative to each other. You don't have to worry about leaving one line, box, or frame behind accidentally. You can also resize a group while maintaining the same relative size and position of the frames within that group. Trust me, this is a heck of a lot easier than resizing and adjusting the position of each object in a group individually and getting the same results.

To group two or more objects, do one of the following:

✔ Select the objects that you want to include in your group and click the Group Objects button that appears at the lower right of the selection's bounding box to create the group. The button changes to resemble locked puzzle pieces. You can even group groups.

✔ Choose Arrange⇨Group Objects or press Ctrl+Shift+G.

To ungroup a group of objects, do one of the following:

✔ Select the group and click the Group Objects button again. The button changes to look like two unjoined puzzle pieces. Figure 5-32 shows you an example of the same figures grouped and ungrouped.

✔ Choose Arrange⇨Ungroup Objects from the main menu or press Ctrl+Shift+G.

Figure 5-32:
Grouped
and
ungrouped
objects.

What you can do to an object in a group depends upon that object's capability. Earlier in the chapter, you see how you can apply borders to several shapes at once in a group. You can also resize a group; if you do, each object resizes proportionally. You can type text in a text or table frame that is part of a group; just click the frame and start typing. You can modify a graphic, a WordArt object, or an OLE object by double-clicking it.

If you want to modify a single object in a group, you need to ungroup the group. For example, to resize a single frame or change one frame's margins, you need to ungroup the frames first. As you ungroup a group of groups, you need to successively apply the Ungroup command to release the objects. The wizards make good use of groups. Don't be surprised if you find yourself doing a lot of ungrouping to get at individual elements if you base your document on a wizard.

Part III
10,000 Words, One Maniac

The 5th Wave   By Rich Tennant

GUS & LILY'S
DOG GROOMING
NOW USING CAD SOFTWARE

In this part ...

Fancy graphics and layouts can draw attention to your publication, but words usually comprise the core of your message. The three chapters in Part III cover working with text in your publication: Where and how do you get it? What do you do to it once you have it? And how do you select type to convey the feeling of what you are trying to say? I don't tell you what to write here — that's up to you. I do tell you how to get information from other Microsoft Office 2000 programs into Publisher 2000. After reading this part, you'll be able to produce a publication that has better-looking text with less effort.

Chapter 6

Getting the Word

*I*n this chapter, I take a closer look at two frame types: text frames and table frames. You use *text frames* to place and manage text in your publication. Microsoft Publisher 2000 has some special features to help you manage text frames across pages: the capacity to flow text automatically between linked frames, and *stories,* which are just blocks of text managed as a single entity. You can even place *continued on* and *continued from* notices in your publication to help your readers follow a story that begins on one page and continues on another.

In addition to regular text frames, Microsoft Publisher 2000 provides two other types of frames for holding text: table frames and WordArt frames. If you've worked in a spreadsheet program such as Microsoft Excel or Lotus 1-2-3, or used a word processor that offers a table feature such as Microsoft Word, the features in Microsoft Publisher 2000's table frames will seem familiar to you. If not, you can find out what you need to know about table frames at the end of this chapter.

WordArt frames enable you to create fancy text by using the WordArt OLE server to manipulate type. I cover WordArt in Chapter 9, as these types of frames are more commonly used for short pieces of decorative text than for the longer text that comprises most people's publications.

More about Text Frames

If you're accustomed to creating text in other computer programs, you may find it odd that you can't just begin typing right away in a Microsoft Publisher 2000 publication. You must first create a text frame to tell the program where to put your text. Chapter 5 shows you how easy creating a text frame is: You simply click the Text tool in the toolbox and then click and drag to create the frame.

After you create a text frame, you can fill it in three ways:

- ✔ You can type text directly into the text frame.

- ✔ You can paste text in from the Clipboard.

- ✔ You can import text from your word processor or text file.

Typing text

Microsoft Publisher 2000 offers a complete environment for creating page layout, so you discover that you can write your text in text frames with little trouble. Microsoft Publisher 2000 is not the most capable text creation tool, and it doesn't have all the bells and whistles that you would expect to find in your word processor, but it has been updated to integrate more closely with the Microsoft Office suite of applications. The idea is to let you leverage skills acquired from other Microsoft programs such as Microsoft Word. In fact, if you are familiar with Microsoft Word 2000, you may recognize some common features:

- ✔ **Similar menus and toolbars:** You may recognize the File, Edit, View, Insert, Format, Tools, and Help menus on the Menu bar. Also, the New, Open, Save, Print, Cut, Copy, Paste, Format Painter, Undo, Redo, Show/Hide ¶, and the Microsoft Publisher Help (called Microsoft Word Help in Word 2000) buttons from Microsoft Word 2000 will seem familiar.

- ✔ **The Office Assistant:** This is the same help system found in Microsoft Office 2000 that lets you ask for help in your own words.

- ✔ **AutoCorrect:** This feature lets you automatically fix some common errors, such as correcting two initial capitals or automatically capitalizing the names of days.

- ✔ **Spell Check:** This feature automatically checks spelling as you type; it flags any misspelled and repeated words by underlining them.

- ✔ **Microsoft Draw:** This is a helpful tool for creating complex art. You can use it to create flowcharts or draw freehand.

If you're used to typing on a typewriter or in a word processor, you may be used to doing some things that you shouldn't do in Microsoft Publisher 2000 — or in any page layout program — when you enter text.

Here are some highlights to keep in mind when you're entering text:

✔ **Turn on the Show Special Characters command.** Choose View➪Show Special Characters or press Ctrl+Shift+Y. Better yet, click the Show Special Characters button (the one that looks like a backward *P*) on the Standard toolbar. Special characters are symbols that represent things such as spaces, tabs, line endings, and so on. These symbols help you figure out why your text appears the way it does. Figure 6-1 shows a text block with special characters turned on.

✔ **Don't press Enter to force a line ending.** Pressing Enter tells the program that you've reached the end of a paragraph. If you press Enter at the end of every line, you won't be able to format the lines of your paragraph together as a unit, which is a bad thing. When you get to the end of a line of text, let Microsoft Publisher 2000 word-wrap the text to the next line for you (which it does automatically). Press Enter only to end a paragraph or a short, independent line of text (such as a line in an address).

Figure 6-1:
Special characters in your text frames help you figure out what's going on.

Here·are·some·highlights·to·keep·in·mind·when·you're·entering·text.¶
¶
→   *   →   Turn·on·the·Show·Special·Characters·command.·Choose·
View@-->Show·Special·Characters·or·press·Ctrl+Shift+Y.·Better·yet,·click·the·
Show·Special·Characters·button·(the·one·that·looks·like·a·backward·*P*)·on·the·
Standard·toolbar.▓Special·characters·are·symbols·that·represent·things·such·as·
spaces,·tabs,·line·endings,·and·so·on.·These·symbols·help·you·figure·out·why·
your·text·appears·the·way·it·does.·Figure·6-1·shows·a·text·block·with·special·
characters·turned·on.¶
→   *   →   Don't·press·Enter·to·force·a·line·ending.·Pressing·Enter·tells·the·
program·that·you've·reached·the·end·of·a·paragraph.·If·you·press·Enter·at·the·
end·of·every·line,·you·won't·be·able·to·format·the·lines·of·your·paragraph·to-
gether·as·a·unit,·which·is·a·bad·thing.·When·you·get·to·the·end·of·a·line·of·text,·
let·Microsoft·Publisher·2000·word-wrap·the·text·to·the·next·line·for·you·(which·
it·does·automatically).·Press·Enter·only·to·end·a·paragraph·or·a·short,·independ-
ent·line·of·text·(such·as·a·line·in·an·address).¶

✔ **If you need to force a line break without creating a new paragraph, press Shift+Enter.** This keystroke creates what is called a *soft carriage return*, and places the symbol ⤸ at the end of the line.

✔ **Don't press the Enter key to create blank lines between paragraphs.** Microsoft Publisher 2000 provides a much better way of creating spaces before and after paragraphs by choosing the Format➪Line Spacing command on the menu bar.

✔ **Don't insert two spaces between sentences.** Use just one. It makes your text easier to read.

✔ **Don't use the Tab key to indent the first lines of paragraphs.** Instead, use the paragraph indent controls explained in Chapter 8. These controls offer much more flexibility than tabs.

✔ **Don't try to edit or format your text as you go.** It's much more efficient to do all your typing first, your editing second, and your formatting last.

If any preceding suggestion seems new to you, I recommend that you consider picking up a copy of one of the typographical style books mentioned near the end of Chapter 2. I am especially fond of *The PC is Not a Typewriter* by Robin Williams (published by Peachpit Press). If you are working in a specific word processing program, you may also want to pick up the ...*For Dummies* book on that program.

As you type, your text begins filling the text frame from left to right, top to bottom. If the text frame isn't large enough to accommodate all your text, you eventually reach the bottom of the frame. When you type more text than can fit into a text frame, the extra text moves into an invisible place called the *overflow area.* You can type blindly into that overflow area; the program keeps track of everything you type. If you're like most people, though, you probably want to see what you're typing as you type it.

The Text in Overflow indicator alerts you to the fact that you have typed more text than can fit into the current frame. This indicator is located near the bottom-right corner of the frame. If you see the Text in Overflow indicator at the bottom of a text frame, you know that the frame is not large enough to contain the text. Figure 6-2 shows a text frame with the Text in Overflow indicator. Although you can view the contents of a text frame's overflow area in several ways, the most straightforward method is to simply enlarge the text frame, as explained in Chapter 5. When you do, the text in the overflow area automatically appears. You can also use the Connect Text Frames button to link text frames together for Autoflow, as described later in this chapter.

Figure 6-2:
Text frame with text in the overflow area.

> This text frame has some text in the overflow area, as is indicated by the Text in Overflow button attached to the bottom of the Text frame.

Text in Overflow indicator

The first thing that you may notice about text in a text frame is that in most views that provide an overview of your publication, the text is much too small to read. If you try to read this small text, you are going to go crazy before your time. So do yourself a favor and press F9 to zoom right in to view your text as you type it into your text frame. Pressing F9 toggles the view between the current magnification and 100% magnification.

Importing text

Placing text created in another program into your Microsoft Publisher 2000 publication, called *importing text*, can be an excellent time-saver — especially when you get someone else to do all the typing for you. In any case, you never want to type the same text into a computer more than once. Have I mentioned saving lately?

Using the Clipboard

You can paste text into a Microsoft Publisher 2000 publication from the Windows Clipboard or import text from a disk file. Here's how:

1. **Highlight the text in the program containing the text that you want to use.**

2. **Select Edit⇨Copy or press Ctrl+C.**

3. **Open your publication, select the Pointer tool, and click in a text frame to set the insertion point at the position where you want your text to be pasted.**

4. **Choose Edit⇨Paste or press Ctrl+V.**

   If you didn't set an insertion point in Step 3 or didn't have a text frame selected, Microsoft Publisher 2000 creates a new text frame and imports the copied text into that frame.

If you can copy formatted text successfully to the Windows Clipboard, the text should paste correctly into your text frame. For more information about using the Windows Clipboard, see Chapter 5.

If the text on the Clipboard can't fit in the text frame that you selected, the program performs an autoflow. First, it displays a dialog box informing you that the inserted text doesn't fit into the select frame, and asks whether you want to use an autoflow. I talk about autoflow in more depth later in this chapter.

Using the Text File command

The Text File command on the Insert menu provides a way to move text between your word processor and Microsoft Publisher 2000 by using an intervening text file. If your computer has sufficient memory, you can also do editing in place by running Microsoft Word as an OLE server inside Microsoft Publisher 2000.

Before you use the Text File command, you must save your text to a file in a format that Microsoft Publisher 2000 can use. Fortunately, Microsoft Publisher 2000 accepts many different file formats. The section on saving files in Chapter 3 covers these formats. Microsoft Publisher 2000 uses the same filters to import text as it does to save the text in your publication. You can use this feature to export text out of Microsoft Publisher 2000, as you find out later in this chapter.

The text file formats that Microsoft Publisher 2000 understands include the following:

- ✔ Other Microsoft Publisher files
- ✔ Plain text or plain text formatted for DOS (plain text is ASCII text)

  Most programs should at least be able to save the text as plain or ASCII text. But ASCII is your last resort. If you save a text file in the ASCII format, you lose all your formatting. Any work that you did bolding, italicizing, underlining, and so on, is lost. Try to avoid this option at all costs.

- ✔ Rich Text Format (RTF) — the Microsoft text-based formatted text interchange format. In RTF, only normal characters are saved in your file. Any formatting such as bold, italic, and so on is indicated with a set of codes of plain text. No special symbols are used.
- ✔ Microsoft Word for Windows 6.0/95 for Windows/Macintosh
- ✔ Microsoft Word (Asian Versions) 6.0/95
- ✔ Microsoft Word 97/2000 for Windows/Macintosh
- ✔ Microsoft Word 2.*x* for Windows
- ✔ Microsoft Word for the Macintosh 4.0 – 5.1
- ✔ Recover Text from Any File
- ✔ Lotus 1-2-3
- ✔ WordPerfect 5.*x* and 6.*x*
- ✔ Microsoft Works for Windows 3.0 and 4.0 word-processing files
- ✔ Microsoft Windows Write

If your word processor doesn't save to one of these file formats automatically, check to see whether it offers an Export command that can translate your word processor file into a form that Microsoft Publisher 2000 understands.

To import a text file into Microsoft Publisher 2000:

1. **Position the insertion point in (click inside) the text frame into which you want to import the text.**

2. **Choose Insert⇨Text File.**

   The Insert Text File dialog box shown in Figure 6-3 appears.

Figure 6-3:
The Insert
Text File
dialog box.

3. **Locate the file of interest, highlight it, and click OK.**

   After a moment, the text appears in your selected text frame.

If you can't find your text file, make sure that you selected the correct import filter from the Files of type list box. To see all files in a folder, type ***.*** into the File name text box and press Enter. If the file still doesn't appear, you're looking in the wrong place. If all the imported text can't fit in the selected text frame, the program opens a dialog box asking whether you want to autoflow the rest of your text into other text frames. I present more information on autoflowing text later in this chapter.

You can view the contents of a text file without importing the file into your publication. Choose File⇨Open (or press Ctrl+O), click the down arrow next to the Files of Type text box, and select All text formats. Find the file you want and click Open. Microsoft Publisher 2000 opens the text or word processor file as a full-page publication that offers the requisite number of pages filled with full-page text frames.

TIP

As an alternative to using the menu commands, don't forget the context-sensitive menus that you can get by right-clicking a text frame, as shown in Figure 6-4. Some people find that using the context-sensitive menu for the Insert Text File task is easier than mousing up to the top of the screen. I think it's a tossup.

2. **Highlight the desired text using your favorite text selection technique.**

3. **Select Edit⇨Copy, press Ctrl+C, or click the Copy button on the Standard toolbar.**

4. **Switch to the Microsoft Publisher window by clicking its button on the Windows taskbar.**

   If the Windows taskbar isn't visible, you can switch applications by pressing Alt+Tab. Hold down the Alt key and press Tab until the Microsoft Publisher icon is highlighted in the Cool Switch box that appears. Release both keys.

5. **Click in the text frame at the location where you want to insert the text from the Microsoft Word document.**

   If the text frame is empty, click anywhere inside the text frame.

6. **Select Edit⇨Paste, press Ctrl+V, or click the Paste button on the Standard toolbar.**

   The text from the Microsoft Word document appears as if by magic. Gotta love that copy and paste.

Let Me Tell You a Story

When you add large amounts of text to a publication, you often have text that doesn't fit in a single text frame. In such cases, the traditional publishing solution is to jump (continue) each article to other pages. Jumps are extremely common in newspapers and magazines: How often each day do you see lines such as "Continued on page 3" or "Continued from page 1"?

The capability of jumping a particular story between text frames and pages is one of the best arguments for using Microsoft Publisher 2000 rather than a word processing program. Although most word processing programs prefer to deal with all the text in a file as one big story, Microsoft Publisher 2000 excels at juggling multiple stories within a single publication. For example, you can begin four stories on page 1 and then jump half those stories to page 2 and the other half to page 3. At the same time, you can begin separate stories on pages 2 and 3 and jump each of those stories to any other page. If there's not enough room on a page to finish a story that you've already jumped from another page, you can jump the story to another page, and another, and another. The sky (or maybe the forest) is the limit.

Forming, reforming, and deforming stories

In its simplest form, a Microsoft Publisher 2000 story is a block of text that exists in a single, self-contained text frame. To enable a story to jump across and flow through a series or chain of several text frames, you connect those frames to each other in the order that you want the story to jump and flow. A chain of connected frames can exist on a single page or across multiple pages. You can even connect text frames that are in the scratch area and then later move those frames onto your publication pages.

Although you can use side-by-side connected text frames on a single page to create snaking columns, where text ends at the bottom of one column and continues again at the top of the next (as you find in a newspaper or magazine), you may find setting multiple columns within a single text frame on a page easier.

How and when you connect text frames depends on your situation:

✔ If you haven't yet typed or imported your text, you can manually connect empty text frames together to serve as a series of ready-made containers for that text. When you then type or import your text, it automatically jumps and flows between frames as water jumps and flows between the separate compartments in a plastic ice-cube tray. Just remember not to put your Publisher files in the freezer.

✔ If you're typing your text in Microsoft Publisher 2000 and don't know how much text you'll end up having, you can manually connect to new text frames as you run out of room in each current frame.

✔ If you're importing text and there's not enough room to fit it in the current frame, you can use the program's autoflow feature to help you connect your text frames. You can even have Microsoft Publisher 2000 draw new text frames and insert new pages as needed to fit all that text.

The next few sections show you how to best handle each of these situations.

Connecting frames

When you select a text frame, you may see one of several items attached to the top or bottom of the frame. The Text in Overflow indicator (refer to Figure 6-2) lets you know that the text won't fit in the frame and has, well, overflowed. The Go to Next Frame and Go to Previous Frame buttons are indicators that the selected frame is connected to at least one other text frame. Clicking one of these buttons takes you to the next or previous connected frame in the chain.

Here's how to connect a text frame to another text frame:

1. **Click the text frame to select it.**

   The Connect Frames toolbar appears docked to the right of the Standard toolbar. If the Connect Frames toolbar doesn't appear when you click a text frame, select View➪Toolbars➪Text Frame Connecting from the menu.

2. **Click the Connect Text Frames button.**

   Your mouse pointer changes from a standard arrow pointer to a cute little pitcher pointer bearing a down-pointing arrow. As you move over a text frame, the pitcher tilts and the arrow points to the right. The metaphor that Microsoft Publisher 2000 is using is that you've loaded the cursor with the text from your overflow area. The pitcher is a very '90s kind of icon; in earlier days, programs often used a loaded-gun icon.

   By the way, anytime you accidentally click the Connect Text Frames button, you can press the Esc key to get rid of the pitcher pointer.

3. **Click the next text frame (even one on another page) to which you want to connect in the sequence.**

   The pitcher pointer now tips sideways, drains its text, and returns to its normal state.

The two frames are now connected; any text in the first frame's overflow area appears in the second frame. Also, as you type or enter additional text into the first text frame, it pushes extra text into the second frame. To create a chain of more than two connected frames, repeat the preceding steps. If a chain is empty, you can link another chain to its first frame to create the combination of the two chains.

As you might guess, you can connect text frames only. If you select another kind of frame, you don't see the Connect Frames toolbar. Also, you can't connect a text frame that's already connected to some other text frame or a text frame that has some text in it already. If you try to do this, Microsoft Publisher 2000 displays a dialog box to complain.

After you connect text frames together, extra buttons appear at the top and/or bottom of each frame when the frame is selected. Figure 6-5 shows examples of three connected text frames on a page in a sequence, with each frame selected. Notice that when the middle frame is selected, two buttons are attached to it: the Go to Previous Frame button on top, and the Go to Next Frame button on the bottom. Think of Figure 6-5 as three separate figures, though, because if you tried to select all three text frames at the same time on your screen, you would see the frames selected as a group with only a single Group Objects button.

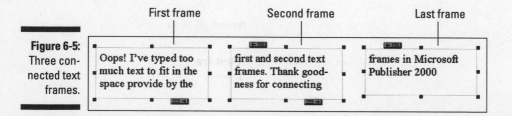

Figure 6-5:
Three connected text frames.

First frame   Second frame   Last frame

Oops! I've typed too much text to fit in the space provide by the

first and second text frames. Thank goodness for connecting

frames in Microsoft Publisher 2000

Don't worry too much about connecting frames in the proper order the first time around. After you connect frames, you can disconnect and rearrange them quite easily. Later in this chapter, the section on rearranging chains tells you how.

Moving among the story's frames

One of the first things to consider when you work with multiple-frame story text is how best to move among the story's frames — and knowing which frame follows which! You can move easily and reliably between connected frames using either the mouse or the keyboard. Both techniques are easy.

To move between connected frames using the mouse:

1. **Click the Go to Previous Frame button to move backward in the sequence.**

2. **Click the Go to Next Frame button to move forward in the sequence.**

These two buttons are shown in Figure 6-5. The button with an arrow at the top of the frame is the Go to Previous Frame button; the button with an arrow at the bottom of the frame is the Go to Next Frame button. The first frame in a chain has no Go to Previous Frame button, whereas the last frame has no Go to Next Frame button. That is, unless you live in Eerie, Indiana.

You can also use the Go to Previous Frame and Go to Next Frame buttons on the Connect Frames Toolbar. They are the second-to-last and the last buttons on the toolbar, respectively. Figure 6-6 shows the Connect Frames toolbar.

Figure 6-6:
The Connect
Frames
toolbar.

To move between connected frames using the keyboard:

1. **Press Ctrl+Tab from a connected frame (that is selected) to move to and select the chain's next frame.**

2. **Press Ctrl+Shift+Tab from a connected frame (that is selected) to move to and select the chain's previous frame.**

If your connected frames are full of text, you can also use many of the keyboard shortcuts for navigating text (listed in Chapter 8) to move between connected text frames. If your insertion point is in the last line of text in a connected text frame, for example, you can press the down-arrow key to move to and select the chain's next frame.

Autoflowing text

Autoflowing text helps you fit long text documents into a series of linked text frames. This feature is handy for automatically managing the flow of text among pages of your publication. To autoflow text into a set of linked text frames, you need to select the first text frame in the chain. When you insert (or copy) text into the frame, Microsoft Publisher 2000 fills your connected frames, beginning with the frame that you selected, with the inserted text. If the inserted text fits in the selected frame or chain of frames, you are done.

If all the text won't fit into the first text frame or the set of linked frames, Microsoft Publisher 2000 posts the autoflow dialog box shown in Figure 6-7. Click Yes to autoflow your text or click No to put the text into the overflow area of the first text frame. Microsoft Publisher 2000 then proceeds to the next text frame in your sequence and posts yet another dialog box to ask your permission to autoflow to that frame. Microsoft Publisher 2000 continues posting this dialog box with every additional frame that it requires.

What happens if you don't have enough linked text frames to take care of the incoming text? The autoflow process continues: Microsoft Publisher 2000 autoflows the extra text into the first empty or unconnected frame that it can find, or, failing that, the first frame of any empty connected series of text frames that exist in your publication. At each new frame, the program asks your permission to use that frame. But wait, there's more!

Figure 6-7:
An autoflow
dialog box.

Publisher
The inserted text doesn't fit in this frame. Do you want to use autoflow?

To have Publisher automatically flow text throughout your publication, asking for confirmation before it flows into existing frames, click Yes. To connect frames yourself, click No. For information on connecting text frames, press F1 now.

Yes   No

If no empty frames are available, Microsoft Publisher 2000 displays a fourth dialog box that asks whether you want to create additional pages at the end of your publication and fill those pages with full-page text frames until the imported text has been placed. If you click Yes, Microsoft Publisher 2000 continues flowing the story to the end, creating new pages and full-page text frames as required. At the end of this process, the program displays a final dialog box that tells you the number of new pages created and your current page location (see Figure 6-8).

Microsoft Publisher 2000 looks for text frames from left to right, then top to bottom, and finally page to page. It even suggests empty text frames that it finds in the scratch area. If you want Microsoft Publisher 2000 to connect your text frames in a different order, forget autoflow and instead connect the frames manually.

The process of autoflow is a lot more complex to explain than it is to do. I find it natural, efficient, and well thought out; I doubt that it will give you pause or worry.

If text already exists in a text frame but you still want to take advantage of Microsoft Publisher 2000's autoflow feature, use this little trick: Right-click in the frame that contains the text, choose Change Text➪Highlight Entire Story, and then cut and paste the story to your target text frame. Microsoft Publisher 2000 treats pasted text just like it does inserted text, and initiates the autoflow process described in this section.

Figure 6-8:
Microsoft
Publisher
2000 lets
you know
how many
pages it
created.

> (i) **Publisher**
> Publisher has inserted 1 new page(s)
> for your text. You are now on page 2.
>
> [OK]

Rearranging chains

Rearranging a chain involves two parts: temporarily breaking the chain (disconnecting two frames in the chain) at the point at which you want to begin rearranging, and reconnecting frames in the desired order.

Suppose that you have a chain, A-B-C-D, and you plan to add a frame X between frames B and C to make the chain A-B-X-C-D. Follow these steps to rearrange the chain:

1. **Click frame B to select it.**

2. **Click the Disconnect Text Frames button (the second button from the left, shown back in Figure 6-6) on the Connect Frames toolbar.**

If the Connect Frames toolbar does not appear when you click frame B, select Frame Connecting from the menu. You now have two chains: A-B and C-D.

3. **Click the Connect Text Frames button (the first button on the left in Figure 6-6) on the Connect Frames toolbar.**

   (Frame B is still selected.) The pointer turns into that cool pitcher again.

4. **Click frame X. Now you have chains A-B-X and C-D.**

5. **Click the Connect Text Frames button on the Connect Frames toolbar.**

   (Frame X is still selected.)

6. **Click frame C.**

   Now you have one chain: A-B-X-C-D.

Voilà! You're now ready to go into the chain-repair business.

If you continue to add new frames and don't reconnect C-D to your chain, eventually your story flows into your new additional frames. Frames C and D are still connected to each other; they just aren't connected to your linked chain.

Frame X in the example can be an empty, unconnected text frame or an empty, connected text frame that's the first frame in another chain. No surprise there. Because you're rearranging a chain, however, frame X also can be any empty frame that was, but is no longer, an original part of the current chain. For example, if you disconnect frames B and C in the chain A-B-C-D, you can then click frame D to make it the third frame in the chain. Connect frame D to frame C to form the chain A-B-D-C.

If you try to type in an empty, connected text frame that isn't the first frame in a chain, Microsoft Publisher 2000 opens a dialog box asking whether you want to begin a new story. Click OK to have the program disconnect that frame from the previous frame in the chain. Any frames farther down the chain are now part of the new story.

You can use this technique only when typing; it won't work when you're importing or inserting a text file. To insert a text file into an empty, connected frame that's not the first frame in a chain, you must first manually disconnect that text frame from the preceding frame in the chain.

After you know how to break a chain temporarily in order to rearrange it, permanently breaking a chain is easy. Just select the frame and click the Disconnect Text Frame button of the last frame that you want to include in the sequence. All text that follows in the next frames disappears from those frames and becomes overflow for the last frame in your sequence. You can place the text where you want it at a later date when you connect this last frame to another frame.

Deleting stories

Connecting text frames makes accidental text deletions a little less likely. Unfortunately, it also makes intentional deletions a little more difficult. Life is full of trade-offs!

When you delete a story's only frame, the story text has nowhere else to go, so it gets wiped out along with the frame. When you delete a frame from a multiple-frame story, however, the story text does have somewhere it can go: into the other frames in the chain. Microsoft Publisher 2000 is also nice enough to mend the chain for you. If you have the chain A-B-C and you delete frame B, for example, the program leaves you with the chain A-C.

If you really want to delete multiple-frame story text, follow these steps:

1. **Click any text frame in the story and choose Edit⇨Highlight Entire Story or press Ctrl+A.**

2. **Press the Delete or Backspace key.**

   The entire story is deleted without deleting the frames.

Editing story text

Cutting and copying connected frames and the story text within them works similarly to deleting connected frames. If you cut or copy a connected text frame, pasting results only in an empty text frame; the story text in the original frame remains a part of the original story. To cut or copy multiple-frame story text, you must highlight the text itself.

Although editing and formatting multiple-frame story text is much the same as editing and formatting single-frame story text, you can suffer a stroke trying to highlight text in multiple text frames by dragging over it with the mouse. Save yourself a visit to the hospital: Use the Shift key together with the keyboard-based movement techniques listed in Table 8-1 in Chapter 8. For example, use Shift+Ctrl+End to extend your selection to the end of the current frame and then press Shift+right-arrow to extend your selection to the next frame in your publication. You also can select all the text in a multiple-frame story by using the Edit⇨Highlight Entire Story command from the menu bar, as mentioned in the preceding section.

If your connected frames are full of text, you can capitalize on the Highlight Entire Story command to zip to the beginning or end of a chain. Just choose Edit⇨Highlight Entire Story and then press either the left- or right-arrow key. Doing this is handy when you want to delete the entire text in a story. (Maybe you have a new version of the story that you want to place in your publication.) Or perhaps you want to edit your story in a word processor: You can export that story to a text or word processor file, open your word processor, open that file, and perform your edits.

If you use Microsoft Word, choose Edit➪Edit Story in Microsoft Word from the menu. (The command also conveniently sits on the context-sensitive menu of the text frame. Right-click a text frame and point to Change Text to see it.) This command launches the Microsoft Word OLE engine and opens the program with your story in a document window, as shown in Figure 6-9. When you are finished making your edits and close the Word window, you're automatically returned to Microsoft Publisher 2000. Except for the title bar in Word, you would never know that Microsoft Publisher 2000 was the OLE client running the session. You just can't beat this kind of integration between these two programs.

Adding continuation notices

Microsoft Publisher 2000 offers you a feature to help your readers locate the next and previous frames in a story in your publication: Continued notices. Publishing professionals sometimes refer to these handy guidance devices as jumplines. They come in two types: a Continued from page notice tells readers where the story left off; and a Continued on page notice tells readers where the story continues.

Figure 6-9: Editing a Microsoft Publisher 2000 story in Microsoft Word's OLE server.

Microsoft Publisher 2000 manages continuation notices for you as an automated feature. To create a Continued notice, just right-click a linked text frame, point to Change Frame on the context-sensitive menu, and select the Text Frame Properties command. Click the Include "Continued on page..." and the Include "Continued from page..." check boxes to turn the notices on (checked) and off (unchecked) for your selected text frame. When you click OK, the program places the notices on your text frame. Figure 6-10 shows you an example.

Microsoft Publisher 2000 displays Continued notices only when it makes sense to display them. A Continued on page notice displays only if the current story jumps to another frame on another page. A Continued from page notice displays only if the current story jumps from a previous frame on another page. If you modify a story such that a Continued notice no longer makes sense, the program automatically hides that notice.

Story jumps are distracting, and after readers jump to a new page, they don't often come back to the page from which they jumped. Use story jumps as little as possible to increase reader comprehension.

Figure 6-10:
A text
frame with
continuation
notices.

(Continued from page 1)
frame; the story text in the original frame remains a part of the original story. To cut or copy multiple-frame story text, you must highlight the text itself.
Although editing and formatting multiple-frame story text is much the same as editing and formatting single-frame story text, you can suffer a stroke trying to highlight text in multiple text frames by dragging over it
(Continued on page 3)

When Continued notices do display, they always contain the proper page reference. If you move or delete the next frame in a chain or add or remove pages between the connected frames, Microsoft Publisher 2000 adjusts the page reference automatically; it certainly is smart when it comes to Continued notices!

If you don't like the wording of a continuation notice, you can edit it as you edit any other text. For example, you can change a Continued on notice to read "See page . . ." or "I ran out of room here so I stuck the rest of the story on page . . ." Don't try to add a second line to a Continued notice, though. If you press Enter while in a Continued notice, your computer just beeps at you. If you add so much text to a Continued notice that it no longer fits on one line, some of the text disappears.

If you accidentally delete a Continued notice's page-reference number, you can replace it by choosing Insert⇨Page Numbers from the menu. Or use the Text Frame Properties command to turn the Continued notice off and then use the command again to turn the notice back on. Your notice comes back as good as new.

Table Frames

As you discover in the next chapter, you can use tab stops and tabs in your paragraphs to create tables in your text frames. But a more elegant way is to use table frames to create a predefined grid of columns and rows that automatically align your text perfectly — and keep it perfectly aligned. Table frames are so easy to create and manage that it makes little sense not to use them throughout your publication whenever you need tabular displays.

Figure 6-11 shows how a plain, unformatted table frame may look after you create it. You can tell by the selection handles that the table frame is selected.

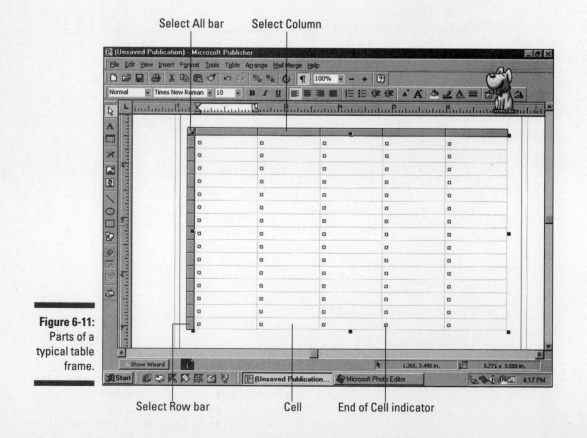

Figure 6-11: Parts of a typical table frame.

Here are some important things to know about table frames:

- ✔ A table frame's selection bars display only when the frame is selected — and they never print.

- ✔ If you can't see the gridlines on-screen, choose View⇨Show Boundaries and Guides or press Ctrl+Shift+O. You can hide the gridlines by choosing the Hide Boundaries and Guides command.

- ✔ If you choose a table format, what appear to be nonprinting gridlines in your table frame may be printing cell borders instead.

- ✔ If you choose to show special characters in your publication (which I recommend), each cell also displays an end-of-cell mark that looks like a small starburst. As with other special characters, end-of-cell marks display on-screen only; they don't print.

Moving around in tables

Microsoft Publisher 2000 has only two navigation techniques specific to table frames:

- ✔ **Press Tab to move to the next cell (to the right).** If there's no cell to the right, the next cell is the first (leftmost) cell in the row immediately below. If you press Tab in a table frame's lower-right cell, however, you create an extra row of cells at the bottom of the table frame.

- ✔ **Press Shift+Tab to move to the previous cell (to the left).** If there's no cell to the left, the previous cell is the last (rightmost) cell in the row immediately above. If you press Shift+Tab in a table frame's upper-left cell, your computer just beeps at you.

If the cell that you move to contains any text, these movement techniques also highlight that text.

Although Tab and Shift+Tab can move you to any cell in a table frame, you may find it convenient at times to use some other movement techniques. As with text frames, you can move anywhere in a table frame simply by clicking at that position. You can also use many of the same keyboard shortcuts to move around in your tables. For information on moving around in text frames, see Chapter 7.

Creating a table frame

Chapter 5 briefly explains how to create a table frame: You click the Table tool in the toolbox and then click and drag your frame outline. Table frames are different from text frames in that after you create your frame outline, you have to make a selection from the Create Table dialog box that then appears, shown in Figure 6-12. You have three selections to make in this dialog box:

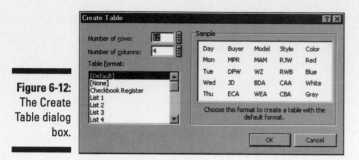

Figure 6-12:
The Create
Table dialog
box.

- ✔ Number of rows
- ✔ Number of columns
- ✔ Table format

Microsoft Publisher 2000 lets you create tables up to 128 x 128 cells large and offers you up to 23 different styles of tables, or formats. As you select a format, the program shows you a sample of the format in the Sample portion of the dialog box. The [Default] and [None] formats usually give you the same thing: a very plain, unformatted table frame. When you click OK in the Create Table dialog box, Microsoft Publisher 2000 creates your table in the frame that you drew.

Each table format has a minimum default cell size. If you select a larger number of cells than can be accommodated, Microsoft Publisher 2000 displays a dialog box asking your permission to resize the frame. If you click No, you return to the Create Table dialog box, where you can then reduce the number of rows and/or columns in your table. If you click Yes, you create a table with the number of rows and columns that you specified using the minimum cell dimensions.

Modifying tables

When a table is selected, the Table menu commands become active. This menu, shown in Figure 6-13, contains commands that you can use to modify the appearance of the table. If you choose the Table AutoFormat command, the Auto Format dialog box appears (see Figure 6-14). This dialog box is almost identical to the Create Table dialog box shown previously in Figure 6-12. The differences are that you can't change the number of rows or cells, but you can control some of the formatting options that you apply to your table.

Although applying manual formatting is a good way to get your table frame to look just the way you want, it sometimes can mean plenty of work. Instead of manually formatting a table frame, use AutoFormat; it can do a lot of work for you. The AutoFormat feature not only applies character and paragraph formatting but also may merge cells and add cell borders and shading. Cell borders overlay table-frame gridlines and, unlike gridlines, actually print. Cell shading, a color or pattern that fills the interior of a cell, also prints.

Figure 6-13:
The Table
menu.

Figure 6-14:
The Auto
Format
dialog box.

Resizing tables, columns, and rows

The structure of a table frame is what really differentiates it from a text frame. Whereas a text frame is one big rectangle into which you dump your text, a table frame is divided into a grid of separate text compartments (cells). After you create a table frame, you're not stuck with its original structure. You can resize the entire table frame; resize, insert, or delete selected columns and rows; merge multiple cells into one; and split a cell into separate cells. In short, you can restructure a table frame just about any way you want.

To resize a table frame:

- Click and drag any of its selection handles. Microsoft Publisher 2000 automatically adjusts the height of each row to fit each row's contents.

- When you narrow or widen a table frame, thus decreasing or increasing the available horizontal area in each cell, Microsoft Publisher 2000 often compensates by heightening or shortening some rows, thus heightening or shortening the overall frame.

- ✔ When you shorten a table frame, Microsoft Publisher 2000 reduces each row only to the minimum required to display the text in each row.

- ✔ Regardless of whether your table frame contains text or not, you can't reduce any cell to less than ⅙-inch square. You can heighten a table frame as much as you want, however; and Microsoft Publisher 2000 heightens each row by the same proportion.

- ✔ If you choose Table➪Grow to Fit Text, the table's row height will expand to accommodate the text that you enter.

To resize a column or row:

- ✔ Move your pointer to the edge of a column or selection-bar button until it becomes a double-headed arrow. Then click and drag until the column or row is the size that you want.

- ✔ You can't shorten a row to less than is required to display its text, and you can't shrink any cell to less than ⅙-inch square.

- ✔ By default, when you resize a column or row, Microsoft Publisher 2000 keeps all other columns and rows the same size. Columns to the right are pushed to the right or pulled to the left, whereas rows below are pushed down or pulled up. The table frame increases or decreases in overall size to accommodate the change.

- ✔ To keep a table frame the same size when resizing a column or row, hold down the Shift key as you resize. You now move only the border between the current column or row and the next. If you enlarge a column or row, the next column or row shrinks by that same amount. If you instead shrink a column or row, the next column or row enlarges by that amount. In either case, all other columns and rows remain the same size, as does the overall table frame.

- ✔ If you use the Shift key when resizing, you face even more limits. Unless you first lock the table frame, you can't shorten the row below the row that you're resizing to less than that lower row requires to display its text. And you can't shrink any adjacent column or row to less than ⅙-inch. In addition, even if you lock the table frame, you can increase a column or row only by the amount that you can take from the next column or row.

- ✔ You can resize multiple columns or rows simultaneously. Just highlight those columns or rows, point to the right or bottom edge of the selection bar button that borders the right or bottom edge of your highlight, and then click and drag. Note that if you use the Shift key to resize, however, the program ignores your highlighting. You resize only the rightmost highlighted column or bottommost highlighted row.

> ✔ If you resize an entire table frame after resizing individual columns and rows, Microsoft Publisher 2000 resizes your columns and rows proportionally. For example, if your first column is 2 inches wide and your second column is 1 inch wide, and you then double the width of the entire table frame, your first column increases to 4 inches wide, and your second column increases to 2 inches.

Inserting and deleting columns and rows

You can insert and delete all the columns and rows you want. If you move to the last cell and press Tab, Microsoft Publisher 2000 adds a new row at the bottom of the table frame and places the insertion point in the first cell of that row. You're now ready to type in that cell. How convenient!

To insert rows elsewhere, or to insert columns anywhere, you need to do only a little more work:

1. **Place the insertion point in the column or row adjacent to where you want to insert a new column or row.**

2. **Choose Table⇨Insert Rows or Columns.**

   Microsoft Publisher 2000 opens the Insert (row or column) dialog box, as shown in Figure 6-15.

Figure 6-15:
The Insert (row or column) dialog box.

3. **Select whether you want Rows or a Columns inserted, type in the Number you want to insert, and select whether the new columns or rows go Before selected cells or After selected cells.**

   Even if your table frame is locked, the program increases the table frame's size to accommodate the new columns or rows.

4. **Click OK to finish inserting your row (or column).**

Deleting a column or row is even easier:

1. **Highlight the entire row or column you want to delete by clicking the row or column selector button.**

2. Choose Table⇨Delete Rows or Table⇨Delete Columns.

If you neglect to highlight entire columns or rows in Step 1, Microsoft Publisher 2000 displays the Delete dialog box. Indicate whether you want to delete rows or columns, and then click OK.

You can't delete an entire table frame by using the Delete Columns, Delete Rows, or Delete Rows Or Columns commands. Instead, choose Edit⇨Delete Object or press Ctrl+Shift+X.

Merging and splitting cells

On occasion, you may want to merge multiple cells so that they become one cell. For example, as shown in Figure 6-16, you may want to merge cells so that you can center a heading over multiple columns.

First Quarter Sales			Second Quarter Sales		
January	February	March	April	May	June

Figure 6-16: Cells merged to create column headings.

▶ To merge cells, highlight the cells that you want to merge and then choose Table⇨Merge Cells. Your highlighted cells now become one. Any text in the individual cells moves into the one merged cell. You now can work with this merged cell as you would work with any other cell.

▶ After you merge a cell, you can split it into individual cells again. Click or highlight the merged cell and select Table⇨Split Cells. (When you're in a merged cell, the Split Cells command replaces the Merge Cells command in the menu.) Your merged cell splits back into the original number of separate cells.

▶ The table's context-sensitive menu contains the commands for inserting and deleting rows and columns and for merging and splitting cells. After you right-click the table, point to Change Table to see them.

Working with table text

As with text frames, you can fill a table frame either by typing the text directly into the frame or by importing existing text from somewhere else. Except for the differences that I point out in the next two sections, typing and importing text into both types of frames is pretty darn similar.

Each cell in a table frame works much like a miniature text frame. For example, when you reach the right edge of a cell, Microsoft Publisher 2000 automatically word-wraps your text to a new line within that cell. If the text that you type disappears beyond the right edge of the cell, you have probably locked the table. Choose Table➪Grow to Fit Text to unlock it. If you want to end a short line within a cell, press Enter. It usually is easiest to fill in your table frame row by row; when you finish one cell, just press Tab to move on to the next one.

If pressing Tab moves you from one cell to the next, how do you insert a tab mark? I don't know why you'd ever need a tab mark in a table frame, but if you do, press Ctrl+Tab.

There is one very important difference between typing in a cell and typing in a text frame: When you run out of vertical room in a cell, Microsoft Publisher 2000 automatically heightens that entire row of cells to accommodate additional lines of text. Should you later remove or reduce the size of some of that text, Microsoft Publisher 2000 automatically shortens that row. Compare this to typing in a text frame: When you run out of room, the text frame remains the same size, and the program sticks that text into an overflow area or, if available, into a connected text frame.

Importing table frame text

Just as you can with text frames, you can paste or insert a text file into a table frame. Some important differences exist, however. If your text is arranged in a table-like manner, such as in a spreadsheet or a word processing table, Microsoft Publisher 2000 senses the arrangement and imports that text across the necessary number of cells in your table frame. If your text isn't arranged in a table-like manner, Microsoft Publisher 2000 imports all text into the current cell.

If no table-like feature is available in your other program, you can use tab marks or commas to indicate column separations (called *delimiters*) and paragraph marks to indicate row separations (called *end-of-row markers*).

Although you may be able to use the Insert➪Text File command to import text into a table frame (as described earlier in this chapter), the Windows Clipboard is much more reliable. Use it whenever possible.

Do one of the following to paste or insert text into a table:

> ✔ **Cut or copy the text to the Windows Clipboard; then, click the cell that is to be the upper-left cell of the range and choose Edit➪Paste or press Ctrl+V.**
>
> ✔ **Choose Insert➪Text File to import text into the table frame.**

When you import text into a table frame, Microsoft Publisher 2000 overwrites (replaces) any text that exists in the cells into which you import. To restore accidentally overwritten text, immediately choose Edit➪Undo Paste from the menu.

Here are some other important things to remember about bringing text into your table:

> ✔ If the copied text is arranged in a table-like manner and the current table frame doesn't have enough cells to accommodate all the copied cells, Microsoft Publisher 2000 opens a dialog box to ask whether it should insert columns and rows as necessary. Click Yes to make sure that you paste all your text.
>
> ✔ If you don't have a table frame selected and if the copied text is arranged in a table-like manner, the program creates a new table frame and places the copied text into that frame.
>
> ✔ Although a table frame can look much like a spreadsheet, Microsoft Publisher 2000 doesn't have the power to calculate numbers. If you want to calculate the numbers in a table, calculate them in a spreadsheet program before importing. If you don't have a spreadsheet program, get out the hand calculator!

> ✔ Although you can't put drawn graphics into a Microsoft Publisher 2000 table frame, here's a trick that you can use to make it look as if your table frame contains graphics. Layer your graphics on top of the table frame, with each graphic completely within the boundaries of a cell. Then group the table frame and graphics together. No one who sees your printed publication will be the wiser.

Editing table-frame text is much the same as editing text-frame text. You need to know just a few extra things to efficiently highlight, move, and copy table-frame text.

You can use all the same mouse techniques to highlight (select) table-frame text as you can to highlight text-frame text: drag, double-click, and Shift+click. You can also highlight table-frame text by combining the Shift key with any table-frame-movement techniques that I mention earlier in this section.

You also can highlight the contents of an entire cell by pressing Tab or Shift+Tab to move to that cell.

When you highlight any amount of text in more than one cell, you automatically highlight the entire contents of all those cells.

Here are some additional ways to select table-frame text:

- ✔ To select the entire contents of the current cell, choose Edit⇨Highlight Text or press Ctrl+A (for All).
- ✔ To select every cell in a column, click the selection bar button above that column.
- ✔ To select every cell in a row, click the selection bar button to the left of that row.
- ✔ To select multiple columns or rows, drag across the appropriate selection bar buttons. Or press the Shift key and click selection bar buttons to extend or diminish a selected range.
- ✔ To select every cell in a table frame, click the upper-left selection bar button or choose Table⇨Select⇨Table.

Moving and copying table text

As with text frames, you can use the Clipboard or drag-and-drop text editing (see Chapter 8) to copy and move text within and between table frames. If you like, you can even copy text between text and table frames.

Working in a table frame has a very important difference, however: Whenever you move or copy the contents of multiple cells into other cells, Microsoft Publisher 2000 automatically overwrites any text in those destination cells. To retain the contents of a destination cell, be sure to move or copy the contents of only one cell at a time. If you accidentally overwrite text when moving or copying, immediately select the Undo-whatever command from the Edit menu (Ctrl+Z).

Because of the way in which Microsoft Publisher 2000 overwrites destination cells, rearranging entire columns and rows of text requires some extra steps. First, insert an extra column or row where you want to move the contents of an existing column or row. Then, move the contents. Finally, delete the column or row that you just emptied. Repeat these steps for every column and row that you want to move.

Two commands on the Table menu, Fill Down and Fill Right, enable you to copy the entire contents of one cell into any number of adjacent cells either below or to the right.

Do the following to fill a series of cells in a row or column:

1. **Select the cell containing the text you want to copy and the cells to which you want to copy the text.**

   To use the fill commands, you must select cells adjacent to the cell containing the text to be copied.

2. **Choose Table➪Fill Down to copy the value in the topmost cell to the selected cells in the column below it.**

   Or, choose Table➪Fill Right to copy the value in the leftmost cell to selected cells in the row to the right.

Formatting table text manually

You can format table-frame text manually to make that information easier to read and understand. You can use all the character- and paragraph-formatting options detailed in the next chapter: fonts, text size, text effects, line spacing, alignment, tab stops, indents, bulleted and numbered lists, and so on. You can even hyphenate table-frame text.

The key difference when applying paragraph formatting in table frames is that Microsoft Publisher 2000 treats each cell as a miniature text frame. Thus, when you align text, the text aligns within just that cell rather than across the entire table frame. And when you indent text, that text indents according to that cell's left and right edges.

To improve the look of cells, you can also change cell margins, thus changing the amount of space between a cell's contents and its edges. To change cell margins, choose Format➪Table Cell Properties. The resulting dialog box is shown in Figure 6-17.

Figure 6-17:
The Table
Cell
Properties
dialog box.

Using Excel tables

Microsoft Publisher 2000 lets you create and edit tables in your publication. It even has that cool Table AutoFormat command. However, if you are a Microsoft Excel user, you may find entering and formatting your tabular data in Microsoft Excel more convenient. Maybe you already have a Microsoft Excel worksheet that contains data that you want to include in your publication. You don't have to waste time and risk data entry errors retyping the information.

Importing an Excel worksheet

If you are a Microsoft Excel user and you don't want to remember all this stuff about working with tables in Publisher 2000, don't. Use Microsoft Excel to enter and format your tabular data and then import the worksheet into Publisher 2000:

1. **In Microsoft Excel, enter and format your tabular data.**

2. **Save your Microsoft Excel worksheet.**

   If you are finished working in Microsoft Excel, you may close it.

3. **Switch to the Microsoft Publisher window by clicking its button on the Windows taskbar.**

   If the Windows Taskbar isn't visible, you can switch applications by pressing Alt+Tab. Hold down the Alt key and press Tab until the Microsoft Publisher icon is highlighted in the Cool Switch box that appears. Release both keys.

4. **Select Insert⇨Object.**

   The Insert Object dialog box, shown in Figure 6-18, appears.

Figure 6-18:
The Insert Object dialog box.

5. **Click the Create from File radio button and then click Browse.**

   The Browse dialog box appears.

6. **Click the Microsoft Excel file that you want to insert into your publication and click Insert.**

   You return to the Insert Object dialog box.

7. Click OK to insert the Microsoft Excel worksheet into your publication.

Figure 6-19 shows an example of an Excel worksheet inserted into a publication.

The Excel worksheet that you insert into your publication isn't really a table. I know, if it looks like a duck, waddles like a duck, and quacks like a duck, then it must be a duck. Well, in Microsoft Publisher 2000, it isn't a duck, er, table. It's an object. If you select the newly inserted Excel worksheet and select Table from the menu bar, you will notice that all the Table commands are unavailable.

Editing an Excel worksheet in Publisher 2000

So, you created that jazzy-looking worksheet in Microsoft Excel, saved it to your hard disk, and imported it into Publisher 2000. Great — until you realize that you spelled the company name incorrectly. Do you have to launch Microsoft Excel, open the worksheet, correct the spelling of the company name, save the worksheet, and re-import it into Publisher 2000? Yes. Okay, just kidding. You do not. Just double-click the worksheet to launch Microsoft Excel inside Publisher 2000. Although the Title bar still proclaims that you are in Publisher 2000, the menu bar and toolbars change to those belonging to Microsoft Excel (see Figure 6-20). Edit the worksheet as you would in Microsoft Excel. When you are finished making changes, just click anywhere outside the worksheet. That's all there is to it!

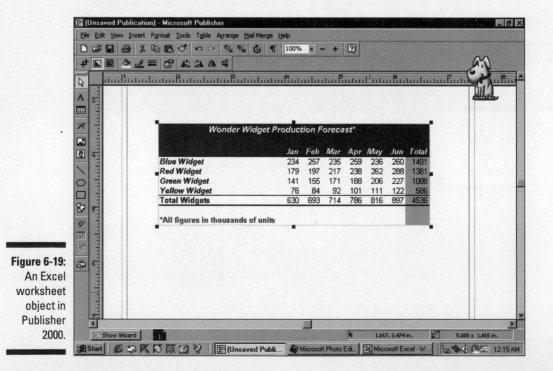

Figure 6-19:
An Excel worksheet object in Publisher 2000.

Accessing tables in Access

For those database die-hards among you who are wondering whether you can use your Microsoft Access tables in your publications, the answer is yes. You can even use your Microsoft Access query results. Essentially, you have two options for getting data from your Microsoft Access tables and query results into Microsoft Publisher 2000. You can bring in the entire table (or query results), or you can select part of the table (or query results) to bring into Publisher 2000. Here's how to bring in an entire table or query results:

1. **In Microsoft Access, open the database that contains the table or query that you want to use in your publication.**

2. **Click the Tables button in the Objects pane of the Database window.**

   To bring in the results from a query, click the Queries button in the Objects pane of the Database window.

3. **Select the desired table or query and then click the Copy button on the Standard toolbar.**

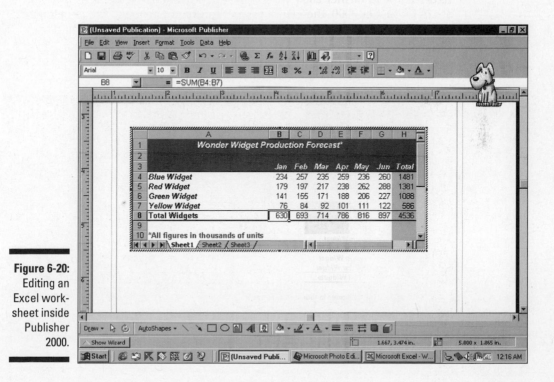

Figure 6-20:
Editing an Excel worksheet inside Publisher 2000.

4. **Switch to the Microsoft Publisher window by clicking its button on the Windows taskbar.**

   If the Windows taskbar isn't visible, you can switch applications by pressing Alt+Tab. Hold down the Alt key and press Tab until the Microsoft Publisher icon is highlighted in the Cool Switch box that appears. Release both keys.

5. **In the Publisher 2000 window, select Edit⇨Paste, press Ctrl+V, or click the Paste button on the Standard toolbar.**

   Microsoft Publisher 20000 creates a new table containing the records from your Microsoft Access table or query.

Microsoft Publisher 2000 creates an honest-to-goodness table from your Microsoft Access table or query. Use the commands on the Table menu to format the table just as you would any other Publisher 2000 table.

If you want to use only a portion of the records in your Microsoft Access table or query, select the desired records before clicking the Copy button in the preceding Step 3.

Chapter 7

Editors Are Bought, Not Born

In This Chapter

▶ Editing, navigating, and generally messing with text

▶ Searching, replacing, hyphenating, and checking the spelling of your text

▶ Formatting each and every character in your document

▶ Formatting paragraphs with style — and with styles

▶ Dressing your text — frame by frame

*I*f you use a word processing or similar computer program, you know that making changes to text (editing) can be a breeze. Delete a word here, insert a couple words there, rewrite a sentence, add a comma, and the program takes care of the rest. The ease with which you can edit text in a computer program is one of the reasons that typewriters are choking landfills worldwide. My typewriter hasn't seen the light of day in years. I keep it just so I can say that I have one.

Editing text in Microsoft Publisher 2000 is easy, too. Almost everything you know about editing text in a word processor applies to editing and formatting text in Microsoft Publisher 2000. Although Microsoft Publisher 2000 doesn't have quite the editing muscle and sophistication of some full-blown word processing programs, it still does a very respectable job.

Microsoft Publisher 2000 is also more than a match for the formatting tools that you find in any word processor. Its many text-formatting features enable you to take control over how your text looks, character by character, paragraph by paragraph, frame by frame. You control the horizontal; you control the vertical.

This chapter focuses on editing and formatting text in Microsoft Publisher 2000. It focuses specifically on working with text in text frames, but you can use most of the techniques shown here to work with text in table frames as well.

Tricks of the Editing Meisters

You probably are an editing master already. If you've been banging away at a word processor for a while, chances are that this section is a review for you. In case it's not, I want to mention some of the tricks that you can use to edit text in a text frame.

To edit text, you first must position the insertion point in the text or highlight the text. If you position the insertion point in the text, you can press Delete to remove any characters to the right of the insertion point or press Backspace to remove characters to the left. You can place an insertion point anywhere in a text frame; when you do, Microsoft Publisher 2000 also selects the text frame for you.

If you highlight text, any character that you type replaces the highlighted text. This works the same way in Publisher 2000 as it does in the other Microsoft Office products. Be careful when selecting text. If you do accidentally replace some text, press Ctrl+Z right away. Have I mentioned backing up lately?

Haven't purchased Microsoft Publisher 2000 yet? Save yourself some money and buy Microsoft Office 2000 Small Business Edition. In addition to Microsoft Publisher 2000, you will also get the following Microsoft applications:

✔ Microsoft Word 2000

✔ Microsoft Excel 2000

✔ Microsoft Outlook 2000

✔ Small Business Tools

Movin' and groovin'

If you are familiar with keys that move your insertion point in Microsoft Word, you find that they all work inside Microsoft Publisher 2000. You can also reposition the insertion point by using your keyboard's movement keys: Home, End, PgUp, PgDn, and the four arrow keys.

Some keyboards offer a separate bank of navigation keys, and some place the keys on the numeric keypad at the right end of the keyboard. To use the keys on the numeric keypad as navigation keys, you must first turn off the Num Lock key on the keyboard. If the Num Lock key is turned on, the keys type numbers rather than move your insertion point. Figure 7-1 shows a classic 101-key computer keyboard.

Table 7-1 lists some of the common movement keys and what they do. Notice that only the numbers on the numeric keypad — and not the ones on the main keyboard — move your insertion point.

Table 7-1	Navigation Keys
Press This	*To Do This*
Home or 7 key	Go to the beginning of current text line
End or 1 key	Go to the end of current text line
Up-arrow or 8 key	Move up one text line
Down-arrow or 2 key	Move down one text line
Right-arrow or 6 key	Move right one character
Left-arrow or 4 key	Move left one character
Ctrl+Home or Ctrl+7	Go to the beginning of current text frame
Ctrl+End or Ctrl+1	Go to the end of current text frame
Ctrl+up-arrow or Ctrl+8	Go to the beginning of current paragraph
Ctrl+down-arrow or Ctrl+2	Go to the beginning of next paragraph
Ctrl+right-arrow or Ctrl+6	Move right one word
Ctrl+left-arrow or Ctrl+4	Move left one word

Numeric keypad

Cursor Control keys

Figure 7-1:
A classic
101-key
computer
keyboard.

If text is highlighted, pressing the left- or right-arrow key positions the insertion point at the beginning or end of the text and then removes the highlighting (deselects the text).

Selection tricks

As mentioned earlier, before you can do any editing or formatting to a piece of text, you must select it. The simplest way to highlight text is to select the Pointer tool in the toolbox and then drag the cursor over the text that you want to highlight. But here are several other ways to highlight text:

- ✔ Double-click a word to select the word and any blank spaces following it.

- ✔ Click at one end of the text that you want to highlight, press and hold down the Shift key, click at the other end of the text, and then release the Shift key.

- ✔ Combine the Shift key with any of the movement techniques listed in the preceding section. For example, to select an entire line of text, move the insertion point to the beginning of the line and then press Shift+End.

- ✔ Choose Edit⇨Highlight Entire Story or press Ctrl+A (for All) to highlight all the text in the current text frame and in any connected frames.

You can also use the Shift key in combination with clicking or any movement technique to extend or reduce an existing highlight.

Drag and drop

Previous chapters in this book illustrate the use of Cut, Copy, and Paste in several different applications. The Cut/Copy/Paste technique is one of the two ways of moving text in text frames. The other is called *drag and drop*, which sounds like a training seminar for airport baggage handlers. By using drag-and-drop text editing, you can move and copy text within and between frames located on any single page or two-page spread without going through all the steps of using the Windows Clipboard. I think of it as a direct form of cut and paste (or copy and paste, if you hold down the Ctrl key as you drag and drop).

To remove text from one spot and place it in another by using drag and drop, highlight the text and move your pointer over it. Your pointer turns into a *T* with the word *Drag* next to it as soon as you move the pointer over the selected text, to indicate that you can drag and drop. Click the highlighted text and drag it to a new location. Your pointer turns into a *T* with the word *Move* next to it as soon as you press the mouse button to indicate that you are moving the text and not copying it.

To copy text by using drag and drop, highlight the text that you want to copy, press Ctrl, and then click and drag the selection to a new location. Your pointer turns into a *T* with the word *Copy* next to it to indicate that you can drag and drop the copy.

If your mouse pointer is a plain, left-pointing arrow, the Use helpful mouse pointers check box is turned off in the Options dialog box (see Chapter 3). Or you may have turned drag-and-drop text editing off, although for the life of me I can't think of why you'd want to do that. I love drag and drop. The Drag and drop text editing check box on the Edit tab of the Options dialog box disables this feature (which is turned on by default) in all your publications.

Drag-and-drop text editing isn't for everyone. My daughter, Rebecca, wrinkles her nose at the mere mention of dragon droppings. If you are mouse challenged, you may want to skip this feature.

Symbols

A big mistake that many new desktop publishers make is failing to use those special typographic characters that are known in Microsoft Publisher 2000 as *symbols.* If you look carefully at this book or almost any well-produced publication, you can see symbols all over the place. These special symbols, which include fractions (such as ¼); special quotation marks (" "); special hyphens, such as en dashes (–) and em dashes (—); ligatures (Æ, œ, æ); and so on are a typographer's stock-in-trade.

Microsoft Publisher 2000 provides two ways to put appropriate typographical symbols in your publications: automatically and manually. As you type, Microsoft Publisher 2000 automatically replaces inch and foot marks (" and '), also known as *straight quotes,* with typographic quotation marks (" ", and ' '), and double hyphens (- -) with em dashes (—). (Typographic quotation marks are often called *smart quotes* or *curly quotes.*) If you import text, punctuation marks in that text remain as they were in your source document.

If Microsoft Publisher 2000 doesn't replace these marks for you as you type, you probably turned off the features. Select <u>T</u>ools⇨AutoCorrect and click the AutoFormat as You Type tab of the AutoCorrect dialog box that appears. In the Replace as you type area, click to place a check mark in both the "Straight Quotes" with "Smart Quotes" and Hyphens (-,—) with en/em dashes (–, —) check boxes to turn these settings on. They apply to all your Microsoft Publisher 2000 sessions.

If you can, try to set up the program that you use to create your text so that it automatically replaces these marks as you type. Microsoft Word offers this feature, for example. Otherwise, you must search and replace the marks manually by using the <u>E</u>dit⇨<u>R</u>eplace command on the menu bar.

What if you *want* to type an inch or foot mark? You must turn the "Straight Quotes" with "Smart Quotes" option off for a moment, then type your inch or foot mark. Don't forget to turn the option on again.

To insert a symbol manually into a publication, choose Insert⇨Symbol and make your selection from the Symbol dialog box, as shown in Figure 7-2.

The Symbol dialog box shows you all the available symbols in your installed system fonts. Your current font appears, but you can switch to other fonts as well — including symbol font. You can find en dashes, fractions, copyright and registration marks, foreign letters and currency symbols, smiley faces, hearts, diamonds, clubs, spades, and even that *é* that you need to type *résumé* correctly. If you are looking for a special symbol, check out the Symbol font by selecting it from the Font list box. The Wingdings font is also a rich source of symbols such as bullets, buttons, and bows.

Don't bother to insert symbols one at a time to create bulleted lists like the ones you see in this book. Instead, use the bulleted or numbered list feature in Microsoft Publisher 2000 to create this special format.

Figure 7-2:
The Symbol
dialog box.

Tools of the Editing Meisters

Any good page layout program comes with a set of basic text management tools. Some of the heavyweight programs come with tools for formatting, text correction, seek and destroy, and other features that any word processor would envy. These tools are important; they increase accuracy and make your text more readable.

Microsoft Publisher 2000 offers the following tools:

✔ Search and replace

✔ A spell checker (including spell check as you type)

✔ AutoCorrect

✔ Automatic hyphenation

Additionally, the Microsoft Publisher 2000 Tools menu offers some other tools that aren't specific to text management. The Design Checker command looks at your document for common printing problems. And the Design Gallery contains such Publisher-designed objects as pull quotes, logos, calendars, and more that you can use in your publication. I discuss the Design Gallery and Design Checker in Chapters 10 and 12, respectively. The sections that follow examine the text tools.

Hide and seek: Find and Replace

Any good word processor has a find feature — a command that enables you to hunt down a specific word or phrase in your document. Okay, even *poor* word processors have a find feature. Microsoft Publisher 2000 has a find feature and even has a replace feature, which enables you to search and replace one word or phrase with another. If you need to correct text at story length, you just can't get by without these search and replace features.

Here's how to find text:

1. **Select a text frame of the story that you want Microsoft Publisher 2000 to search.**

   Before finding and replacing text, press F9 to view your text at a readable size.

2. **Choose Edit⇨Find or press Ctrl+F.**

   The Find dialog box, shown in Figure 7-3, appears.

3. **In the Find what text box, type the text that you want Microsoft Publisher 2000 to find, using wildcard symbols, if desired.**

   If you've ever worked in MS-DOS, you probably know about wildcards. One wildcard, the question mark (?), works in the Find dialog box. If you use a question mark in your search criteria, any character can be a match for the character in the question mark position. For example, if you ask Microsoft Publisher 2000 to search for the text *no?,* it finds the words *not, now, nod,* and so on. If you need to search for actual question marks, type a caret (^) before the mark, as in ^?. And to find a caret, ask a rabet. No, that's not right. To find a caret, type ^^. Table 7-2 that appears shortly lists codes that you can use to find other special characters.

Figure 7-3:
The Find
dialog box.

4. **Click the Match whole word only and/or the Match case check box if you want those options.**

   The Match whole word only option finds any occurrence of your search string that is surrounded by spaces or punctuation marks. It ignores any matches that are part of larger words. With the option on, for example, a search for *publish* ignores the word *publisher*.

   The Match case option searches your document for an exact match of your search string's characters, using upper- and lowercase characters as filtering criteria. With this option on and the Match whole word only option off, for example, a search for the word *publish* ignores any occurrence of *Publisher;* a search for the word *Publish,* however, finds *Publisher.*

5. **Click the Up or Down radio button to specify the direction of the search.**

   If you choose the Up radio button, Microsoft Publisher 2000 searches from the location of your cursor up to the beginning of the text frame or story. If you choose the Down button, it searches from the cursor location to the end of the frame or story.

6. **Click the Find Next button.**

If you have used Microsoft Word, all this finding and replacing may look familiar to you. The Find and Replace procedures work the same in Microsoft Publisher 2000 as they do in Microsoft Word.

Microsoft Publisher 2000 scampers off to look for your text, and one of four things happens:

✔ Your text is found and highlighted. Microsoft Publisher 2000 even scoots the Find dialog box out of the way if it is covering the text you are looking for. Good program, nice program.

✔ Microsoft Publisher 2000 finds your text, but not the occurrence for which you were looking. Click the Find Next button to continue the search.

✔ Microsoft Publisher 2000 gets to the beginning or end of the text without a match and opens a dialog box asking permission to continue looking from the other end. After Microsoft Publisher 2000 searches the entire story, it displays a dialog box saying that no matching text was found. Sorry!

Microsoft Publisher 2000 can't find text in a WordArt frame.

Microsoft Publisher 2000 can't find your remote control or your cordless phone, either.

Sometimes, you may want to search for special characters, such as an end of paragraph mark or a tab space. You can do so by using the codes listed in Table 7-2.

Table 7-2	Find and Replace Codes for Special Characters
To Find This	*Use This Code*
Two spaces	(type two spaces)
Optional hyphen	^-
Nonbreaking hyphen (a hyphen that doesn't break across a line ending)	^~
Line break	^N
End of paragraph mark	^P
Nonbreaking space (a space that doesn't break across a line ending)	^S
Tab space	^T
White space (a tab character or space between words)	^W

Having Microsoft Publisher 2000 help you find text is great, but getting it to replace unwanted text is an even bigger labor-saving device. To both find and replace text, use the Edit➪Replace command. Here's how:

1. **Select the story containing the text that you want Microsoft Publisher 2000 to replace.**

2. **Choose Edit➪Replace or press Ctrl+H.**

   The Replace dialog box, as shown in Figure 7-4, appears. It is very similar to the Find dialog box and remembers the last text that you typed in the Find dialog box during your current Microsoft Publisher 2000 session.

Replace

Find what: `Dole wins by a landslide!`

Replace with: `Clinton re-elected!`

☐ Match whole word only

☐ Match case

[Replace] [Replace All] [Find Next] [Close]

Figure 7-4:
The Replace
dialog box.

3. **Type the text that you want to find in the Find what text box and the text that you want to replace it with in the Replace with text box.**

   You can also set the same Match options described in the preceding set of steps.

4. **Click Find Next.**

One of three things happens here:

- ✔ A match is found. To replace the found text, click the Replace button. Microsoft Publisher 2000 then searches for the next occurrence of the text in the Find What text box. Microsoft Publisher 2000 even scoots the Replace dialog box out of the way if it is covering the text you are look-ing for. Good program, nice program.

- ✔ A match is found, but not the match that you want. Click the Find Next button to continue the search.

- ✔ Microsoft Publisher 2000 gets to the beginning or end of the text without finding a match, so it opens a dialog box asking permission to continue looking from the other end. Click the Yes button to continue the search or No to end the search. If Microsoft Publisher 2000 still can't find your text, it opens a dialog box to say that no matching text was found.

If you click the Replace All button, Microsoft Publisher 2000 replaces all occurrences of the matching text with your replacement text in one fell swoop. Take care when using the Replace All button; unless you are careful, you may replace matches that you didn't intend to change. Mistakes are hard to catch in large stories.

The Replace command is an excellent way to repair text that wasn't prepared the correct typographical way. For example, you can use the command to replace all double spaces with single spaces. Replacing other things such as double dashes and old-fashioned fractions with their correct typographic counterparts also is possible. Use the Symbol dialog box (refer to Figure 7-2, shown previously) to insert the correct symbol into your text. Cut or copy the symbol to the Clipboard, choose the Edit⇨Replace command, and type the old-fashioned mark that you want to replace in the Find what text box. Then click the Replace with text box and press Ctrl+V to insert the symbol there. The symbol may appear as some bizarre shape totally unrelated to what you copied from the publication, but don't pay any attention to that. The symbol appears correctly again after it's back in the publication. Now you're ready to replace at will — but just to be safe, always test things out by replacing a single match before using the Replace All button to apply the replace universally.

Can you check my spelling?

No doubt about it: Spalling errors make you look bad. To begin checking your spelling, select a text frame and then choose Tools⇨Spelling⇨Check Spelling or press F7. Microsoft Publisher 2000 immediately searches for the first word that it doesn't recognize; if it finds one, a Check Spelling dialog box similar to the one in Figure 7-5 appears. Microsoft Publisher 2000 places that word in the Not in dictionary text box. You can correct the word in the Change to text box, and the spell checker even makes suggestions of close matches in the Suggestions list box.

Microsoft Publisher 2000 can't check spelling in WordArt frames.

The spell checker is one of those "shared tools" in the Microsoft arsenal. Know one, know them all. Like other Microsoft programs with spell-checking capabilities, Microsoft Publisher 2000 doesn't find misspelled words per se. It actually compares every word it comes across against its own 100,000-word electronic dictionary. It considers anything between two spaces or similar delimiting characters to be a word. If a word doesn't match, Microsoft Publisher 2000 points it out. That's why the dialog box has a Not in dictionary box rather than a Misspelled word box.

Figure 7-5:
The Check Spelling dialog box.

You have several choices for dealing with each word that Microsoft Publisher 2000 finds:

- ✔ If the word is incorrect and you can find the correct word in the Suggestions list box, double-click that correct word.

- ✔ Alternatively, you can single-click the correct word and then click Change All to have Microsoft Publisher 2000 automatically fix every occurrence of the incorrect word as it finds it.

- ✔ If the word is incorrect and you can't find the correct word in the Suggestions list box, enter the correct word in the Change to text box and then click the Change or Change All button.

- ✔ If the word is correct but it's not a word that you use very often, click the Ignore button to leave the word as is. Or click Ignore All to leave every occurrence of the word that Microsoft Publisher 2000 finds in this spelling check as is.

- ✔ If the word is correct and it's a word that you do use often (such as your own name), click the Add button to add the word to the Microsoft Publisher 2000 dictionary. Be careful with this button, though, because if you add an incorrect word to the dictionary, Microsoft Publisher 2000 never points out the word again, in this or any other publication!

After you tell Microsoft Publisher 2000 what to do with the first word, the spell checker continues on until the end of your highlighted text or to the end of the story. Microsoft Publisher 2000 then asks whether you want to continue checking the rest of the current story. If you have more than one story in your publication, Microsoft Publisher 2000 checks the current story first and then asks whether you want to check the next story (unless the Check all stories check box is checked, in which case Microsoft Publisher 2000 goes ahead and checks every story without asking). When it comes to checking spelling, Microsoft Publisher 2000 is as relentless as my editor. Eventually, though, Microsoft Publisher 2000 runs out of words to check and closes the Check Spelling dialog box.

You've typed a word, but you aren't sure whether you've spelled it correctly? Double-click the word and press F7.

What are those squiggly red lines in your text frame? Microsoft Publisher 2000 can check your spelling as you type. When you misspell a word, it gets a squiggly red underline to let you know that you made a boo-boo. Select Tools⇨Spelling⇨Spelling Options and click to place a check mark next to the Check spelling as you type option. This option is on by default.

A spell checker is not a substitute for proofreading. Don't believe me? Ask my editor. Just because all the words are spelled correctly doesn't mean that they're the correct words. Did you know that *spalling* (which I misspelled for *spelling* a couple of pages ago) is actually a word? In case this is news to you (it was to me), it means "to break up or reduce by chipping with a hammer" as in "I'll be out in the garage spalling the old computers, honey. . . ."

Hyphenation

To fit more text in a given space or to make justified text easier to read, you can have Microsoft Publisher 2000 hyphenate your text, automatically breaking words in two at line endings. This process is automated, so Microsoft Publisher 2000 continually removes and adds hyphens as needed as you type, edit, and rearrange text.

To have Microsoft Publisher 2000 hyphenate your text automatically:

1. **Select the text frame or story that you want to hyphenate.**

2. **Choose Tools⇨Language⇨Hyphenation or press Ctrl+Shift+H.**

   The Hyphenation dialog box, as shown in Figure 7-6, appears.

Figure 7-6:
The
Hyphenation
dialog box.

3. **Verify that Automatically hyphenate this story is selected and then click the OK button.**

Your text is now hyphenated. Should you later change the text in any way, Microsoft Publisher 2000 automatically rehyphenates the text.

If you don't trust Microsoft Publisher 2000 to hyphenate your text for you or if you want to manually control where a hyphen in a word occurs, you can click the Manual button. Then, when Microsoft Publisher 2000 finds a word appropriate for hyphenating, it shows you that word and how it wants to hyphenate it. You can either approve, modify, or reject this hyphenation. If you use this option, though, Microsoft Publisher 2000 doesn't rehyphenate your text for you; you have to issue the Hyphenation command again.

Another control that you have in adjusting hyphenation is the setting in the Hyphenation zone text box. The smaller the hyphenation zone, the more hyphens Microsoft Publisher 2000 uses and the more even the right edge of your text is.

To remove automatic hyphenation, choose the Tools⇨Language⇨ Hyphenation command again. Click the Automatically hyphenate this story check box to remove the check mark. You can set up Microsoft Publisher 2000 to hyphenate all text by default. To do this, select Tools⇨Options and click the User Assistance tab. Click the Automatically hyphenate in new text frames check box if it's not already selected — it's on by default — and then change the setting in the Hyphenation zone text box if you want. For any text frame that you now create in any publication, Microsoft Publisher 2000 automatically hyphenates the frame's text. Microsoft Publisher 2000 doesn't change the hyphenation in any existing frames, however.

Text Formatting

If you've worked in a word processor, you've formatted your share of text. Perhaps you are a text formatting meister. Even so, you may learn a trick or two in the sections that follow. If you don't, reward yourself with three gold asterisks and move on down the line.

Modern word processors and page layout programs divide the formatting that you can apply to text into three levels:

- **Character formats:** Formats that you can apply to each character in your text: type styles, fonts, sizes, cases, and so on.
- **Paragraph formats:** Default formats that apply to your paragraph. Some of these formats, such as styles, you may be able to change. Others, such as line spacing, may not be changeable, depending on the program that you are using.
- **Document formats:** Formats that usually apply to the entire document. Page margins are an example of a document format. Because Microsoft Publisher 2000 treats stories as if they are documents, document formats apply to text frames and connected text frames with a story in them.

If you understand which formats belong to which category, you can quickly apply the format that you desire to get very professional results — often with dramatic time savings.

The Formatting toolbar

After you have selected text, a Formatting toolbar appropriate to text appears under the Standard toolbar. Figure 7-7 shows the Formatting toolbar for text. Most of the elements of the toolbar should be familiar to you if you have worked in a word processor.

Figure 7-7:
The
Formatting
toolbar.

The formatting options on the toolbar are (from left to right):

- ✔ **Style list box:** A *style* is a set of formats that apply to a paragraph, as explained later in this chapter. This list box enables you to choose a style and apply it to your selection.

- ✔ **Font list box:** This shows your current font and enables you to select a different font.

- ✔ **Font Size list box:** This box shows your current font size and enables you to enter a new one.

- ✔ **Bold, Italic, and Underline buttons:** These buttons set the font style.

- ✔ **Align Left, Center, Align Right, and Justify buttons:** These buttons apply text justification, which is a paragraph-level setting.

- ✔ **Numbering button:** This button accesses a paragraph-level setting that enables you to automatically number your paragraphs.

- ✔ **Bullets button:** This button accesses a paragraph-level setting that enables you to automatically place bullets at the beginning of paragraphs.

- ✔ **Decrease Indent button:** This button moves the selected paragraph to the previous tab stop.

- ✔ **Increase Indent button:** This button moves the selected paragraph to the next tab stop.

- ✔ **Decrease Font Size button:** This button changes the selected text to the next smaller font size listed in the Font Size list box.

- ✔ **Increase Font Size button:** This button changes the selected text to the next larger font size listed in the Font Size list box.

- ✔ **Fill Color button:** This button lets you apply color to the background of a text frame.

- ✔ **Line Color button:** This button opens the color selector pop-up menu, which enables you to change the color of the selected line.

- ✔ **Font Color button:** This button opens the color selector pop-up menu, which enables you to change the font color of selected text.

- ✔ **Line/Border Style button:** This button enables you to place borders around your text frames.

- ✔ **Text Frame Properties button:** This button accesses the Text Frame Properties dialog box, where you can perform such wonders as changing the margins, setting up margins, wrapping text around pictures, and including Continued notices.

> ✔ **Rotate Left button:** This button lets you rotate the selected text frame left — counterclockwise — 90 degrees with each click.
>
> ✔ **Rotate Right button:** This button lets you rotate the selected text frame right — clockwise — 90 degrees with each click.

It's important to realize that the toolbar offers you only highlights of what's possible format-wise. Many of the Format menu commands that the buttons duplicate provide access to dialog boxes containing lots of additional options. Still, the buttons are a convenient, quick way to apply basic formatting.

Character formatting

Character formatting enables you to change the appearance of individual characters. Character formatting is most often used for emphasis, to set text apart from the text surrounding it. For example, words are often italicized to make them stand out in a block of plain text.

One of the really confusing aspects of formatting text is that you can format the text in your paragraphs at the paragraph level and also format individual characters in that paragraph any way that you want. You can think of paragraph formatting as a default format that you can override as needed.

Character formatting can make your text look great, but for even fancier text, try out WordArt, as described in Chapter 8.

Choosing a font

Perhaps the most noticeable character format is the *font* (also known as the *typeface*) of your text. The font determines each character's basic shape. Microsoft Windows and Microsoft Publisher 2000 together offer you lots of fonts. Text always uses some font or another; by default, it's Times New Roman. Some of the fonts, such as Vacation MT, Webdings, and Wingdings, are symbol fonts and aren't used for regular text.

As if the fonts that come with Microsoft Publisher 2000 and Microsoft Windows weren't enough, you may have even more available to you. Other Windows programs may have installed additional fonts on your computer, and your printer may have its own set of built-in fonts. If you become a raving font addict, rest assured that you can buy and install even more fonts.

As Roger C. Parker says in *Desktop Publishing & Design For Dummies* (published by IDG Books Worldwide, Inc.): "He who dies with the most fonts wins."

Do one of the following to change the font for selected text:

- ✔ Select the font name from the Font list box in the toolbar.

- ✔ Select Format⇨Font to open the Font dialog box, shown in Figure 7-8. Click the font name in the Font list box.

  If no font name appears in the Font box, you've probably highlighted text that is currently formatted with more than one font. You can still use the Font list box to apply the font that you want.

Font

General

Font:
Times New Roman

Font style:
Regular

Size:
32

Underline:
(none)

Color:

Effects

☐ Superscript ☐ Outline ☐ Small caps ☐ Shadow
☐ Subscript ☐ Emboss ☐ All caps ☐ Engrave

Sample

Times New Roman

☐ Mark colors that will not print well on my printer

OK Cancel Apply

Figure 7-8:
The Font
dialog box.

Press Ctrl+Shift+F to activate the Font list box and then press the up- or down-arrow keys to move to the font that you want. Press Enter to select the highlighted font.

When you open the Font box's drop-down list, you see an icon next to each font name. The two *T*s icon means that the font is a *TrueType font,* an outline font that any Windows program can use. The little printer icon means that the font is a *printer font,* built into the current publication's target printer. No symbol means that the font is a *system font,* one that Windows itself uses to label windows, dialog boxes, options, and so on.

Which type of font should you use? TrueType is generally the most hassle-free font type, but you may want to go with printer fonts if you're having your publication printed by a printer service. Many printer services use Postscript fonts that require printer descriptions.

Note that if you *do* use printer fonts, those fonts may look bad on-screen. Because Windows has only sketchy information about any given printer font, your on-screen characters may be misshapen and lines of text may appear clipped off in certain views. Everything should look fine when you print your publication, though. Chapter 8 explains fonts and typography in detail.

Changing the font size

There must be something about publishing professionals that makes using standard English terms difficult for them. Even when it comes to measuring the size of text, they can't stick with inches, centimeters, or any other measurement that the rest of the world uses. Instead, they measure the height of text in *points*. A point is approximately $\frac{1}{72}$ of an inch, and you can make text any size from 0.5 point to 999.9 points, in 0.1 point increments. In inches, that translates from $\frac{1}{144}$ inches to almost 14 inches high — that's quite a range! Unless you're making banners, though, you probably want to keep your text somewhere between 6 and 72 points.

With typography, nothing is as simple as it seems. Even a standard point size changes depending on the font selected. These and other mysteries of life are explained in Chapter 8.

To change the size of selected text:

- ✔ Select the size from the Font Size list box in the toolbar or enter your own size into the list box.

- ✔ Alternatively, you can choose Format⇨Font to open the Font dialog box, as shown back in Figure 7-8, and enter the font size there.

- ✔ If no font size appears in the Size list box, you've probably highlighted text formatted with more than one size. You can still use the Size list box to apply the size you want.

Press Ctrl+Shift+P to activate the Size list box. Use the up and down arrows to increase or decrease the font size, or type any size — between 0.5 and 999.9 — you wish and press Enter.

With TrueType fonts, you can enter any font size that you want (in the allowed range), even decimal numbers. Some printer fonts support only a limited set of sizes, however. If you plan to use printer fonts, consult the printer's documentation to see whether this limitation applies.

Applying a type style

The last important character format is type style, which Microsoft Publisher 2000 refers to as *Effects*. Want to make a word or two stand out? Then apply text effects such as **boldface,** *italics,* or underlining. You can apply these effects to selected text by using toolbar buttons or from the Font dialog box.

You can specify whether you want to underline all the selected text or just the individual words and not the spaces between them. You can choose a double underline, a wavy underline, or a dotted or dashed underline. Go ahead, take a peek at the Underline list box in the Font dialog box. You can also create superscripts or subscripts, all caps, small caps, outline, shadow, emboss, and engrave effects in the dialog box.

TIP

I think that you will want to know the keyboard shortcuts for these text effects cold: Press Ctrl+B for bold; Ctrl+I for italic; Ctrl+U for underline; Ctrl+= for superscript; Ctrl+Shift+= for subscript; Ctrl+Shift+K for small caps, and, most important, Ctrl+Spacebar for plain text (removes all style formats from selected text). With the exception of Ctrl+Spacebar, all these keyboard shortcuts are toggles. Press the shortcut once to turn the effect on; press the shortcut a second time to remove the effect.

As with font and font size, you can use either the toolbar buttons or the Font dialog box (more generally) to make your type style selections. When you select text to which the bold, italic, or underline effect has been applied, the corresponding button on the toolbar shows a pushed-in look. It is possible to simultaneously select both text that has one of these effects applied and text that does not. When you do this, you may notice that the corresponding toolbar button does not have the pushed-in look. If you click the button once, you remove the effect from all the highlighted text. Click again to apply the effect to all the selected text.

Some fonts (not common Windows ones, though) don't support boldface and/or italics. For these fonts, the B (bold) and I (italic) buttons are useless. You can click them all you want, but your text doesn't change.

Getting the yearn to kern

If you're really picky about how your text looks, you can even control the amount of horizontal space between characters, either squishing text together or spreading it apart. Publishing professionals call this *kerning*. (Don't confuse kerning with line spacing. Kerning controls the amount of *horizontal* spacing between characters, whereas line spacing controls the *vertical* spacing between lines of text.)

By default, Microsoft Publisher 2000 automatically kerns between relatively large characters — anything 14 points or larger. To get Microsoft Publisher 2000 to kern even smaller characters, choose the Format➪Character Spacing command from the menu and change the setting in the Kern text at scroll box. Microsoft Publisher 2000 then adjusts the spacing between letters based on a list of letter pairs that are part of a font's definition.

Microsoft Publisher 2000 does a good job of automatic kerning, but if you have some specific text that you want to kern manually, you have two choices. You can use the Tracking option for large selections of text, or the Kerning option to fine-tune the spacing between two characters. Select Format⇨ Character Spacing from the menu. This command opens the Character Spacing dialog box, as shown in Figure 7-9, where you can adjust the spacing for large selections (Microsoft Publisher 2000 calls this *tracking*) or fine-tune the spacing between two characters (Microsoft Publisher 2000 calls this *kerning*). Perfect kerning is one of those power features that desktop publishers crave.

Figure 7-9:
The
Character
Spacing
dialog box.

Character Spacing	? ☒

Scaling
△→ Shrink or stretch selected   [100 %]

Tracking
Use this option to adjust the spacing for a highlighted block of text.
[Normal ▼]   By this amount: [100 %]

Kerning
Use this option to fine-tune the spacing between two characters.
[Normal ▼]   By this amount: [0 pt]

Automatic pair kerning
☑ Kern text at: [14 pt] and above

Sample
Times New Roman

[Show Toolbar] [Apply] [OK] [Cancel]

To quickly adjust the spacing of selected text, press Ctrl+Shift+[to move characters closer together or Ctrl+Shift+] to spread them apart.

Don't bother spending much time kerning small text. Kerning is best done on large text, particularly headline text. Figure 7-10 shows you the difference between tight and loose kerning.

Figure 7-10:
Expanded
versus
condensed
kerning.

The Yearn to Kern
The Yearn to Kern

Paragraph formatting

Whereas character formatting enables you to control text one character at a time, *paragraph formatting* controls entire paragraphs. Paragraph formatting includes line spacing, alignment within a frame, tab stops, indents, and formatting text as bulleted or numbered lists.

You probably discovered in grade school that a paragraph is a group of sentences that form a complete thought. Well, forget it! In Microsoft Publisher 2000, regardless of complete thoughts, a paragraph is anything that ends with a *paragraph mark,* one of those special characters that you create every time you press the Enter key. Thus, if you type a three-line address, pressing Enter to begin each new line, that address consists of three separate paragraphs. If you want, you can format each of those paragraphs differently.

With character formatting, you must select all the text that you want to format. But you don't need to bother highlighting entire paragraphs to apply paragraph formatting. To mark a single paragraph for paragraph formatting, just place the insertion point anywhere in the paragraph or highlight text anywhere in the paragraph. To mark multiple paragraphs for formatting, just highlight some text in each of those paragraphs. Keep this in mind during the next few sections whenever I tell you to "mark the paragraph(s)."

Here's a weird one: Microsoft Publisher 2000 and word processors store the paragraph format and any variation that you apply to characters in that paragraph in the paragraph mark itself.

Adjusting line spacing

You can control the amount of space that appears above and below each paragraph. This option is important for making headings stand out and for many other purposes.

To change the paragraph(s) line spacing:

✓ Select the paragraph(s) that you want to affect and then choose Format➪Line Spacing. The Line Spacing dialog box appears, as shown in Figure 7-11.

✓ You can set the Between lines spinner to control the amount of space between lines within a paragraph. Use the Before paragraphs and After paragraphs spinners to add space before the first line of a paragraph or after the last line. The Sample box shows you the result of your settings.

✓ Alternatively, you can press Ctrl+1 for single space text; Ctrl+2 for double space; Ctrl+5 for 1½ line space; and Ctrl+0 (zero) to remove the space before a paragraph.

Figure 7-11:
The Line
Spacing
dialog box.

It is considered good typographical practice to set line spacing rather than insert additional paragraph marks to create spacing. Then, if you decide to change the spacing between the paragraph later, you need to work with the attributes of only the paragraphs that contain your content. You don't need to add or delete paragraphs that you use as space holders.

You can specify any and all line spacing settings in terms of inches (in), centimeters (cm), points (pt), picas (pi), or the Microsoft Publisher 2000 special space (sp) measurement. One space in Microsoft Publisher 2000 always equals 120 percent of the current text size — an ideal size-to-spacing ratio for single spacing. If you use the sp measurement — 1 sp for single-spacing, 2 sp for double spacing, and so on — your line spacing changes as your text size changes. If you use any other measurement, your line spacing remains the same when you enlarge or reduce your text size, even if the result is wildly squished or spaced out text lines.

Setting paragraph alignment

By default, Microsoft Publisher 2000 lines up paragraphs along the left edge of the text frame that holds them. Text aligned in this manner is said by typographers to be *ragged right* or *left justified*. To instead push text to the right edge (ragged left or right justified), center it between the edges (fully ragged), or stretch it from edge to edge (fully justified), you change its *alignment,* also called *justification* in publishing lingo.

Here are some ways to set paragraph alignment for your selected paragraph(s):

✔ Click one of the four alignment icons on the Formatting toolbar. These are, from left to right across the tool bar, Align Left, Center, Align Right, and Justify.

✔ You can also use the following keystrokes: Ctrl+L for left justified; Ctrl+R for right justified; Ctrl+E for center (think *even!*); or Ctrl+J for fully justified. Press Ctrl+Q to return your paragraph to the default format.

✔ You can also align paragraphs using the Indents and Lists command on the Format menu, but using an Alignment toolbar button is much easier.

Justified text can stretch your text out so far that it's difficult to read. To remedy this, try hyphenating the text, as described earlier in this chapter.

The justification that you use, hyphenation, the amount of line spacing, and other paragraph-level formats are important determinants in how your publication looks. They "color" your text and make it either more or less readable. A full explanation of this topic would require more space than I have available. But you should really take the time to visit the style guides that I recommend to you at the end of Chapter 2. See Chapter 12, too, for more information on hyphenating and justifying text.

Setting tab stops

When you press the Tab key in a text frame, Microsoft Publisher 2000 inserts a special character called a *tab mark*. How a tab mark affects the text following that mark depends on the *tab stops* set for the paragraph.

By default, left-aligned tab stops are set every half-inch on the horizontal ruler. (When you're working in a text frame, a special subsection of the horizontal ruler measures distances from the frame's left edge.) Thus, each tab mark that you create usually causes the text following that mark to left-align with the next available half-inch mark. For example, if your text is 1¼ inches from the left edge of a frame and you insert a tab mark before that text, the text left-aligns with the 1½-inch ruler mark.

By setting your own custom tab stops, however, you can get tab marks to align a number of other ways. Microsoft Publisher 2000 supports four different kinds of tab stops:

- ✔ **Left tab stop:** This setting is the default, and a tab moves text to the right of the tab mark so that it aligns flush left to the tab stop.

- ✔ **Center tab stop:** A tab moves text so that it aligns centered on the tab stop.

- ✔ **Right tab stop:** A tab moves text so that it aligns flush right to the tab stop.

- ✔ **Decimal tab stop:** A tab moves text so that any decimal point aligns to the tab stop. This tab is useful for aligning numeric data in tables.

You can quickly set a tab stop for your selected paragraph(s) by clicking the Move Both Rulers button at the intersection of the two rulers until the type of tab that you want appears. Then, click at the place on the horizontal ruler where you want the tab to go. To remove a tab stop that you have set, simply drag it from the horizontal ruler.

But sometimes you may want to use a tab leader. In that case, you need to set tabs by using the Tabs dialog box, as explained in the following steps:

1. **Select the paragraph(s) that you want to affect.**

2. **Choose Format⇨Tabs.**

   The Tabs dialog box, as shown in Figure 7-12, appears.

Figure 7-12:
The Tabs
dialog box.

3. **In the Tab stop positions list box, specify a position for your tab stop.**

   This position is the distance between the frame's left edge and the tab stop.

4. **Under Alignment, choose how you want text to align to your tab stop.**

5. **If desired, set a tab leader.**

   A *tab leader* is a set of characters that fill any gap created by a tab mark. Dotted tab leaders are commonly used together with right-aligned tab stops in tables of contents (as in the beginning of this book). The dots connect the titles on the left with the page numbers on the right.

6. **Click the Set button.**

   Your tab-stop position now appears in the Tab stop positions list box.

7. **If desired, set additional tabs by repeating Steps 3 through 6.**

8. **Click the OK button.**

After you set custom tab stops, the horizontal ruler displays those stops, using symbols for the four kinds of tab stops. If you're fairly adept with the mouse, you can fine-tune the position of a tab stop by dragging it back and forth on the ruler. Be careful to point directly to the tab stop that you want to move, however, or you may accidentally create a new stop.

Here are some helpful shortcuts for working with tab stops:

✔ To delete a tab stop, drag it down off the horizontal ruler. Or use the Tabs dialog box's Clear and Clear All buttons.

✔ Notice that the Tabs dialog box provides an option for changing the Default tab stops from every half inch to any other increment you like.

✔ To modify the alignment or leader of an existing tab stop, open the Tabs dialog box and click the stop that you want to change in the Tab stop positions list box. Then, set the desired alignment and/or leader, click Set, and click OK.

Remember that tab stops are paragraph specific. If you click or highlight text in another paragraph, the horizontal ruler displays any custom tab stops set in that new paragraph. If the tab stops on the horizontal ruler are gray, you've probably highlighted text in multiple paragraphs that use different tab stops.

Tab stops can be a pain. If you get frustrated working with them, remember that just about anything you can accomplish with tab stops you can often more easily accomplish with indents, table frames, and multiple text frames.

Setting paragraph indents

Indents are like margins that affect only individual paragraphs. By default, all indents are set to 0, which makes paragraphs align with the text frame's margins. By increasing the indent setting, you can move paragraphs in from those margins.

If you want to move every line of text in a text frame, you needn't bother with indents. Instead, just resize or move the frame.

To set indents, follow these steps:

1. **Mark the paragraph(s) that you want to affect.**

2. **Choose Format⇨Indents and Lists from the menu bar.**

   The Indents and Lists dialog box, as shown in Figure 7-13, opens.

Figure 7-13:
The Indents and Lists dialog box for a normal paragraph.

[Indents and Lists dialog box]

Indent settings
⦿ Normal   ○ Bulleted list   ○ Numbered list

Indents
Preset: Flush Left

Left: 0"
First line: 0"
Right: 0"

Alignment: Left

Line Spacing...   OK   Cancel

Sample

3. **Under Indent settings, verify that <u>N</u>ormal is selected.**

4. **From the <u>P</u>reset drop-down list, choose the type of indent that you want.**

5. **If desired, use the <u>L</u>eft, <u>F</u>irst Line, and <u>R</u>ight options to fine-tune the preset indent.**

   Left indents the left edge of every paragraph line. First Line indents the left edge of just the first paragraph line, and Right indents the right edge of every paragraph line.

   The Sample box shows the effect of your choices.

6. **Click OK.**

After you set custom indents, *indent markers* — those little black triangles on the horizontal ruler — move to reflect the indenting. If you want, you can change the indents by dragging the indent markers back and forth:

- ✔ The top-left indent marker controls the left edge of the first line in the paragraph.

- ✔ The bottom-left marker controls the left edge of every line in the paragraph but the first line.

- ✔ The right indent marker controls the right edge of every line in the paragraph.

- ✔ The rectangle under the bottom-left marker controls both the first line and left indents.

Be careful to point directly to the indent marker that you want to move, however, or you may accidentally create a tab stop. If the indent markers on the horizontal ruler are gray, you've probably highlighted text in multiple paragraphs that use different indents. You can still use the markers to adjust your indents.

It is considered good typographical practice to use a first-line indent rather than tab marks to indent the first lines of paragraphs.

As an example of how indents are used, consider the *hanging indent* shown in Figure 7-14. You create a hanging indent by setting the left indent larger than the first-line indent. Hanging indents are generally used to create bulleted and numbered lists, as described in the next section.

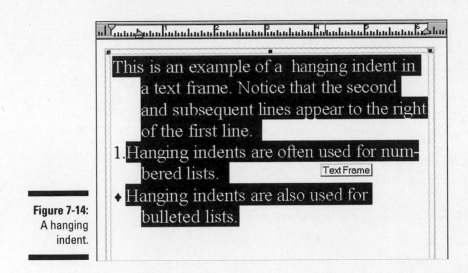

Figure 7-14:
A hanging
indent.

Unlike some word processors, Microsoft Publisher 2000 doesn't allow you to set negative indents. That is, your text can't extend beyond a frame's margins. You may, however, be able to get text to move closer to the edge of a frame by reducing the frame's internal margins. To do this, use the Format⇨Text Frame Properties command on the menu bar.

Using paragraph styles

You may not want to get into this subject, but many hard-core desktop publishers prefer to use text styles to apply text formatting. (If you've used a modern word-processing program, you may already be familiar with text styles.) A *text style* is a named set of attributes that you can apply to a paragraph.

I use text styles extensively because they are a terrific labor-saving device. For example, if you want all your body text to be double-spaced, 12-point Arial italic text with a ¼-inch first-line indent, you can create a text style that contains all those formatting instructions. When you then apply that style to a paragraph, all the text in that paragraph instantly takes on each formatting option specified by the style. Should you later decide to change a text style, all the paragraphs that bear that style change instantly — quite the time-saver! So, most experienced authors, editors, layout artists, and publishers start the text-formatting process by creating a style sheet of all the allowed paragraph types in their document. Then they apply these styles to their work.

To create, change, rename, delete, and even import styles, select Format⇨Text Style. The Text Style dialog box, as shown in Figure 7-15, appears.

Figure 7-15:
The Text
Style dialog
box.

Make your selections by clicking one of the Click to buttons in the dialog box. These buttons lead to other dialog boxes that lead you to the various character and paragraph formatting dialog boxes covered earlier in this chapter. You can set the following properties as part of a text style:

- ✔ Character type and size
- ✔ Indents and lists
- ✔ Line spacing
- ✔ Character spacing
- ✔ Tabs

The Sample box in the Text Style dialog box shows you a graphic indicating the effect of your selections.

To apply text styles to selected paragraphs, select a style from the Style list box at the left end of the Formatting toolbar, or change the selection in the Text Style dialog box.

Press Ctrl+Shift+S to activate the Style list box in the Formatting toolbar and then use the down- or up-arrow keys to move to the style that you want.

I think that the import feature of the Text Style dialog box is particularly helpful. I write almost all of my work in Microsoft Word and import the text into Microsoft Publisher 2000. (Remember that you can also do editing-in-place with Microsoft Word, as explained in Chapter 6.) I can import my styles from Word when setting up my document inside Microsoft Publisher 2000.

Using the Format Painter

Microsoft Publisher 2000 offers a feature called the Format Painter. The Format Painter enables you to copy the format of an object to another object. It is particularly useful when applied to text. It works generally with any object, however.

To copy and paste the formatting of selected characters or a paragraph:

1. **Highlight the text with the formatting that you want to copy.**

   Select the characters or any part of a paragraph that contains the paragraph mark.

2. **Click the Format Painter button on the toolbar.**

   Your pointer turns into a paintbrush that looks like the Format Painter button.

3. **Click and drag the pointer over the characters or paragraph mark that you want to change.**

To apply the format to multiple selections, double-click the Format Painter button in Step 2. When you are done applying the format to your text, click the Format Painter button again.

Frame formatting

Two text formatting features affect entire frames:

✔ Hyphenating text

✔ Arranging text in snaking columns

Because these features affect entire frames, it doesn't matter whether you highlight text before you apply them.

The section "Hyphenation," earlier in this chapter, discusses the Microsoft Publisher 2000 hyphenation feature. (Chapter 12 discusses this feature more fully.) In many programs, hyphenation is done at the paragraph level, but in Microsoft Publisher 2000, hyphenation is done an entire frame at a time.

In publications such as newsletters, text is often laid out in *snaking columns,* where text ends at the bottom of one column and continues again at the top of the next. You can create snaking text columns by laying down text frames side by side and then connecting those frames, as described in Chapter 6. But that's the hard way of doing things. If you wanted to do things the hard way, you probably wouldn't be reading this book.

To set multiple columns within a text frame:

1. **Select the text frame.**

2. **Choose Format⇨Text Frame Properties.**

   The Text Frame Properties dialog box appears, as shown in Figure 7-16.

Figure 7-16:
The Text
Frame
Properties
dialog box.

3. **In the Columns Number spinner, enter the number of columns that you want.**

   You can have up to 63 columns in one frame.

4. **In the Columns Spacing spinner, set how much space you want between your columns.**

   Publishing professionals call this space a *column gutter*. The Sample section shows you an example of the division of your text frame.

5. **Click the OK button.**

   The text in your frame rearranges itself into multiple, snaking columns.

Microsoft Publisher 2000 automatically ends one column of text and begins the next after it runs out of room at the bottom of a frame. To lengthen a column, try decreasing the frame's top and bottom margins or resizing the frame.

To force Microsoft Publisher 2000 to end a column before it reaches the bottom of a text frame, place the insertion point where you want the column to end, and then press Ctrl+Shift+Enter. This keyboard shortcut is the same one that Microsoft Word uses to specify the end of a section, and this keystroke is imported from Word as a column end.

For nonsnaking columns, as in this book's tables, consider using table frames.

Chapter 8

Vintage Type:
The Corkscrew, Please

I think that choosing fonts for your publication is like decorating your house. It's great fun, and it is important in giving your publication a personality. Just as some people like art deco whereas others like Bauhaus decor, different designers prefer different fonts. Although you *can* decorate your house with purple velvet wallpaper or alternate orange and black paint on the bedroom walls, chances are that you want to choose more conventional design themes. The same is true in your publications.

In this chapter, I tell you how to buy, install, and use fonts. Some of the chapter deals with the common practices that most desktop publishing experts recommend, and some sections give you the technical details, such as how to work with fonts, what font files are, and how to best use them.

About Type and Fonts

I was at a client's office recently doing some consulting work when I saw the most amazing thing. The client's secretary was busy typing a letter on an old IBM Selectric typewriter. Okay, I know. That isn't so amazing. The amazing part is that the typewriter was sitting next to his brand-new PC! Let's see . . . type a letter on this typewriter and choose any typeface as long as it is Courier, or type the letter on a PC and choose from hundreds of typefaces?

Tough call! Of course, I smugly informed him of the superiority of the computer's technology over the typewriter. His response? "That old typewriter never locks up on me when the boss wants something typed in a hurry!"

Now don't get me wrong. I actually like Courier. It is an extremely attractive font and its widespread use is a testament to its durability. I think that Courier's main problem is that it is overused. And certainly, using the same typeface every day gets old fast, no matter how great the typewriter.

The point of this typewriter story is to introduce a basic term of typography: *font.* A font is one typeface, in one style. The print ball for that typewriter contained one font: Courier.

Of course, you can go out and buy other fonts for the typewriter I mentioned. When you get to the point in your document at which you need another font, you simply replace the ball and carry on. Compare that time-consuming process with creating text on your computer: With a computer, you can have as many fonts as you want, and switching to a different font is as simple as making a menu selection. Until you print your document, you can go back and reformat your document to your heart's content — something that you'd need gallons of correction fluid and unending patience to do on a typewriter. It's no wonder that few people buy typewriters anymore.

Font styles

The fonts used today come in four main styles:

- **Serif fonts:** A *serif* is a small line that hangs off the upper and lower ends of the strokes that make up a text character. Serifs help guide the reader's eye, which is why serif fonts are typically used in body copy. (Body copy, or body text, makes up the majority of the paragraphs in a publication.) Examples of common serif fonts are Benguiat, Bodoni, Bookman, Courier New, Galliard, Garamond, Goudy, Jenson, Palatino, and Times New Roman. Many of these fonts are named after the designers who either created or inspired them.

- **Sans serif fonts:** Sans serif fonts don't have serifs (*sans* is French for *without*) and are typically square and plainer than serif fonts. In older days, these fonts were described as either *gothic* or *grotesque* faces. They are more commonly used in headlines, in which a limited number of characters need to be read. Examples of sans serif fonts in common use are Arial, Helvetica, Optima, Tekton, and Univers.

- **Decorative fonts:** Decorative fonts are used to present letters in stylized form. Usually, they are thematic; a set of fonts may be created out of pictures of jugglers and clowns or use cowboy motifs, for example. Great for kids' birthday party invitations, not so great for your annual report to the Board of Directors.

TECHNICAL STUFF

Sizing up your font

You can make a font virtually any size you want. The size of a font is normally measured in points. A point is approximately ½ of an inch, but varies somewhat from typeface to typeface. The normal font size used in correspondence is 12 points, but 8, 10, and 11 points are also common.

It's important to remember that the size of a point depends on what font you're using; 12-point type in one font can be substantially different in size from 12-point type in another font, for example. (Figure 8-1 shows you samples in various faces at the same size.)

Not only do the fonts have different vertical dimensions, but their widths are different as well. Font height is usually gauged by the height of the lowercase x, whereas the width is usually gauged by the width of the lowercase m. For this reason, a font's vertical dimension is referred to as its x-height, and its horizontal size is referred to as its m-width.

✔ **Symbol fonts:** This font style presents symbols as a character set. Earlier chapters show examples of the Symbol and Wingdings fonts that are installed in Windows 98. Vendors also sell symbol sets for maps (Adobe's Carta) and for music (Adobe's Sonata).

Figure 8-1:
Examples of fonts in various styles.

Serif fonts
Bookman
The quick brown fox jumps over the lazy dog. 0 1 2 3 4 5 6 7 8 9

Courier New
The quick brown fox jumps over the lazy dog. 0 1 2 3 4 5 6 7 8 9

Garamond
The quick brown fox jumps over the lazy dog. 0 1 2 3 4 5 6 7 8 9

Goudy
The quick brown fox jumps over the lazy dog. 0 1 2 3 4 5 6 7 8 9

Times
The quick brown fox jumps over the lazy dog. 0 1 2 3 4 5 6 7 8 9

Sans Serif fonts
Arial
The quick brown fox jumps over the lazy dog. 0 1 2 3 4 5 6 7 8 9

DESDEMONA
THE QUICK BROWN FOX JUMPS OVER THE LAZT DOG. 0 1 2 3 4 5 6 7 8 9

Impact
The quick brown fox jumps over the lazy dog. 0 1 2 3 4 5 6 7 8 9

Univers
The quick brown fox jumps over the lazy dog. 0 1 2 3 4 5 6 7 8 9

Symbol fonts
Symbol
Τηε θυιχκ βροων φοξ φυμπσ οϖερ τηε λαζψ δογ. 0 1 2 3 4 5 6 7 8 9

Wingdings

Fixed fonts

The first computer fonts emulated those found in older typesetting equipment or in typewriters. Each font was a single typeface designed for a specific size. Most of these fonts were designed as bitmapped descriptions (that is, comprised of a collection of dots) and so were called *bitmapped fonts*. You could install Courier 8, 10, and 12 on your computer in plain (roman), italic, bold, and bold italic styles, with one font file each for your screen and for your printer. All together, you would have installed 12 separate files for these three sizes. What a mess!

As time went by, type vendors produced font descriptions that let you create a fixed font in any size from a single description. Today, the use of fixed fonts is extremely limited.

Fixed fonts are usually sold in pairs that contain a *screen font* (used to display the font on your computer screen) and a *printer font* (used to actually print out your text). In Windows 98, an *A* icon in the Fonts folder indicates a fixed font. Click Panel; then double-click the Fonts icon to see the fonts that are installed on your computer.

When you use a fixed screen font at the size that it was designed to be used, the results look as good as with any font you can use. You also get the added performance advantage of not having to have the font description *rasterized* (that is, converted to a bitmap for display or output), which isn't much of an advantage in these days of very fast computers.

If you use a fixed font at some perfect multiple of the size it was designed for — for example, at $\frac{1}{2}$ or $\frac{1}{4}$ size — you also get perfect results. You can even get reasonable results when using a fixed font at two times or four times its intended size. Your screen font looks distorted at other sizes, however, even though your printed material often looks perfect.

Some printers come with their own printer fonts. If Windows isn't familiar with your printer's printer font, it will substitute some other font to display the document on-screen. Although you won't see a realistic display of how your document prints, it prints just fine by using the fonts contained in the printer. Most people have given up on fixed fonts at this point.

TrueType fonts

TrueType is one of two popular font formats (the other is *PostScript,* discussed in the next section). Unlike fixed fonts and PostScript fonts, TrueType fonts do not require separate screen and printer font description files — Windows can use the same description file to display the font on-screen and to print your publication. Because the font information is contained in one file, you have half the file management chores that you do with fixed fonts and PostScript fonts, which is a major benefit of using TrueType fonts. In addition, Windows versions 3.1 and later contain built-in support for TrueType fonts. Without getting into all the technical background, this support results in smaller font file sizes and somewhat faster font display and printing.

PostScript fonts

Adobe PostScript fonts have been available since the middle 1980s. Most service bureaus and professional designers favor PostScript fonts because of their high quality and large library of available font descriptions. I've seen estimates that more than 10,000 typefaces are available in PostScript form. Sorry, but my editor won't let me list them for you.

PostScript fonts come in two types: Type 1 and Type 3. The difference between the two types is that Type 3 doesn't contain special instructions — called *hinting* — that alter the appearance of fonts at small point sizes (11 point and below) to make them more readable both on-screen (if you have the Adobe Type Manager installed) and in your printed matter. Type 1 fonts (as well as TrueType fonts) come with hinting built into their descriptions.

PostScript fonts require a special font rasterizer to convert them to bitmaps that can be displayed on the screen or printed by your printer. For a long time, PostScript fonts required a PostScript printer to print properly. PostScript printers contained a ROM chip that stored the PostScript interpreter that did the bitmap conversion for output. In 1989, under pressure from other vendors who finally cracked the technology of Adobe hinting, Adobe released Adobe Type Manager and published the specifications of PostScript type encryption and hinting.

Adobe Type Manager (ATM) displays PostScript fonts well and makes printing the fonts to non-PostScript printers possible. Your computer's processor takes the place of the processor in a PostScript printer. Thanks to ATM, you can get great-looking output even from inkjet printers.

Choosing between TrueType and PostScript fonts

In regard to performance and quality, no one has yet been able to show me to my satisfaction that there is much difference — or, in fact, any difference — between TrueType and PostScript fonts. Of course, you get some TrueType fonts free with the installation of Windows and other Microsoft products such as Publisher. You can't beat that.

The best advice that I can give you regarding fonts is the following: If you are an occasional desktop publisher, choose either TrueType or PostScript, but try not to use both. If you do use both, pay particular attention to making sure that you don't use a font with the same name in both styles. In other words, if you set certain body text in TrueType Times Roman, don't set other body text in PostScript Times Roman. Easier said than done.

If you are a professional desktop publisher, you may have no choice but to use both typeface descriptions (TrueType and PostScript). The people who are my gurus of type favor PostScript type. I think that this is largely due to the extremely large library of high-quality fonts available in Postscript, the fact that many printer services can't work with TrueType, and the bias of many years of usage. DTP professionals collect type like some people collect wine and toss around the same nonsense about flavor, bouquet, body, and so on.

I remain unconvinced. I like the convenience of TrueType and think that PostScript is worth the additional trouble only when a typeface exists in PostScript that doesn't exist in TrueType.

A primer on buying fonts

You buy fonts in sets. At a minimum, fonts are sold as a single typeface, usually in different sizes and styles. Fixed fonts are sold as individual font files. TrueType and PostScript fonts are sold without regard to font size.

Initially, font vendors sold fonts in a general package meant to serve a variety of needs. The first Apple LaserWriter collection of 35 fonts in 7 typefaces was this kind of package. I've seen a movement afoot for the last few years to sell fonts in related families for a related purpose. Now you can buy packages meant for newsletters, faxes, correspondence, and decorative purposes, to name but a few. Typically, these packages offer three or four typefaces in several styles. If you are font-minded (and who isn't these days!), you can buy many vendors' entire font libraries on CD-ROM. The fonts on the CD-ROM are usually encrypted, and you need to obtain a serial number from the vendor in order to "unlock" the fonts so that you can install them. The vendor gives you the serial number for a particular font when you buy that font.

The Bézier versus the Spline

TrueType fonts are outline fonts based on the mathematical B-Quadratic Spline curve. These curves are similar to the Bézier curves upon which Adobe PostScript fonts are based. Unlike PostScript fonts, TrueType fonts do not require separate screen and printer fonts. The rasterizing software in Windows contains the necessary interpreter to output the same file description to your printer as it does to your monitor — with excellent results to both. This is TrueType's major advantage; you have less file

management to worry about with TrueType fonts.

TrueType fonts are rasterized — converted to a bitmap for display or output using software built into Windows versions 3.1 and later. Macintosh System 7 and later also contains a TrueType rasterizer. The advantage of using a built-in rasterizer may be seen in reduced font file sizes for TrueType fonts, and somewhat faster display and print times.

Buying fonts in families is a great way to add to a collection. Most designers recommend that you be conservative in your use of fonts, so a collection of fonts in the same family makes sense. It's better to collect one typeface in many styles — even to collect special character sets such as Small Caps for a font such as Times — than it is to have an incomplete collection of several faces.

Without a doubt, font technology has undergone an explosion since the introduction of the personal computer. More and better fonts have been created in the last ten years than in all of the previous five centuries of type design. I won't say that the best type designers are alive today, as that would be presumptuous of me. But I wouldn't be surprised if that were true. And certainly the most prolific designers are out there working in their studios today.

I'd like to mention some recent developments in font technology because they are important and valuable. First, several typefaces have been created that contain both sans serif and serif members. My favorite of this ilk is the Adobe Stone family, designed by noted type designer Sumner Stone.

Another development is the introduction of "intelligent font technology." Adobe has introduced a family of typefaces called *Multiple Masters*. These fonts can be varied infinitely over a range through three or four axes, so that you can have a single font description yielding plain, condensed, expanded, italic, bold, or different-sized characters. These fonts require Version 2.6 or later of the Adobe Type Manager.

Most computer stores and computer direct-marketing catalogs sell fonts in packages from one vendor or another. What you can find in these mass-market outlets are the most well-known and commercial font packages. These sources are adequate for the occasional desktop publisher.

For more complete collections of fonts, you should contact the font vendors themselves. Each of the vendors in the following list publishes very attractive magazines with samples of all their fonts. Adobe's *Font and Function* appears quarterly, for example. The magazines also highlight new fonts that appear. Addresses are as follows:

Adobe Systems, Inc., 345 Park Ave., San Jose, CA 95110-2704 USA; phone 408-536-6000; Internet: www.adobe.com

Agfa Division, Bayer Corp., 100 Challenger Rd., Ridgefield Park, NJ 07660-2199; phone 201-440-2500; Internet: www.agfahome.com/agfatype

Bitstream, Inc., 215 First St., Cambridge, MA 02142-1270; phone 617-497-6222, 800-522-3668; Internet: www.bitstream.com

Casady & Greene, Inc., 22734 Portola Drive, Salinas, CA 93908-1119; phone 408-484-9228, 800-359-4920; Internet: www.casadyg.com

The Font Bureau, Inc., 326 A St., Suite #6C, Boston, MA 02210; phone 617-423-8770; Internet: www.fontbureau.com

FontHaus, Inc., 1375 Kings Highway E., Fairfield, CT 06430; phone 203-367-1993, 800-942-9110; Internet: `www.fonthaus.com`

International Typeface Corporation, 228 East 45th St., 12th Floor, New York, NY 10017; phone 212-949-8072; `www.itcfonts.com`

Esselte Letraset USA, 40 Eisenhower Dr., Paramus, NJ 07653; phone 201-845-6100, 800-343-8973; Internet: `www.letraset.com`

Monotype Typography, Inc., 20005 Busse Rd., Elk Grove, IL 60007-2400; phone 800-666-6897; Internet: `www.monotype.com`

Our apologies to the many other fine typographers whose firms I couldn't list here. Picking up a book of typestyles, such as *Typestyle,* by Daniel Will-Harris (Peachpit Press) and *The Electronic Type Catalog,* by Steve Byers (Random House) also wouldn't be a bad idea.

If you still don't have enough fonts or haven't found just the right font for your publication, try searching the Internet. Go to your favorite search engine, such as Yahoo!, Excite, Altavista, InfoSeek, Lycos, and so on, and search on the word *fonts.* You will find more font resources than Carter has pills.

Selecting fonts in your publication

In Chapter 8, I explain that you set the attributes for your selected characters and paragraphs from either the Font list box in the Format toolbar or the Font dialog box (Format➪Font). Figure 8-2 shows you the Font dialog box again with the Font list box open.

Another thing to notice about the Font dialog box is that when you have a TrueType font selected, it offers you four different font styles:

- Regular
- *Italic*
- **Bold**
- ***Bold Italic***

You also have access to eight different effects:

- Super$_{script}$
- Sub^{script}
- Shadow
- Outline
- Emboss
- Engrave

Figure 8-2:
The Font
dialog box.

   ✔ Small caps

   ✔ All caps

And you have 17 different underline options:

   ✔ Single

   ✔ Words only

   ✔ Double

   ✔ Dotted

   ✔ Thick dot

   ✔ Thick

   ✔ Dash

   ✔ Long dash

   ✔ Thick dash

   ✔ Thick long dash

   ✔ Dot dash

   ✔ Thick dot dash

   ✔ Dot dot dash

   ✔ Thick dot dot dash

   ✔ Wave

   ✔ Double wave

   ✔ Thick wave

You can mix and match styles, effects, and line placement options. As you may have figured out by now, the TrueType font rasterizer synthesizes these various options from the single TrueType font description.

Printing with fonts

When you print a publication that contains fonts found in the printer's ROM (permanent memory), the printer uses those hard fonts. Many printers allow you to attach a hard drive or CD-ROM drive that you can use as secondary storage for font descriptions. Then that printer knows about a lot more fonts. When you print a document with fonts that aren't in a printer's ROM, a couple of different things can happen.

First, your computer can rasterize the font and send the converted font information to the printer's RAM. This process, known as *downloading,* converts the font to a bitmap that the printer requires and puts the bitmap in the printer's temporary memory. The font descriptions are stored in the printer's RAM until the print engine needs them — which makes it obvious why having a lot of RAM in a printer is valuable. Alternatively, the printer may be able to do the bitmap conversion on its own, freeing up your computer for other work. PostScript printers have this capability.

If your document contains more fonts than can be contained in the printer memory, your computer may store them in a *font cache.* You can change the size of the font cache in the Adobe Type Manager — if you have it installed on your computer — and thus improve printing performance. After a font is rasterized and stored in the cache, it doesn't have to be rasterized again.

Typography 101

I don't have room here to tell you everything about typography that you should probably know. Typography is a big topic and one with a fascinating history. That history has generated more jargon than you could shake a stick at, so to speak. If you want an in-depth background in typography, I refer you to the references mentioned previously, or to *Desktop Publishing & Disign For Dummies* by Roger C. Parker (published by IDG Books Worldwide, Inc.). For now, though, a rundown of some basic terminology is in order. Figure 8-3 shows you a sample font with some of its features called out.

Most designers recommend that you choose a serif font for your body copy. You can add some variety and visual interest to your pages by using sans serif fonts for headlines and subheads. A classic combination is to use the sans serif font Arial (also called Helvetica) for heads and the serif font Times Roman for body copy. This pairing (like Courier), however, has been overused. For that reason, you may want to try other combinations.

The font that you use for the body copy of a long piece is of particular importance. It colors your work and affects readability. Serif fonts have letters that are different sizes, which makes it easier for the eye to recognize words. For this reason, italics, scripts, and sans serif fonts are typically reserved for headlines or captions. Try taking a look at a page of body copy in several fonts to see which one works best with your piece.

The typographical size of a font varies according to its design. If you need to fit a lot of copy onto a single page, select a compact font. Many of the leading fonts were designed for these special purposes. For example, the omnipresent Times New Roman font was created in the 1920s as part of a redesign of *The Times* of London. The intent was to make copy readable but very compact — the better to sell advertising space, my dear. Other fonts, such as Bookman, were created with a more open typestyle to make novels and other books easier to read. Most font catalogs offer suggestions as to how particular fonts are best used and recommend fonts that go well with them as body or display fonts.

Figure 8-3:
Typographic
terms.

The one overriding piece of advice that most designers give is to avoid using too many fonts on your page. Too many fonts make your publications seem cheap, poorly designed, confusing, and hard to read. I've all seen those "ransom note" designs where each letter is in a different font. Most people's sensibilities are better than that — especially because we've been bombarded with well-designed printed material for our entire lifetimes.

The best way to impose good type practice in a publication is to create and manage your publication with style sheets, as described in Chapter 6. Or better yet, use one of the many wizards that Publisher 2000 provides to give your publication a consistent and professional look.

You have a lot of control over the way the type looks on your page. You can adjust the following characteristics to open up your text:

✔ Use bigger font sizes

✔ Adjust letter spacing or kerning

✔ Add additional line spacing

✔ Add spacing between paragraphs

✔ Use paragraph indents

✔ Shorten the length of your lines by adjusting your frame width

✔ Change the justification of your text frame

In regard to the last point, left-justified text is generally considered the most readable text and is most often seen. Right-justified and center-justified text is much less common and is generally used for special purposes such as headlines, captions, or pull quotes. Fully justified text works reasonably well for line lengths of about 10 to 12 words and is commonly used in dense newspaper or newsletter pages.

Using display text for headlines is a great way to pull a reader's eye to a section of a page. Often, headlines use larger and bolder fonts, display fonts, or some other special font treatment. Because the headline is the thing that most people see first on a page, it pays to be particularly attentive to the selection of font and font size. Also, proper kerning of a headline is well worth the additional effort. See Chapter 7 for details on kerning. It's also worthwhile to adjust the line spacing of a headline so that the words seem to clearly belong together. I like to use mixed casing in my headlines unless the headline is very short. In that event, I sometimes use all caps or small caps. When I use scripts in headlines (infrequently), I tend to use them in mixed case only.

WordArt frames often give you an effective way of creating attractive headlines. (See the next section for more information.)

Another way to set off headlines and sections of your documents is to use *rules*. Rules are lines, either horizontal (for headlines) or vertical (for columns). Rules are very effective and they don't have to be thick, either. A single-point rule will suffice in most cases except for separating the headline of your page.

No matter how much time you take designing your publications, you can always learn something from other people's work. When you are doing a project, take a look at the best examples that you can find of similar pieces and see which fonts were used, and how.

WordArt

Microsoft WordArt enables you to create especially fancy text objects, called — pause for effect — _WordArt objects_. Microsoft Publisher 2000 provides WordArt frames for the very purpose of creating and holding WordArt objects. When you draw a WordArt frame, Microsoft Publisher 2000 automatically loads the Microsoft WordArt program, which is an OLE server program. When you create a WordArt object, you insert a special OLE object into your publication. (See Chapter 1 for a discussion of using OLE objects.) To make this particularly easy, the toolbox contains a tool for a WordArt frame.

Figure 8-4 shows you a WordArt frame in the editing-in-place mode typical of some OLE objects in Microsoft Publisher 2000.

Figure 8-4: A sample WordArt object.

Your WordArt text appears in the fuzzy box on your screen, and you enter and edit the actual text in the Enter Your Text Here window that appears below it. Notice the completely new menus and toolbars. Even though it sort of looks like you're in Microsoft Publisher 2000, you're actually in the Microsoft WordArt program, ready to create a WordArt object.

You will want to explore the use of the tools in the Format toolbar when WordArt is open. Figure 8-5 shows you a labeled WordArt toolbar. Table 8-1 describes these tools and what they do. You should note that WordArt comes with its own online Help system. To get more information about using WordArt, select the WordArt Help Topics command from the Help menu.

Figure 8-5: The labled WordArt toolbar.

Follow these steps to create a WordArt object in a WordArt frame:

1. **Click the WordArt Frame tool in the Objects toolbar.**

2. **Click and drag to draw the WordArt Frame.**

3. **In the Enter Your Text Here dialog box, type the text that you want to be your WordArt object.**

   If you want multiple-line text, press Enter to create new lines.

4. **In the Enter Your Text Here dialog box, click the Update Display button.**

   The WordArt object on your publication page now displays the text that you typed.

5. **Use any or all of the Microsoft WordArt tools to fancify your WordArt object.**

   As you use each tool, the WordArt object automatically changes to show the effect you set.

6. **When your WordArt object looks the way you want, press Esc.**

   This step exits Microsoft WordArt and returns you to Microsoft Publisher 2000.

Table 8-1	Microsoft WordArt's Toolbar Tools
Tool	*Purpose*
Shape	Opens a list that enables you to fit your text to a specific path or shape
Font	Opens a list of installed fonts
Size	Opens a list of text sizes (when in doubt, leave this set to Best Fit)
Bold	Boldfaces the text, making each character thicker
Italic	Italicizes the text, slanting each character to the right
Even Height	Makes all characters the same height
Flip	Changes a line of text from horizontal to vertical alignment
Stretch	Stretches text in all directions to make it completely fill the WordArt frame
Align	A pop-up menu with three flavors of justify plus center, left, and right
Spacing Between Characters	Opens a dialog box that enables you to adjust the amount of spacing between characters

Tool	Purpose
Rotation	Opens a dialog box that enables you to rotate and skew your text
Shading	Opens a dialog box that enables you to set a pattern or color for your text
Shadow	Opens a list of shadow effects that you can place around your text
Border	Opens a dialog box that enables you to change each character's outline

The Enter Your Text Here dialog box disappears, Microsoft Publisher 2000 takes back control of the menu bar and the top toolbar, and the WordArt frame loses its fuzzy edge and gains regular selection handles.

If you inadvertently click the publication window when you're working in Microsoft WordArt, you may end up back in Microsoft Publisher 2000 with little warning. You can tell you're back when your WordArt frame loses its fuzzy border. To return to Microsoft WordArt, just double-click the WordArt frame.

Some WordArt effects can cancel out other effects. For example, if you have Best Fit set in the Size box, the Align options have no effect. Just experiment a while. And have fun!

To modify an internal component of a WordArt object after you return to Microsoft Publisher 2000 — for example, if you want to change a character or fit the text to a different path — you must first reload Microsoft WordArt. To do this, double-click the WordArt object. The WordArt frame regains its fuzzy border, Microsoft WordArt once again takes over the menu bar and top toolbar, and the Enter Your Text Here dialog box reopens. You are in the edit-in-place mode for an OLE server.

Microsoft Publisher 2000 treats the WordArt object as a picture. You can move, resize, and crop it just as you can any picture (see Chapter 9).

Be careful of your typing in Microsoft WordArt. The WordArt program doesn't have a spell checker, and because Microsoft Publisher 2000 treats a WordArt object as a picture rather than as text, it won't check the object's spelling, either.

Creating an electronic watermark

If you hold expensive typing paper or foreign currency up to a light, you sometimes can see a watermark, an almost transparent image of a company logo, some dead king's portrait, or whatever. A very cool effect!

You can use Microsoft WordArt to create a similar effect electronically. Draw a full-page WordArt frame, use Microsoft WordArt to create an attention-getting message such as Confidential or Important Notice, and then format the message as you'd like. Now, use Microsoft WordArt's Shading tool to make the object a very light color or shade of gray. Press Esc to return to Publisher, and layer your WordArt object behind all other page objects or place the object on a background so that it appears on every publication page.

If you did everything just right, you now should be able to see your electronic watermark behind your other objects. Way cool!

Other Special Text Effects

Many publications use special large letters to start off a text block. When this letter extends below the top line of the text, it is called a *drop cap*. A large letter that appears above a line of text is a *raised cap*. Figure 8-6 shows you an example of each: The top *L* is an example of a drop cap, whereas the bottom *L* is an example of a raised cap. The shaded box between them is a *pull quote*.

Figure 8-6: A drop cap (top) and raised cap (bottom).

Many people use drop caps in place of smaller headlines. It's a good idea to spread these effects about your page and not to put them on the same line as the actual headline. Typically, I try to use only one of these caps on a page at a time.

To add a fancy first letter:

1. **Click the paragraph that is to contain the fancy first letter.**

2. **Choose Format⇨Drop Cap.**

   The Drop Cap dialog box, shown in Figure 8-7, appears.

3. **If you want to create your own drop cap, click the Custom Drop Cap tab of the Drop Cap dialog box.**

   The Custom Drop Cap tab of the Drop Cap dialog box, shown in Figure 8-8, appears. On this tab, you can select the number of special characters, their position with reference to the first line, the font, and font size.

4. **Click a Choose letter position and size button to set a drop cap or a raised cap; choose a font; and/or select the number of letters that you want to stylize.**

5. **Click the OK button.**

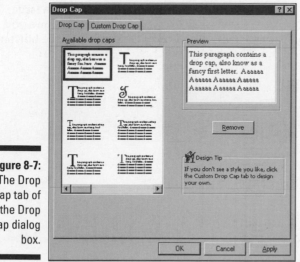

Figure 8-7:
The Drop Cap tab of the Drop Cap dialog box.

Figure 8-8:
The Custom
Drop Cap
tab of the
Drop Cap
dialog box.

Part IV
A Picture Is Worth $3.95

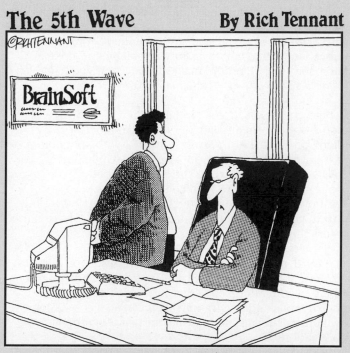

The 5th Wave — By Rich Tennant

BrainSoft

"Our new program has been on the market for over 6 months, and not one intellectual property lawsuit brought against us. I'm worried."

In this part ...

Reading a publication without graphics or pictures is like listening to a basketball game on the radio. Sure, it can be interesting, but something seems to be missing. Microsoft Publisher 2000 lets you include graphic images in your pages to make them more visually appealing and to convey your message in a more compact form. In the three chapters that comprise this part, you can see the various ways of incorporating graphics as a design element in your publication. Microsoft Publisher 2000 helps you import photographs, drawings, paintings, and even animated GIF's and video clips directly into your work with ease. You can also use a library of clip art or work with a library of design elements supplied by Microsoft Publisher 2000 to create snappy, sophisticated layouts. Microsoft Publisher 2000 makes it easy, and you'll find it a lot of fun to work with this aspect of the program.

Face it, color sells. Color can highlight a section, set a mood, or perform any number of design functions. Microsoft Publisher 2000 lets you work with spot colors one at a time, or create colors from the whole universe of colors in a full-color page. The second chapter in this part is a primer on working with color. You can see what colors are, how they are represented, how to match colors, and how to get the best and most accurate output of the colors that you want.

The third, and last, chapter in this part gives you a brief introduction to Microsoft PhotoDraw 2000. This program, included with Microsoft Office 2000, enables you to edit photographs and illustrations. You can also create your own graphic images for use in your printed or on-line publications.

Chapter 9

You Ought to Be in Pictures

At the risk of repeating an old cliché, singing an old song, seeing an old saw, a picture really can be worth a thousand words. Why use dozens of paragraphs explaining what an Aurora X-100 looks like when you can just show your readers a picture of one?

Although Microsoft Publisher 2000 really isn't the place to draw complex pictures, it's mighty flexible when it comes to importing pictures created elsewhere. Some desktop publishers rely heavily on collections of electronic clip art and libraries of photographs, whereas others are daring enough to create their own pictures using specialized graphics programs. Whether you're working from a clip art collection or creating your own pictures, this chapter shows you how to get pictures into and out of your publications and how to work with pictures after they're in Microsoft Publisher 2000.

This chapter also shows you how to use some related tools that come with Microsoft Publisher 2000. You find out how to use Microsoft Draw to create your own drawings, use the Design Gallery to obtain publication elements, apply border art, and even use your own scanner from within Microsoft Publisher 2000 to bring images directly into the program.

Understanding More about Picture Frames

Microsoft Publisher 2000 uses picture frames to display graphics on a layout. A picture frame can contain either drawings or images. The differences between drawings and images are described later in this chapter.

You don't create graphics inside a picture frame; they must be created elsewhere. The graphic contained in a picture frame can either be a data file or an OLE object that is managed by another program.

You can create picture frames in two ways. You can draw them yourself or have the program create them for you when you insert or import a graphic of some kind. Which method is best depends upon your purpose:

✔ When you need to place a picture frame of a specific size at a specific position in your layout, draw the frame with the Picture tool (in the toolbox) and fill the frame with a picture manually.

✔ When the content and size of the graphic determine the size of the frame, have Microsoft Publisher 2000 create the frame for you as you bring in the picture. You can always adjust the frame's size and position later on.

Getting Yours

Microsoft Publisher 2000 provides five ways to insert or import pictures:

✔ Copy a graphic from another Windows program onto the Windows Clipboard and then paste it into a picture frame.

✔ Use the Insert➪Object command to fill a picture frame with any OLE object.

✔ Choose Insert➪Picture➪Clip Art to open the Microsoft Clip Gallery, which provides easy access to the thousands of pieces of clip art that you can install with Microsoft Publisher 2000.

✔ Choose Insert➪Picture➪From File to import any picture that is saved in a format that Microsoft Publisher 2000 can recognize.

✔ Choose Insert➪Picture➪From Scanner or Camera to scan a hard copy of an image or capture an image from a digital camera.

If you don't want to make a trip to the Insert menu to choose the last three commands, you can also get to them by right-clicking a picture frame, which displays the context-sensitive menu shown in Figure 9-1. Point to Change Picture, then Picture to see the selections. The context-sensitive menu also offers the Windows Clipboard commands: Cut, Copy, and Paste.

I assume that you know how to use the Windows Clipboard at this point, although you may want to know more about what kinds of graphic formats the Clipboard supports. The four other methods for bringing pictures into a picture frame are discussed in the sections that follow.

Figure 9-1:
A picture
frame's
context-
sensitive
menu.

No matter how you put a graphic into a picture frame, you can use any of the methods to replace that picture.

Using the Microsoft Clip Gallery

Microsoft Clip Gallery is a visual showcase of thousands of pieces of clip art that you can install along with Microsoft Publisher 2000. The Gallery itself is actually a piece of software — an image browser — that lets you view your clip art collection. Rather than use the Insert⇨Picture⇨From File command to insert a clip art file — which requires you to remember the name and location of the picture file (files are stored in the Clip Art folder) — you simply click a miniature version of the picture in the Gallery.

The clip art contained in the collection that Microsoft gives you is saved in the Computer Graphic Metafile (CGM) format, which can be edited in Microsoft Draw. A metafile format lets you save both drawn and painted images in the same file; however, CGM is almost always used for drawings. The files that have the extension PCS contain the thumbnail versions of the clip art pictures; don't try to open or edit these files.

To insert a picture using Microsoft Clip Gallery:

1. **If you want to import the picture into a specific picture frame, select that frame.**

   Otherwise, make sure that no frame is selected — Microsoft Publisher 2000 creates a frame for you in this case.

2. **Choose Insert⇨Picture⇨Clip Art.**

   The Insert Clip Art dialog box, shown in Figure 9-2, appears. Microsoft Clip Gallery is actually a self-contained program and not a dialog box.

Figure 9-2:
The Insert
Clip Art
dialog box.

3. **Click a specific category in the list box located to the left of the pictures, if you want.**

   If you don't find the image you are looking for in the category you selected, you can return to the list of categories by clicking the All Categories button at the top of the Insert Clip Art dialog box. For you keyboard fans, press Alt+Home.

4. **Scroll as necessary and then click the picture that you want.**

5. **Click the Insert Clip icon in the pop-up menu that appears.**

   If the Clip Gallery completely covers your publication, it appears that nothing happens. Click the Close button in the Insert Clip Art dialog box to dismiss the Clip Gallery and return to you publication. If you selected a picture frame in Step 1, the picture completely fills that frame. Otherwise, Microsoft Publisher 2000 creates a picture frame for you in the center of the current view and places the picture in that new frame.

If you draw a picture frame before you import a picture from Microsoft Clip Gallery, Microsoft Publisher 2000 automatically resizes the frame to keep the inserted image in proper proportion. After the image has been inserted into the frame, you may resize it to your heart's content. It's very easy to replace the picture from the clip art collection with another picture. Just double-click the existing picture to reopen the Microsoft Clip Gallery dialog box. Click a different picture and then click the Insert Clip icon. You also can replace an existing picture by using the context-sensitive menu to open the Microsoft Clip Gallery. Right-click the picture that you want to replace. Point to Change Picture, then Picture, and finally Clip Art. I find that double-clicking the picture is much faster. If you have other Microsoft programs on your computer (such as PowerPoint or other Microsoft Office components), they also share the Microsoft Clip Gallery. (In fact, you can access the Microsoft Clip Gallery from almost any modern Windows program, if you know how.) So, you may find more than just Microsoft Publisher 2000 pictures there; you may also find pictures installed by Word, Excel, and so on.

You can do a couple of cool things with Microsoft Clip Gallery that many people never check out. One is to search for pictures by description, file-name, or file format. Type a word that describes the clip art you are looking for in the Search for clips box. Press Enter to have the Clip Gallery search for images that match the word you typed.

Here's how to add pictures to the Microsoft Clip Gallery:

1. **Click the Import Clips button in the Insert Clip Art dialog box.**

   The Add Clip To Clip Gallery dialog box, shown in Figure 9-3, appears.

Figure 9-3:
The Add Clip to Clip Gallery dialog box.

2. **Find and select the picture of interest and click the Import button.**

   Make sure that the Copy into Clip Gallery option, located in the Clip import option section, is selected before clicking the Import button.

   (You are not limited to CGM files; you can select files in TIF, BMP, JPG, GIF, and other formats that Microsoft Publisher 2000 understands.) The Clip Gallery adds your picture and opens the Clip Properties dialog box, shown in Figure 9-4.

3. **Fill out the Clip Properties dialog box.**

   Type a brief description of the picture in the Description of this clip in the Buttons & Icons category text box. Click the Categories tab and click to put a check mark next to each category that will contain this picture. Finally, click the Keywords tab; then click the New Keyword button and enter a keyword for this picture. Click OK to close the New Keyword dialog box. You can enter as many keywords as you like.

Figure 9-4:
The Clip
Properties
dialog box.

4. **Click OK to add the image to the Gallery.**

   You return to the Insert Clip Art dialog box with your newly imported image selected. Click the Close button to dismiss the Clip Gallery.

It may seem like whimsy or technobabble to walk you through the process of adding pictures to the Gallery. If you manage large numbers of images, however, you find this process a valuable one.

One other aspect of all this deserves mentioning: If the 225 megabytes of clip art and images that come with the Microsoft Publisher 2000 CD aren't enough for you, check out the Microsoft Web site for even more. Click the Clips Online button in the Insert Clip Art dialog box. There you find additional clip art images, sounds, videos, and photos. Any clips that you select from this Web site are automatically added to the Clip Gallery. Need I mention that you must have an Internet connection to use this feature? By default, Microsoft Clip Gallery offers only those pictures that install with Microsoft Publisher 2000 and other Microsoft programs. Thus, if you create a picture yourself or get it from some non-Microsoft source, you won't find the picture in Microsoft Clip Gallery. (That is, unless you *import* your picture to the Microsoft Clip Gallery.)

Inserting picture files

The Insert⇨Picture⇨From File command imports a picture stored on disk into your publication. When you find a picture of interest and highlight it in the Insert Picture dialog box shown in Figure 9-5, Microsoft Publisher 2000 builds a preview of the picture for you in the dialog box.

One downside of using the Insert⇨Picture⇨From File command is that you must concern yourself somewhat with picture file formats. Microsoft Publisher 2000 understands 17 of the most commonly used graphics file formats and is a very capable program for importing a wide variety of graphics.

To insert a picture using the Insert➪Picture➪From File command, follow these steps:

1. **If you want to import the picture into a specific picture frame, select that frame.**

   Otherwise, make sure that no frame is selected — Microsoft Publisher 2000 creates the frame as needed.

2. **Select Insert➪Picture➪From File.**

   The Insert Picture dialog box appears, as shown in Figure 9-5.

3. **Find the file that you want to insert and click Insert.**

   The picture is inserted into your publication. If you select a picture frame before importing a picture from a file, Microsoft Publisher 2000 changes the frame to maintain the picture's correct proportions. You can always resize the frame later, manually or by using the Scale Picture command described later in this chapter.

Figure 9-5:
The Insert
Picture
dialog box.

If you import a picture and later decide that you want a different picture, just double-click the existing picture. The Insert Picture dialog box reopens. Click a different filename and then click Insert.

If Microsoft Publisher 2000 doesn't understand the format of the picture that you're trying to import, it whines: `Cannot convert this picture`. If you have access to the program that created that picture, try saving the picture in a different format. Or, if you can open the picture in any other Windows program, try copying the picture to the Windows Clipboard and pasting it into your picture frame.

If you import a picture using the Clipboard and later want to change internal components of that picture, try double-clicking it in your publication. Depending on how your computer is set up, your double-click may load the program that created the picture. Make your changes in that program and then exit the program. Your changes display in Microsoft Publisher 2000.

Scanning pictures

Yet another way of getting a picture into Microsoft Publisher 2000 is to scan the image into your computer or capture the image with a digital camera. Of course, you'll need a scanner or digital camera and some software to run it. Don't have one of these? My brother Kevin just picked up a 24-bit flatbed color scanner for $49. Not that long ago, a scanner with those specs would have cost hundreds of dollars. (When I was a kid, I had to walk five miles through the snow, uphill both ways, to get to school. . .)

Where was I? Oh, yes. Scanning pictures into your computer. Select Insert⇨Picture⇨From Scanner or Camera⇨Acquire Image. What happens next depends on whether you are using a scanner or digital camera, and what software you use for your device. Click Scan or something similar and, after a few moments, the image will appear in your publication. You may resize the scanned picture just as you would any other picture in your publication.

Double-clicking an image that you scanned into your publication brings up the Insert Picture dialog box. To replace the image with a new scanned image, click the picture frame and select Insert⇨Picture⇨From Scanner or Camera⇨Acquire Image. (I discuss scanned images in depth later in this chapter.)

Modifying pictures

After you import a picture, you can adjust it in Microsoft Publisher 2000 in several ways: You can resize it, chop off parts of it (called *cropping*), and add some space between the picture and its frame to create a border. These changes apply to the format of the frame and not to the picture itself. A picture frame can only display graphics, not change them.

If you want to edit the internal components of a picture — for example, to change a zebra's black-and-white stripes to purple and green or to add extra hair to a digital photograph of yourself (not that I have ever done this!) — forget Microsoft Publisher 2000. You need to use a specialized graphics program. If you used the Clipboard to import the picture, you may be able to load the appropriate program just by double-clicking the picture. If that doesn't work, try using the Clipboard to export the picture to the graphics program, make your changes there, and then re-import the picture.

Try using Microsoft Paint or Microsoft PhotoDraw to edit your image. One of these two programs should enable you to open and modify most images. If you know the picture's file type, consult the last section in this chapter to find out what kind of image it is.

Resizing a picture

To resize a picture, you resize its frame. By default, both the picture and its frame are the same size and proportions. You can resize a picture frame much as you would resize any other frame: by dragging any of its selection handles.

To maintain the proportions of a picture and its frame, hold down the Shift key as you drag a corner selection handle.

If Microsoft Publisher 2000 distorted your picture when you imported it, holding down the Shift key as you drag a corner selection handle simply maintains that distortion. To undistort a picture, try using one of the Scale commands described next. (*Scaling* in Microsoft Publisher 2000 is just another term for *resizing*. Scaling in snakes and pipes is another thing entirely.) The Format⇨Scale Picture command is also a way to resize a picture without using the mouse.

Here's how to resize a picture using the menu command:

1. **Select the picture that you want to resize and/or restore.**

2. **Select the Scale Picture command from the Format menu or select Change Picture⇨Scale Picture from the picture's context-sensitive menu.**

   The Scale Picture dialog box, shown in Figure 9-6, appears.

Figure 9-6:
The Scale
Picture
dialog box.

> **Scale Picture** ? ✕
>
> Scale height: `100` %
> Scale width: `100` %
>
> ☐ Original size
>
> [OK]   [Cancel]

You may notice that when you resize your picture, the title of the Scale Picture dialog box reads Scale Object instead. What this is telling you is that the picture is a registered file type of an OLE server. In all other regards, these two dialog boxes work equivalently.

3. **Enter numbers in the Scale <u>h</u>eight and Scale <u>w</u>idth text boxes to set the percentages to which you want to resize your picture.**

   These percentages vary according to the picture's original file size. Use the same percentages in the Scale height and Scale width boxes to retain the figure's proportions.

   To see the picture at its original file size, click the Original size check box.

4. **Click OK.**

   Both the picture and its frame resize accordingly.

Don't forget that resizing a bitmap graphic will lower the quality of the image. You can, however, resize vector graphics (drawings) to your heart's content without doing any damage.

Cropping a picture

Publishing professionals who still assemble publications *without* a computer often remove unwanted edges of a picture by lopping off those edges with a pair of scissors. In the publishing world, editing a picture in this way is called *cropping*. Why bother with scissors, though? As shown in Figure 9-7, you can use Microsoft Publisher 2000 to crop a picture *electronically*.

Figure 9-7:
The left picture is the original; the right picture was cropped to focus in on those angelic faces.

To crop a selected picture:

1. **Click the Crop Picture button on the Formatting toolbar.**

2. **Point to one of the picture frame's selection handles.**

   Your mouse pointer changes to a *cropper pointer* — two scissors with the word *Crop*.

3. **Drag inward until you exclude the part of the picture that you don't want and then release the mouse.**

Cropping a picture doesn't permanently remove any picture parts; it only hides them from view. To restore a picture part that you've cropped, repeat the preceding steps, but drag outward. Regardless of whether you've cropped or not, you can drag outward on any picture to *reverse crop,* thus adding space between the picture and its frame. (You also can add space between a picture and its frame by increasing the picture frame's margins in the Picture Frame Properties dialog box.)

Here are a few more cropping tips to keep in mind:

- ✔ To crop or reverse crop the same amount at each edge — thus keeping the picture in the center of its frame — hold down the Ctrl key as you drag a corner selection handle.

- ✔ By default, Microsoft Publisher 2000 enables you to crop only in a rectangular fashion. For more customizable, irregular cropping, apply the Wrap Text to Picture option and then click the Edit Irregular Wrap button to create and/or modify the adjust handles. See Chapter 5 for details.

- ✔ If you want to resize a picture immediately after cropping, click the Cropping tool again to turn off the cropping option. You can also turn off the cropping option by deselecting and then reselecting the picture.

- ✔ To remove all cropping and reverse cropping from a selected picture with the least amount of effort, select the Scale Picture or Scale Object command from the Format menu, check the Original size check box, and click OK.

Working with captions

Sometimes, pictures are not enough. They require an explanation. You can create captions for your pictures and have them move with their respective pictures in travels across your layout. Unlike the high-priced layout programs, Microsoft Publisher 2000 doesn't automate the process of creating and renumbering captions for you. But you already possess the skills required to create a caption and attach it to a picture.

To create a caption, follow these steps:

1. **Draw a text frame and enter the text of your caption into it.**

2. **Move the text frame next to the picture and select both the picture and the frame.**

3. **Click the Group Objects button to lock it and create a group.**

   Figure 9-8 shows you an example of a figure with a caption.

Figure 9-8:
A figure
with a
caption.

Team McCarter at play

Hey, that's it! What do you think this is, rocket science? Well, there is one trick that you can apply to make a caption even better. Select your text frame and then select the Text Frame Properties command from the Format menu. In the Text Frame Properties dialog box, set all the margins to 0. Then your captions can get up close and personal with your graphics.

Want a fancy caption? Use a WordArt frame rather than a text frame.

Applying borders and BorderArt

You can give your picture frame a border by using the Line/Border Style command's dialog box or the pop-up menu of the Line/Border Style button on the Format toolbar. If the picture frame is a regular rectangle, you can also apply BorderArt to it. (You can't apply this feature to irregular picture frames.) You can also apply BorderArt to text frames, table frames, and even WordArt frames. Here's how to apply BorderArt to a selected frame(s):

1. **Select Format⇔Line/Border Style⇔More Styles.**

   The Border Style dialog box appears, as shown in Figure 9-9.

Figure 9-9:
The Line
Border tab
of the
Border Style
dialog box.

2. **Click the BorderArt tab of the Border Style dialog box.**

   The BorderArt tab of the Border Style dialog box appears, as shown in Figure 9-10.

Figure 9-10: The BorderArt tab of the Border Style dialog box.

3. **Make your selection from the Available Borders list box, set a Border size and Color (if desired), and click the OK button.**

   The Border Style dialog box is one of those simple features that's so well implemented that using it is a breeze. Simply use the arrow keys to move through the list of borders in the dialog box. As you scroll through the list, the Preview section displays the different borders. This dialog box offers tons of fun borders for you to try, and you'll definitely enjoy playing with it.

Working with Different Picture Types

Computers use two types of graphics: drawn graphics and painted graphics. The type of graphic that you are using determines many features about how a graphic displays on your screen and the quality of the printed output. The two types use different file formats and require different types of programs for creating and editing graphics. But Microsoft Publisher 2000 can work with both types of graphics, even in the same publication.

Painted versus drawn graphics

Painted graphics are also referred to as *images* or *bitmapped* or *raster* graphics. In painted graphics, the image is composed of a set of tiny dots, called *pixels* or *pels,* that forms a mosaic. The image is two-dimensional, although the manner in which the image is painted can give the effect of three dimensions.

A painted image is akin to a mosaic of tiles that you might see in a Roman temple. The smaller the tiles, the more realistic the image looks. The size of the tile — or in the case of a computer image, the size of the pixel — is called the *resolution* of the image. This value is often given in *dots per inch* or *dpi.* Because a bitmap is designed for a specific resolution, it looks great at that resolution. It can also look great at larger or coarser resolutions (smaller dpi) because you have more data than you need. Painted graphics do not scale up well, however. For example, a 72-dpi image that displays perfectly on a screen would not print well on your laser printer at 300 dpi.

Programs that create painted images are either paint programs such as Microsoft Paint or image-editing programs such as Adobe Photoshop. I take a look at Microsoft Paint in a moment — because it comes bundled with Windows, it's there for you to use, gratis. At the very highest end of the spectrum, images can be photorealistic and can be rendered to show textures, reflections, and shadings. The file size of a bitmap image is directly related to the size of the image, the number of colors stored, and the resolution.

Drawn graphics are referred to as *vector* or *object-oriented* art. With a drawing, the lines, arcs, and other elements that make up a graphic are stored as mathematical equations. Because drawings are created in this way, they are resolution independent. They are calculated to display or print at the best capability of the output device — which is why they are referred to as *device independent.* This feature makes using drawings generally (but not always) preferable to using paintings in desktop publishing applications.

Here's an important point, though: Regardless of how a drawing is stored, it must be converted to a bitmap when it is printed or displayed on-screen. This process is referred to as *raster image processing (RIP)* and it is done to display graphics to any output device. When you RIP a bitmap image, the only conversion required is the resampling of the bitmap to either throw away or interpolate data from the bitmap.

When you RIP a drawing, the processing can be simple (for lines and simple drawing primitives) to very complex (for sophisticated descriptions of fill patterns). Thus, a complex PostScript drawing with many, many features and complex fills and strokes may take a really long time to calculate and process. These types of drawings may also require large file sizes — thus defeating their advantage over painted images. The crossover point is reached when you attempt to create a natural image as a drawing. Such graphics are better stored as a bitmap.

Paint with Microsoft Paint

You can buy very expensive paint and image-editing programs as a supplement to Microsoft Publisher 2000. Still, if your needs are reasonable, you can create nice bitmapped images (or edit the ones you have) in Microsoft Paint. Microsoft Paint is one of the "accessories" that is installed with Windows 95.

To create a Microsoft Paint OLE object in Microsoft Publisher 2000, do the following:

1. **Select the Insert⇨Object command from the menu. The Insert Object dialog box appears, as shown in Figure 9-11.**

Figure 9-11:
The Insert
Object
dialog box.

2. **Click the Create New radio button and select Bitmap Image in the Object Type box. Click OK.**

   The Microsoft Paint OLE engine opens on your screen, as shown in Figure 9-12.

3. **Create your painting by using the paint tools in the toolbox at the left and the color palette at the bottom of your screen.**

4. **When you are done, click outside the frame to return to Microsoft Publisher 2000.**

The connection of your painted object to Microsoft Paint is an intimate one. To edit the image in place again, simply double-click it. The image is actually part of the Microsoft Publisher 2000 file, however, and does not have an outside or independent existence. That is, you can't open the image as a file from within Microsoft Paint.

You often can use Microsoft Paint to edit images from other sources. To do this, create a Microsoft Paint frame on your layout. Then switch to the picture frame that contains your bitmapped image. Copy that image and paste it into your Microsoft Paint frame. When you double-click the Microsoft Paint frame now, it opens with your image in it.

Figure 9-12:
A Microsoft
Paint OLE
object being
edited in
place.

Microsoft Paint has many features and tools that I don't have room to tell you about here. It's also useful for adjusting image colors. You may want to consult its online Help system for instructions.

Microsoft Paint is based on one of the earlier versions of ZSoft's Paintbrush, which was one of my favorite paint programs a number of years ago. If you open the Paint OLE engine inside Microsoft Publisher 2000, you need never worry about file formats. If you travel from the Start menu to the Programs folder and into the Accessories folder to find and launch Microsoft Paint, however, you can open and work with two important bitmapped file formats. Microsoft Paint can open the two most common bitmapped image file formats around: PCX files (the ZSoft format), and Window's native BMP format. That makes Microsoft Paint a very good program to use to edit and print these kinds of images.

Draw with Microsoft Draw

I have almost no drawing talent whatsoever, so I avoid drawing programs like the plague. I am, therefore, fond of clip art and opt for collections such as the one that comes with Microsoft Publisher 2000. If you, however, are able to draw a horse that looks more like a horse than a cat, you may want to create your own pictures from scratch. Although you certainly can go out and buy a full-blown professional graphics program, a very nice graphics program — Microsoft Draw — installs (free!) along with Microsoft Publisher 2000.

Anytime that you want to create a picture, you can load Microsoft Draw from within Microsoft Publisher 2000, use Microsoft Draw's specialized tools to create that picture, and then exit Microsoft Draw. Your picture automatically becomes part of your current publication. The process is similar to the process described in the preceding section for Microsoft Paint.

To create a Microsoft Draw OLE object in Microsoft Publisher 2000, do the following:

1. **Select Insert➪Picture➪New Drawing from the menu.**

   The Microsoft Draw OLE engine opens on your screen, as shown in Figure 9-13.

Figure 9-13:
A Microsoft Draw OLE object being edited in place.

2. **Create your drawing using the draw tools in the Drawing toolbar at the bottom of your screen and the AutoShapes in the floating AutoShapes toolbar.**

3. **When you are done, click outside the frame to return to Microsoft Publisher 2000.**

To modify an internal component of a Microsoft Draw object, reload Microsoft Draw. To do this, double-click the Microsoft Draw object. After you complete your editing and return to Microsoft Publisher 2000, the program treats the object just like any other picture. You can move, resize, and crop it at will.

Don't use Microsoft Draw to draw very simple graphics such as lines and boxes. Instead, use Microsoft Publisher 2000's own limited drawing tools. These tools create graphics that have smaller file sizes and are more compactly described than a Microsoft Draw frame with objects in it.

You often can use Microsoft Draw to edit the internal components of a drawing created by another program. If you've already imported a drawing into Microsoft Publisher 2000, select that picture and copy it to the Clipboard. Then open a Microsoft Draw window and paste the drawing into it. You can then double-click the drawing to edit it in Microsoft Draw.

Avoid using Microsoft Draw to edit image files whose filenames end with BMP, JPG, PCD, PCX, or TIF. Instead, try to edit the picture with a paint-type program such as Microsoft Paint. Similarly, avoid using Microsoft Paint to work with files that use the EPS, CDR, DRW, or WMF formats. Use Microsoft Draw for those file types. Mixing the wrong format and program results in garbage being displayed on your screen, if anything displays at all.

The next section in this chapter explains how to load other Windows programs from within Microsoft Publisher 2000.

Say OLE!

You've now seen four examples of using OLE servers in Microsoft Publisher 2000: WordArt (in the previous chapter), Clip Gallery (earlier in this chapter), Paint, and Draw. You should be an OLE meister at this point in the book. But you've just started to scratch the surface of the programs that are out there at your service. Many more OLE server programs get installed when you install Windows or other programs.

Before you know it, you'll have sound servers, video servers, coffee servers, and more. (*More* is the operative word here.) To see what you have installed in your system at the moment, select the Insert➪Object command from the menu. The Insert Object dialog box shown in Figure 9-14 appears. The servers are listed in the Object Type list box. You have the option of creating a new data object that is part of your Microsoft Publisher 2000 publication or inserting an object contained in a data file. If you want other programs to access the data object, use the Create from File radio button. If you want the object managed inside your publication, click the Create New radio button. The Display As Icon option lets you display the icon for each object type that you select.

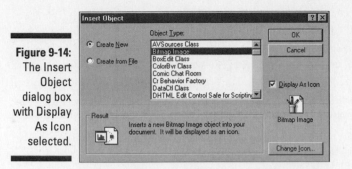

Figure 9-14:
The Insert
Object
dialog box
with Display
As Icon
selected.

I think that Microsoft Chart is one of the OLE servers that you may find most useful. It can take Excel or Works spreadsheet data and create charts and graphs from it.

Did you notice that Clip Gallery loads very differently from Microsoft Draw? Whereas Clip Gallery opens in its own, separate window, Microsoft WordArt takes over part of the Microsoft Publisher 2000 window and fuzzies up your WordArt frame. The term *open editing* describes how Clip Gallery loads: Each program displays in its own window. The term *editing-in-place* describes how Microsoft WordArt loads: The fuzzy-bordered object remains in place while the original program's window adjusts accordingly. In-place editing is one of OLE's newer features, so you'll see it more and more as you begin to use newer programs on your computer.

We are at the beginning of the era of compound documents or rich data type documents. Here, small programs manage your data within a file. Our publications will be all-singing, all-dancing wonders.

Using the Design Gallery

One feature that you should definitely visit in your page layout work is the Design Gallery. The Design Gallery is not a graphics creator per se, although it does rely on graphics in many instances. The Design Gallery is a browser that displays a collection of page layout parts that you can use inside your document to create even more compelling publications. The original categories of parts that you can use include Mastheads, Tables of Contents, Reply Forms, Sidebars, Pull Quotes, Picture Captions, Phone Tear-Off, Calendars, Logos, Advertisements, Coupons, Attention Getters, Barbells, Boxes, Checkerboards, Dots, Accessory Bar, Accent Box, Borders, Linear Accent, Marquee, and Punctuation. The Design Gallery offers you 28 different styles including Arcs, Kid Stuff, Marble, Nature, and Waves. As with the Clip Gallery, you can add selections to the Design Gallery and use them in other publications.

Follow these steps to insert a Design Gallery object into your layout:

1. **Click the Design Gallery Object button in the toolbar.**

   The Design Gallery dialog box appears, as shown in Figure 9-15.

2. **Click either the Objects by Category tab (to view objects organized by type) or the Objects by Design tab (to view objects that share common design elements).**

3. **Click an item in the Categories list (on the Objects by Category tab) or the Design Sets list (on the Objects by Design tab), and then click the object you want to insert in the right pane.**

4. **With your object selected, click the Insert Object button to have the object appear on your layout in a new frame.**

Figure 9-16 shows you a sample pull quote from the Design Gallery placed on a layout, with its text selected for editing.

If you create something in your work or see something that someone else created that you want to save in the Design Gallery and reuse, that's easy to do. Just follow these steps:

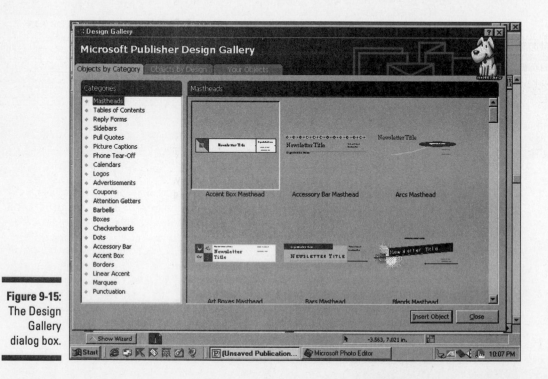

Figure 9-15: The Design Gallery dialog box.

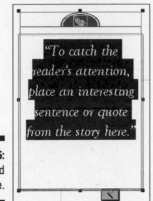

Figure 9-16:
An inserted
pull quote.

1. **Select the object or group of objects and then click the Design Gallery Object button to open the Design Gallery dialog box.**

2. **Select the Your Objects tab.**

   Unless you have previously added some objects to the Design Gallery, the Categories pane will be empty and the right pane will display a message stating `This publication has no saved objects.`

3. **Click the Options button at the bottom-left of the dialog box and select the Add Selection To Design Gallery from the menu that pops up.**

   The Add Object dialog box appears, as shown in Figure 9-17.

4. **Enter a name in the Object name box and a category in the — you guessed it! — Category box and click the OK button.**

   The object is added to the Your Objects tab of the Design Gallery. If you want the objects that you add to the Design Gallery to be available to other publications, be sure to save the current publication.

Between the Clip Gallery and the Design Gallery, Microsoft Publisher 2000 gives you two very powerful methods for managing a collection of graphics and page layout parts to speed your work.

Figure 9-17:
The Add
Object
dialog box.

Tracking Down Other Picture Sources

With Microsoft Publisher 2000, you have just scratched the surface of available picture sources for your work. If you go online, either on the Internet or commercial online services, you discover an almost unlimited number of images that you can use. Many of these images are freely distributed and of high quality. Even most user group bulletin boards have graphics sections with images that you can download. Many images that aren't free are very reasonably priced — or are free if you use them for noncommercial work.

Make sure that you check any downloaded files with virus detection software. Most services do a good job of checking files, but the Internet is wide open to viruses.

You can also find many commercial sources for images. I am inundated with brochures from companies that want to sell me commercial clip art. Chances are that if a company is in the business of creating the images, the images that they sell are of high quality. If a company is in the business of harvesting images from other sources, as you often find in low-priced CD-ROMs, you can be less sure of quality. One good place to look for image sources is *Canned Art: Clip Art for the Macintosh,* by Fenton and Morrissett. Most of the collections referenced in the book are available for the PC as well as for the Mac — or are easily converted.

To the companies 3-D Graphics and Image Club for drawn graphics, I would add the names of Adobe (Mountain View, CA, 800-344-8335) for excellent collections of patterns and fills, and Multi-Ad Services (Peoria, IL, 309-692-1530) for business graphics. The Dover Publications image books (Mineola, NY, 516-294-7000) are also great sources of images that you can scan into your publication.

Try to buy your drawn graphics in either the CGM or WMF formats, as they are the easiest to work with. If you need very high-quality drawn images, then use EPS graphics.

For image collections, PhotoDisk (Seattle, WA, 800-528-3472) is excellent. I am also impressed with the selections from Image Club, which was recently bought by Adobe. You can see selections of photos from the latter catalog in the Adobe Web site at www.adobe.com. Kodak also offers a service that can be used to preview and download (for a fee) images from an image server. The software is called Kodak's Picture Exchange, and it's really practical for people who use and need high-quality images frequently — such as advertising agencies. You may want to visit the Kodak Web site to see what's available there.

Inserting PowerPoint Slides into Publisher

You've created a killer slide presentation in Microsoft PowerPoint and would like to use some of the slides in Microsoft Publisher 2000. No sweat:

1. **In Microsoft PowerPoint, open the presentation file that contains the slide you want to use in your publication.**

2. **Click the Slide Sorter View button and then click the slide you want to use in your publication.**

3. **Choose Edit⇨Copy, press Ctrl+C, or click the Copy button on the Standard toolbar.**

4. **Switch to the Microsoft Publisher window by clicking its button on the Windows taskbar.**

   If the Windows taskbar isn't visible, you can switch applications by pressing Alt+Tab. Hold down the Alt key and press Tab until the Microsoft Publisher icon is highlighted in the Cool Switch box that appears. Release both keys.

5. **In the Publisher 2000 window, select Edit⇨Paste, press Ctrl+V, or click the Paste button on the Standard toolbar.**

   Your PowerPoint slide appears in your publication.

The slide you inserted can be moved and resized just like a picture frame. If you want to edit the contents of the slide, just double-click it. PowerPoint opens inside Publisher 2000. Make the desired changes; then click outside the slide to close PowerPoint.

Scanning the Picture

If you can see it on paper, you can get it into Microsoft Publisher 2000. The ultimate way to bring images into Microsoft Publisher 2000 is by using a scanner. A *scanner* is a machine that digitizes images into bitmapped files. You can buy scanners that can read film or slides; you can also find related equipment for video digitization.

The most popular devices for desktop publishers probably are flatbed desktop scanners. You can get a medium-quality, full-color desktop scanner such as a Mustek 600 III EP Plus Scanner for about $100. These scanners create files in 24-bit (full) color at 600 x 600 dpi. Images of this type are adequate for medium-quality magazine work.

You can also rent scanners at printer services or have them scan your images for you. In the latter case, the equipment used can be high quality, but the charges are greater.

Scanners can create digital images in the following modes:

- ✔ **Black-and-white scans:** This mode creates images with only black or white pixels. It is suitable for images that are predominantly white or black and don't have much detail, but not for art with patterns or textures that you want to preserve. This mode creates very small file sizes.

- ✔ **Line art scans:** This mode is used for finely detailed artwork done in black and white. Turn the brightness up when you scan line art.

- ✔ **Grayscale scans:** This mode preserves any shades of gray in a black-and-white photograph or converts color values in a color image to shades of gray. It gives photographic results and preserves patterns and textures. The eye can see about 80 shades of gray, but it is typical for most people to scan at up to 256 shades of gray for higher-quality work, because that is what computer monitors can display. File sizes can be large but are still only a third of the file sizes of color scans.

- ✔ **Color scans:** This mode is used to create images with pictures in full color. File sizes can be extremely large. Pay particular attention to minimizing the file size when creating these images and to making sure that the color fidelity is correct.

Many printed materials are printed as *halftone images*. In a halftone image, black-and-white images are created with spots, dots, lines, or other repeating patterns. These images don't offer true black and white and, therefore, scan poorly. Scanner software often has special facilities to handle halftones in order to get adequate scans. Chances are that scanned halftones will result in images called *moiré patterns,* which are very unattractive. Often, you can avoid moiré patterns by reducing image size, positioning the picture in your scanner at an angle, and applying filtering in an image-editing program to the image. Then, if you're lucky, moiré patterns don't print. But your best bet is to avoid scanning halftone images if you can.

Large scanned images can take a really long time to display on your layout. They can make scrolling about painful to do. Microsoft Publisher 2000 has a feature that helps you by reducing the detail of your pictures or hiding pictures on a layout from view. You can also display your pictures in a reduced form, which results in a slight improvement in performance.

To hide pictures on a layout, select View⇨Picture Display. The Picture Display dialog box (shown in Figure 9-18) opens, where you can click the Hide pictures radio button.

Image ethics

You need to pay particular attention to the source of any image that you intend to use in your work. Someone created the image, and someone owns it. The two "someones" aren't always the same person. Whoever the owner is controls the use of the image and can let you freely use it, let you use it for noncommercial use, or charge you a fee.

Don't be fooled into thinking that just because an image is a picture of something well known in the public domain — for example, a picture of the Statue of Liberty — it doesn't belong to the person who took the picture. It does.

Microsoft Publisher 2000's license allows you to freely use its clip art in your publications. You cannot sell the clip art electronically as software, either individually or in a collection. This is a generous license. Other companies let you use low-resolution images freely, but charge for the use of high-resolution images. You must check out the license that comes with the image. The problem is, though, that many images don't come with a license. In that case, it is better to err on the side of caution and use an image whose source and conditions of use are known.

Just to muddy up the waters, an aspect of copyright law allows for the "fair use" of text and images in some instances. If you are using a piece of a document or an image for journalistic criticism, you are free to use the work of others. The restriction is that the piece you use must be a small part of the work and not something central to the use of the work. For example, you could use a still frame from a movie or a short video clip, but not a long one. The fair use doctrine has not yet undergone long scrutiny of the law (something that could be said of much of our current copyright law). Each country also has its own copyright laws.

Figure 9-18: The Picture Display dialog box.

When you have the Hide pictures option turned on, your picture frames have an X through them to indicate that they contain a picture. Frames without content appear without an X.

Scanners can be used to import not only pictures but also digitized images of any object: paper, marble, cloth, and so on. You can get great and creative graphics by using scanned images in your work.

Scanning is a complex topic and one that requires specialized knowledge to get just so. I would like to recommend one outstanding book on the topic of scanners and digital imaging technology: *Real World Scanning and Halftones* by David Bladner and Steve Roth. This book is both technically excellent and well written with a sense of humor.

The most important thing that you can remember about the process is that you should scan your images with the purpose of the image in mind. If you are scanning an image for screen display, a resolution of 72 dpi is sufficient. For a laser printer, you don't want to scan at more than 300 dpi; anything more is wasted and can't be used. Similarly, although you can scan any image size to great color depth and your image can be reduced, it is a waste of resources to do so. Use a color and image size appropriate to your work. For example, an 8½ x 11-inch, 24-bit color image at 300 dpi (150 lines per inch or medium-quality magazine printing at full color) consumes about 25MB of disk space! So it pays to save.

For example, if you are printing only in black and white, then scan in black and white — or better still, in shades of gray. You can get great results from 256 shades of gray, and very good results from 64 shades of gray, with enormous file size reductions. You just have to know the intended use of the graphics.

Microsoft Publisher 2000 lets you directly incorporate scans using software that supports the TWAIN standard. This standard is scanner driver software that installs into the Microsoft Publisher 2000 Insert menu as a set of menu commands. If your scanner doesn't support this standard, you find that the From Scanner or Camera command on the Insert⇨Picture menu is grayed-out. If the From Scanner or Camera command on the Insert⇨Picture menu is grayed-out, then all is not lost. Many scanner manufacturers upgrade their software, and you may want to check with your manufacturer to see whether an upgrade exists. Also, third-party software that supports your scanner may be available. For example, the highly regarded Ofoto software supports many common scanners and offers advanced features.

Reviewing File Formats

Graphic image file formats are a rat's nest of acronyms — a veritable alphabet soup. Unfortunately, you have to know something about each format in order to decide which format you want to import a file from. File formats come in three basic types: paint or bitmapped image files, drawing or vector image files, and metafiles, which let you store either type of picture. A file's extension tells you the format of the file. This section describes in brief the file formats that Microsoft Publisher 2000 is capable of importing.

You can't save a picture from Microsoft Publisher 2000 directly. You can copy and paste a picture from Microsoft Publisher 2000 into another program and save it there, however.

The following formats are bitmapped or painted image file formats supported by Microsoft Publisher 2000:

- **JPEG Filter:** Files in the JPEG format take the JPG file extension. These files are very high-quality color files that offer advanced file compression techniques for reducing their image files. JPEG is one of the best choices for full-color images. Most image-editing programs save to JPEG. You will also find JPEG images in scientific work and as a standard file format on the Internet because the format is cross-platform.

- **PC Paintbrush:** ZSoft's PC Paintbrush was a popular early paint program. The program saves its files using the PCX file extension. Originally, this file format was strictly for black-and-white images, but it was extended to include full-color images as well. PCX has been very widely adopted on the PC and is one of the favored bitmapped file formats. Most paint and image-editing programs support this format, and many screen captures are done in PCX.

- **Tagged Image File Format 5.0:** This format, also known as TIFF, is an industry standard file format that creates files that use the TIF extension. The format was created by Microsoft and Aldus and is openly published and supported. TIFF creates files with very high-quality images. The specification is up to level 6, but level 5 was the first that supported file compression. All paint and image-editing programs open and save to TIFF. TIFF is probably the favorite bitmapped file format for desktop publishing applications.

Several variations of TIFF exist, so you can have problems opening TIFF files.

Many programs, such as Photoshop, read one flavor of TIFF and save out to another. So if you are having trouble with a TIFF file, try converting it through a program such as Photoshop or a file-conversion program.

- **Kodak PhotoCD:** The PhotoCD standard produces files with the PCD file extension. This is a very high-quality photographic image storage file format. You can go to a processing center and have your pictures converted to the PCD standard and placed on a CD-ROM disc. Most modern CD-ROM drives read this format. The standard saves images in several sizes and resolutions so that you can use the images for a variety of purposes. PCD is a favored format for use in high-quality image work. It is a cross-platform standard.

- **Windows Bitmaps:** These files are painted images in the Microsoft Paint format and can be either black and white or color. They take the BMP file extension. You can open and edit these files in Microsoft Paint. BMP files are simple ones. They work well for lower-quality paint images, but are not commonly used for images.

TIFF, JPEG, and PCD files are the favored high-quality image file formats.

You can import the following formats for drawn or vector images:

- **Encapsulated PostScript:** Files in this format end with the EPS file extension. EPS files are written in the PostScript language using plain text to indicate graphics and text with formatting. EPS files can be displayed, but require the creator application to alter. You need a PostScript printer to print EPS files correctly.

  EPS files often import incorrectly and appear as a black or gray box in a picture frame, but print correctly. EPS is a very high-quality format that many service bureaus favor. You often find high-quality clip art stored in this file format. When you send an EPS file to a service bureau, it is complete. That is, it contains all the font information it needs and doesn't require the printer service to set up its computer to print your EPS file.

- **WordPerfect Graphic:** This is a proprietary format used for drawings inside the WordPerfect word processor and related products from WordPerfect (now owned by Corel). Otherwise, this file format is infrequently used.

- **Corel Draw Picture:** This is the proprietary drawing format for the very popular CorelDRAW! illustration program. Its files take the CDR file extension. CDR files are of good quality, but EPS is favored for high-quality draw output.

- **Micrografx Designer/Draw:** This format is another popular software vendor's proprietary drawing format. Files take the DRW file extension. The preceding comments about CDR files apply to DRW files, too.

Microsoft Publisher 2000 can import the following metafiles:

- **Computer Graphics Metafile:** This standard produces images with the CGM file extension. CGM is widely used for drawn images and almost never contains bitmaps. CGM is used by many IBM PC clip art collections. This format is never used on a Macintosh.

- **Windows Metafile:** This is the native file format for the Windows Clipboard. It creates files with the WMF file extension. Because WMF is specified by a single vendor (Microsoft), you encounter few difficulties with it. WMF files are nearly always drawings; it is rare to find a file of this type with a bitmap in it. Many PC clip art collections now use the WMF format, as it produces good results.

- **Macintosh PICT:** The PICT format is the native file format of the Macintosh Clipboard. In earlier days, the Macintosh was the source of many illustrations used on the PC. These days, this is much less true. PICT files often contain either bitmaps or drawn images, or both. Images are of moderate quality, and PICT is not a favored high-quality format. The files take the PCT file extension.

Phew! I told you that the world of file formats was a rat's nest. Still, Microsoft Publisher 2000 is blessed with a large and varied collection of file format import filters. All the popular ones are included, so you should have little trouble working with images from outside sources.

Chapter 10

Color by the Numbers

● ●

In This Chapter

▶ Using color in your publication to get your message across

▶ Printing spot colors or process colors

▶ Matching the colors on your monitor to colors on your printer

▶ Marking colors that cannot print on your printer

● ●

Color sells. What once appeared to be dull, listless text looks like super-text when you add color. Microsoft Publisher 2000 makes incorporating color into your publications easy. Some of its features are close to those found in the high-priced spreads.

In this chapter, I tell you how to use color in your publications. I also give you theories on color usage and enough information about color modeling to get you started. I help you get more color in your publications for less money by explaining how to apply color in a cost-effective way.

How Color Improves Your Page

Which would you rather look at: a black-and-white photograph or a color photograph? A black-and-white movie or a color movie? Most people prefer color, even though black and white has its artistic merit.

Color creates highlights, blocks sections of your page, and draws the eye to important sections. Studies show that when color is used correctly, the average reader spends more time on a page and has a higher comprehension of its contents. When color is used badly — an easy thing to do — the average reader finds something better to look at. Studies show that, too.

Following are the keys to using color well:

✔ Don't go overboard when using color.

✔ Choose complementary colors. (More about this later.)

✔ Be consistent in your use of color in a publication; use the same color for the same page elements.

✔ Create a color scheme and then stick to it.

By following these suggestions, you help your reader stay focused on the content of your page without being distracted by the color that you put there. (If you think that these suggestions about not overdoing it with color sound a lot like the suggestions I made to not overdo it with type in Chapter 8, you're right.)

What Is Color?

In technical terms, color is a reaction of the receptors in the eye, the optic nerve, and the human brain to different wavelengths of light. Color also has a certain strength, measured by the amplitude of its wavelength. If a color has no amplitude, it is black and you can't see it. Any color with a strong enough amplitude appears white.

If you mix a color with black, that color darkens and the resulting color is called a *shade*. If you mix a color with white, the color lightens and the result-ing color is called a *tint* of your original color.

So far, so good. The color that an object appears to be is affected by whether the object is a source of light and transmits light (such as a colored piece of glass), or whether the light is reflected from its surface (such as printed paper). This feature affects not only the *range* of color but also the *intensity* of the color. Transmitted light has a greater range and is usually more intense than reflected light. That's why you can get better scans from slide scanners than from desktop scanners that are scanning colored paper. It's also the major reason why output on your computer monitor looks great but printed output sometimes doesn't. Even great-looking printed output doesn't hold a candle to your computer monitor.

Color Models

If your computer has a color monitor, open the Display Properties dialog box by right-clicking on the Desktop and selecting Properties from the pop-up menu. Select the Appearance tab (see Figure 10-1) and then click the Color sample box (you'll find it in the lower right of the dialog box). From the resulting pop-up menu, click the Other button. The Windows 98 Color dialog box appears. Now I can talk a little about color theory and the various models of color.

Anytime that you select color in a Windows 98 program, this Color dialog box (shown in Figure 10-2) may open. Microsoft Publisher 2000 tries very hard to shield you from this monstrosity, but if you keep clicking "More Colors!" — as in "I must have MORE colors!" — eventually you open something that looks similar to the Windows 98 Color dialog box, or selector. Oh, well.

Figure 10-1:
The
Appearance
tab of the
Display
Properties
dialog box
and its color
sample box.

Figure 10-2:
The
Windows 98
Color dialog
box.

To select a color in the selector, click it or drag the crosshair. When you do, you see the values change for a color's hue (Hue) and saturation (Sat), as well as all three values for red, green, and blue. *Hue* is the name of the color; *saturation* is the intensity of the color. The third value, which doesn't change, is the *luminosity,* or lightness. To change the luminosity value, you move the color in the bar to the right of the Color selector box.

In one model, the HSL color model, these three values — hue, saturation, and luminosity — uniquely identify a particular color. In the second model, the RGB model, represented in the Color selector, any color is seen as a combination of three values of red, green, and blue (the *primary* colors). Values in the RGB model can range from 0 to 255, thus describing 256 colors per primary color or 16.7 million possible colors in the spectrum. That 16.7 million is a number that computer programs and manufacturers often toss about.

Remember the color wheel? It's a representation of all the colors. (No, it doesn't actually show all 16.7 million.) Using the primary colors, the sequence around the wheel is red-orange-yellow-green-blue-violet.

You can describe four basic color schemes based on the position of the colors on the color wheel, as shown in Figure 10-3:

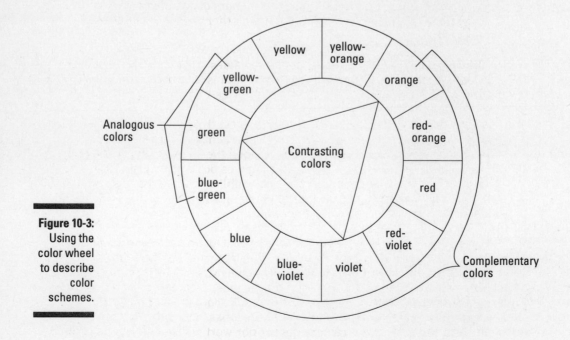

Figure 10-3:
Using the color wheel to describe color schemes.

- ✔ **Monochromatic:** A single color on the color wheel. Monochromatic schemes appear uniform.

- ✔ **Analogous:** Colors that are close to each other on the color wheel. Analogous colors create color schemes that are soothing and harmonious.

- ✔ **Complementary:** Colors that are directly opposite each other on the color wheel. Complementary colors attract the most attention of all color schemes.

- ✔ **Contrasting:** Color combinations that consist of at least three colors that are an equal distance from each other on the color wheel. Contrasting colors are balanced.

I want to pass along some good recommendations for establishing color schemes. When using one color, create a monochromatic scheme by using that color's shades or tints. When using complementary colors, use one dominant color and shades or tints of its complement. When using contrasting colors, use the brightest color as a highlight and the palest color as the background.

Here's a piece of trivia about complementary colors. People who are color impaired are most often color impaired in pairs of complementary colors: Some people are red-green color impaired; others are yellow-blue color impaired.

The RGB color model represented by the values in the Windows 98 Color selector is called a *computer color model*. That is, it represents color as if the human eye were a perfect measurement device — but it is not.

After having said all that about color, I suggest that you do yourself a favor and choose one of the more than sixty color schemes that Microsoft Publisher 2000 offers. Select Scheme to open the Color Scheme dialog box. Click a color scheme in the Available schemes box and then click OK. The selected color scheme is applied to your publication. Microsoft spent a lot of money on talented designer types to come up with these color schemes. No sense reinventing the (color) wheel!

Perhaps the most widely accepted perceptual model of color was developed by the Commission Internationale de l'Eclairage (CIE) in the 1920s, based on populations of people matching a color to mixtures of three primary colors. The results of this model are probably the most accurate indication of true perceived color that we now have. In the *CIE space model*, similar colors appear near each other, and the CIE space looks like a set of hyperbolas with white at the center. Any paint or ink vendor worth its salt calibrates colors to one CIE space or another. Most advanced computer color-matching schemes are based on CIE space as well.

Printing in Color

Printers can print color in one of two ways: by using a specific colored ink or by creating a color using a mixture of other colors. To assign color in a computer program, you specify a color either as a specific ink *(spot color)* or as a process mixture *(process color)*. You can use either, neither, or both in your work.

To print color correctly, you have to tell Microsoft Publisher 2000 which print process you are going to use — spot color or process color — as well as the printer that you are going to use. Microsoft Publisher 2000 lets you print to a desktop color printer using a local print driver at low to medium resolution (up to 600 dpi).

If you are going to create a print-to-disk file for your local copy shop or commercial printer, you need to find out whether the shop has any special requirements. Ask your commercial printer to loan you a copy of its printer driver to work with, if you don't already have it. (Windows 98 ships with many types of printer drivers.) Printer drivers affect not only color fidelity but also margins and other features. See Chapter 13 for more about printer drivers.

Microsoft Publisher 2000 also has an outside printer option. Using this option, you can specify process color or spot color. Spot color can print at high resolution, which can be 1,200 dpi or greater. (High-resolution imagesetters go as high as 2,800 dpi, with 2,400 dpi being common.) Process color prints at medium resolution. I have more to say on this topic in Chapter 13.

Process color (full-color) printing

Microsoft Publisher 2000 refers to process color printing as *full-color printing*, and supports output to color printers with up to 600 dpi resolution. With process color selected, you see 6 colors in the color palette of the Text Color and Object Color toolbar buttons. If that is not enough, you can click the More Colors button. The Colors dialog box then appears with the Basic colors option selected. In that mode, you see 12 shades of 7 colors (purple, blue, green, yellow, orange, red, and black).

Figure 10-4 shows the Basic color selections. If you click the All colors radio button, you see the Colors dialog box that Windows 98 makes possible in Microsoft Publisher 2000, as shown in Figure 10-5.

You can create colors with gradient patterns (that vary from light to dark or from one color to another in steps) by making selections from the Patterns dialog box. Doing so creates striking results.

Because of imperfections in the properties of CMY (cyan, magenta, and yellow) inks, they do not blend to form black. Instead, you get a dark brown. For this reason, and because process black requires more ink than most papers can absorb, black ink is used as a fourth color.

Process color may be applied in two ways. In the first, the inks are applied one on top of another and blended into a *contone,* or continuous tone, image. In the other scheme, color spots are placed side-by-side to create a halftone pattern. With well-crafted halftone patterns, the viewer's mind blends the colored spots to create the color.

Figure 10-4:
The Basic
colors
selector
radio button.

Figure 10-5:
The All
colors
selector
radio button.

Spot color printing

With the spot color option selected for an outside printer, you can see only black, shades of gray, and your selected spot colors in the color palette (see Figure 10-6). You can't see the colors here, but the top two rows are black and grays; the middle two rows are shades (actually tints) of blue; and the bottom two rows are shades of red. Note that the same palette appears under the Font Color button on the toolbar. In either case, your selection of colors is always the same.

Figure 10-6:
The Fill Color dialog box with two spot colors selected.

A spot color adds an additional color to the black ink that is normally used in printing. Adding a single spot color to black is referred to as *two-color printing,* because black ink is also a color. Some commercial print equipment can print two, three, or four colors, including black, in a print run. You can specify any number of spot colors, but because each color must be set up by your printer service, it may be more cost-effective at some point to switch to full-color (or process color) printing. (Microsoft Publisher 2000 recommends that you consider process color at the two-color stage, which is probably too conservative.) The number of copies being printed is also a factor in whether to use spot color or process color. Discuss color options with your commercial printer for the best deal.

When you use spot colors, you have the opportunity to mix your color with blacks (shades) or whites (tints) and thus extend the range of colors. You can also replace black ink with another color and use colored paper rather than white to further introduce color into your work. Be careful, though, because the color of the paper affects the appearance of the color of the ink.

Microsoft Publisher 2000 has an option that lets you print color separations as proof pages that you can hand to your printer when you use spot color. Proofs serve as a check to see that color is being applied to your document in the right places for each colored ink; the term *separations* refers to the fact that each proof is a separate color. Each spot color prints as a separate sheet in black, as does the color black itself. To enable this option, click the Print Color Separations check box in the Print Proof dialog box before a print run.

You must have a color printer selected or use the Outside Printing option with spot color selected to see the Print Proof command on the File menu in place of the Print command.

Because of the high cost of full-color printing, I nearly always prefer spot color to process color. You can get good results by printing spot colors at high resolution and making good use of shades and tints. I often substitute another color for black ink and use colored paper for an additional color.

Color Matching

Every device that can display color also has a range of colors that it can create. That range is called its *color gamut*. Computer monitors have a color gamut, as do desktop scanners and printers. Because color monitors emit light, their color gamut is larger than the color gamut of printers. That's why the color that prints on your color printer often does not match the color that you see on your color monitor. *Color matching* is a process that attempts to match the colors on one device to the nearest color available on another. The results are often less than satisfying.

Matching process color

It's likely that your computer monitor displays fewer than 16.7 million colors, and therefore, a number of colors are unavailable on your screen. Windows shows an unavailable color as a dithered pattern of two colors in the Color sample box of the All colors mode of the Color selector dialog box. The nearest pure color displays in the Solid color sample box. Dithered color happens quite a lot if your system (like ours) has 256 on-screen colors.

When the object can be displayed in the dithered or "true" color that you have selected, Microsoft Publisher 2000 does so. Colored text and objects with fill patterns cannot use dithered color (the text and fill patterns would drop out); for those objects, Microsoft Publisher 2000 uses the closest matching color.

In some printing processes, different color inks are applied one on top of the other to produce a color of any kind. Three inks are used to create process colors: cyan, magenta, and yellow (CMY). These are complementary colors that should theoretically result in a process black (but don't, as I noted earlier).

Microsoft Publisher 2000 can mark colors that fall outside a particular printing device's color gamut. It refers to this process as *marking colors that print poorly*. Before Microsoft Publisher 2000 will mark colors that print poorly on your color printer, you must make sure that the Improve screen and printer color matching setting is enabled (has a check mark next to it) on the General tab of the Options dialog box.

To mark all colors that print poorly, do the following:

1. **Click the object to which you want to apply a color.**

2. **Click the Object Color button to display the color selection menu; then select the More Colors button from that menu.**

3. **Click the check box labeled Mark colors that will not print well on my printer.**

   All colors that will not print well are marked with an X.

For a monitor or printer to use this system, it must ship with a display driver or print driver that uses the Image Color Matching (ICM) standard. If this option is not available to you, get an updated driver from the manufacturer. The ICM system was first included in Windows 98. (Of course, black-and-white printers such as laser printers cannot use this system.) You do not see this option enabled if you run the Prepare File for Printing Service command and then choose Print Proof. Chapter 13 describes outside printing in detail.

If you want to match the colors that you see on your monitor with the colors that you can print, Microsoft Publisher 2000 has a setting in the Options dialog box (selected from the Tools menu) called Improve screen and printer color matching. The match, although not perfect, is at least close.

Even when the color values on a monitor exactly match what a printer is capable of, most printed color output looks pale and washed out in comparison. Most times, special paper made for a particular printer dramatically improves print quality. You can choose from a wide variety of color inkjet printers that provide great quality for under $200.

Most print shops will correct a piece for poor color, provided that you have made it clear that color matching is important. You should have reasonable expectations, though.

Matching spot color

If you print a spot color, you get a color that is uniform but perhaps not exactly the color you intended. If you need to match a particular spot color exactly, you must specify it by using a color matching system, available with many computer programs.

Several color paint matching systems are in use today; the best known is Pantone. The Pantone company produces about 900 standard color swatches that printers can match their printing to. Many ink manufacturing companies match their inks to Pantone colors. Microsoft Publisher 2000 does not offer Pantone matching (or any other kind) in its current version.

You can buy a swatch book of Pantone inks at design retail stores and through most desktop publishing catalogs. With swatch book in hand, you can select the Pantone color that you want and mark that color on each separation. Give those marked pages to your printer and that should do the trick.

When you specify that a color in a publication should be a Pantone match, it is up to the printing service to match that color as part of its contract with you. The results vary, but not nearly as much as when you specify process color printing. Expect to pay more for Pantone inks due to the extra care necessary in their preparation.

I prefer Pantone colors to custom colors that your printer can blend. Custom colors are cheaper, however, and may be worthwhile if you don't mind some variance from print run to print run. Custom colors work best when you do a single print run and don't have to do any matching.

Pantone has created a computer matching system that breaks apart standard colors into component inks so that they can be created with process inks. Some programs, such as Adobe Illustrator, can specify Pantone inks in terms of their color values. Pantone uses a mixture of up to seven ink color components to do its color matching. Pantone is not the only matching system, just the most commonly used.

Color Resources

Color is such a complex topic that I want to recommend some other books on the subject:

- *Using Computer Color Effectively,* by L. G. Thorell and W. J. Smith, 1990, Prentice Hall, Englewood, New Jersey

  This book tells you more than you would ever want to know about the subject and is chock-a-block with great illustrations. It's the best book I've seen on the subject of color and computers.

- *The Color Resource Complete Color Glossary,* by Miles Southworth, Thad McIlroy, and Donna Southworth, 1992, The Color Resource, San Francisco, California

- *Pocket Guide to Color Reproduction,* 2nd Edition, by Miles Southworth, 1987, Graphic Arts Publishing Co., Livonia, New York

✔ *The Desktop Color Book,* by Michael Gosney and Linnea Dayton, 1995, MIS Press, New York, New York

✔ *The Gray Book,* by Michael Gosney, 1990, Ventana Press, Chapel Hill, North Carolina

✔ *Understanding Desktop Color,* by Michael Kiernan, 1994, Peachpit Press, Berkeley, California

You can also get lots of tips on color and other design issues in *Desktop Publishing & Design For Dummies,* by Roger Parker, from IDG Books Worldwide, Inc.

Chapter 11

Photo Finishing with PhotoDraw

● ●

In This Chapter

▶ Maneuvering in the PhotoDraw window

▶ Producing pictures

▶ Moving stuff around

▶ Transforming your pictures

▶ Making fancy text

▶ Choosing Graphic File Formats (choosy moms choose GIF)

● ●

Microsoft PhotoDraw combines the ability to edit photographs and create drawings in one program. The idea is that you can create images for your projects without having to switch back and forth between two or more programs. Microsoft created this program with the nongraphic artist in mind. You don't need to have used a graphics program before to create some very cool-looking pictures. You just have to read this book — to get started, at least.

PhotoDraw has a complete set of drawing tools and photo retouching tools. It even comes with an online tutorial. Because this book is about Publisher 2000, not PhotoDraw 2000, I can't tell you about all the cool features that PhotoDraw 2000 has to offer. I can — and do — give you enough information to get you started along the path to stunning graphics creation.

Deciphering the PhotoDraw Workspace

Before you wander off to become the electronic version of Picasso, you should acquaint yourself with the PhotoDraw workspace. Figure 11-1 shows you a PhotoDraw window with the various parts labeled.

Here is the lowdown on the parts pointed out in Figure 11-1:

- **Menu bar:** You know this one. Click a menu to reveal its commands.

- **Visual menu:** This guy is a cross between a toolbar and a menu. It is intended to provide fast access to the PhotoDraw design features that you use the most.

- **Standard toolbar:** Another familiar one. Click a button to perform an action. Hover the mouse pointer over a button to see a ScreenTip describing the button.

- **Text workpane:** Workpanes contain the tools that you need to work on the various parts of your picture. Depending on what you have selected, the name of the workpane will vary.

- **Picture list:** This list shows you thumbnails of all the pictures that are open during your current PhotoDraw session.

- **Picture area:** The white piece of "paper" in the middle of the screen where you draw your picture.

Figure 11-1:
The
PhotoDraw
screen.

✔ **Scratch area:** The gray area that surrounds the picture area. Think of the scratch area as a staging ground for objects that you will use in your picture.

✔ **Status bar:** The status bar shows the size and position of selected objects — same as in Publisher 2000 — and contains buttons that let you hide or show the workpane or picture list.

Getting Acquainted with the Toolbars and Menus

You should be well acquainted with the way menus work in most Microsoft Windows applications. PhotoDraw holds no surprises in this area. Click a menu name, such as File, and select a command from the menu that drops down.

Menu commands that end in an ellipsis — those three periods — summon a dialog box.

PhotoDraw 2000 has two main toolbars: the Standard toolbar and the Formatting toolbar. Other free-floating toolbars may appear, depending on the task you are performing.

Most of the buttons on the Standard are by now familiar, but a few are probably new to you. Here are the Standard toolbar buttons from left to right, as shown in Figure 11-2:

✔ **New:** Creates a new, blank picture.

✔ **Open:** Summons the Open dialog box.

✔ **Save:** Saves the current picture. Will summon the Save As dialog box the first time you save a picture.

✔ **Print:** Prints your picture to the default printer.

✔ **Print Preview:** Switches to Print Preview mode.

✔ **Scan Picture:** Lets you scan a picture.

✔ **Digital Camera:** Lets you download pictures from a digital camera.

✔ **Cut:** Cuts the current selection to the Windows Clipboard.

✔ **Copy:** Copies the current selection to the Windows Clipboard.

✔ **Paste:** Pastes the contents of the Windows Clipboard into the picture.

✔ **Replace:** Replaces the selected object with another of your choosing.

✔ **Undo:** Undoes the last action.

✔ **Redo:** Redoes the last action.

✔ **Select:** Changes the mouse pointer to the selection arrow.

✔ **Order:** Lets you change the layering order of the selected object.

✔ **Custom Rotate:** Opens the Arrange workpane, where you can specify an amount to rotate the selected object.

✔ **Line:** Allows you to draw a line.

✔ **Curve:** Allows you to draw a curved line or a freeform shape, or just scribble.

✔ **Arrow:** Allows you to draw an arrow.

✔ **Rectangle:** Allows you to draw quadrilaterals.

✔ **Ellipse:** Allows you to draw ovals and circles.

✔ **AutoShapes:** Allows you to draw AutoShapes.

✔ **Insert Text:** Yep, allows you to insert text.

✔ **Zoom:** Changes the current magnification from the drop-down list, or you can type your own amount between 10% and 600%.

✔ **Pan and Zoom:** Opens the Pan and Zoom window, which allows you to zoom in on and center any part of your picture.

✔ **Help Contents and Index:** Opens the Microsoft PhotoDraw Help window.

Figure 11-2:
The Standard toolbar.

Just in case some of the Formatting toolbar buttons — shown in Figure 11-3 — are new to you, here's the up and up on what they do:

✔ **Font:** Allows you to choose a font. This control is available only when you have text selected.

✔ **Font Size:** Allows you to set the font size. This control is available only when you have text selected.

✔ **Bold, Italic:** The old stand-bys. These two buttons let you bold and italicize selected text. These buttons are available only when you have text selected.

TIP

The Formatting toolbar doesn't have an Underline button. If you want to underline text in PhotoDraw, you must draw the line separately. You can then group the line and the text so that they are treated as one object.

✔ **Align Left, Center, Align Right:** Change the alignment of your text. These buttons are available only when you have text selected.

✔ **Fill Color:** Changes the color of the selected object.

✔ **Line Color:** Changes the line color of the selected object.

✔ **Line Width:** Changes the line width of the selected object.

✔ **Line Style:** Changes the line style of the selected object.

✔ **Shadow:** Displays the Shadow workpane so that you can apply a shadow to the selected object.

✔ **3-D:** Opens the 3-D workpane so that you can apply a 3-D effect to the selected object.

✔ **Crop:** Lets you crop an object.

✔ **Brightness and Contrast:** Opens the Color workpane, where you can adjust the brightness and contrast of the selected object.

✔ **Transparency:** Displays the Transparency workpane, which lets you set how transparent or opaque an object is.

✔ **Group:** Groups selected objects so that you can manipulate them as a single object.

✔ **Ungroup:** Ungroups grouped objects so that you can manipulate them separately.

Figure 11-3:
The
Formatting
toolbar.

Then there is the Visual menu. Is it a toolbar or a menu? You decide. Figure 11-4 shows the Visual menu. The commands on the Visual menu are available from the standard menu bar. The Visual menu just organizes them a bit better. For example, if you click the Text menu button on the Visual menu, you will see the following commands: Insert Text, Format Text, Bend Text, 3-D Text, and Designer Text. These commands — with the exception of Insert Text — are available from the Format⇨Effects menu. You can insert text by selecting Insert⇨Text.

Figure 11-4:
The Visual
menu.

Producing New Pictures

You have essentially two ways to create a new picture in PhotoDraw 2000. The first is to start with a clean slate and invent the whole thing yourself. This is the method that I most often use. The other way is to fill in one of the more than 300 professionally designed business templates in PhotoDraw.

Starting from scratch

To create a new picture from scratch:

1. **Launch PhotoDraw 2000 by choosing Start➪Programs➪Microsoft PhotoDraw.**

2. **Make sure the Blank picture option button is selected in the Microsoft PhotoDraw dialog box that you see when you first start the program, and click OK.**

   The New dialog box appears.

3. **Click OK to create the default size blank document.**

   You may elect a different size for your new picture. Just click the icon representing the type of blank picture you want to create on the Pictures or Labels tab of the new dialog box, and click OK.

If you are already running PhotoDraw, skip the preceding steps and click the New button on the Standard toolbar.

Filling in a template

Filling in a template is fairly straightforward. Just select a category — choose from Web Graphics, Business Graphics, Cards, Designer Edges, and Designer Clip Art — and template to use. Then follow the on-screen instructions. As an example, here are the steps to create a Circular Button from the Web Graphics category:

1. **Launch PhotoDraw 2000 by choosing Start⇨Programs⇨Microsoft PhotoDraw.**

   If you are already running PhotoDraw 2000, select File⇨New Template and skip Step 2.

2. **Click the Design template option of the Microsoft PhotoDraw dialog box and click OK.**

   PhotoDraw opens with the Templates workpane displayed on the right portion of the screen. Figure 11-5 shows PhotoDraw with the Web Graphics category open in the Templates workpane.

3. **Select a category in the Templates workpane, and then click a template.**

4. **Click Next.**

   PhotoDraw prompts you to replace the image in the template with one of your own choosing.

5. **Click Browse to select an image of your own for the button.**

   When you find the image that you want to use, select it and click Open. Your image replaces the template's default image.

Figure 11-5:
Select a
category
and
template.

6. **If necessary, click Picture Position to adjust the position of your newly inserted image on the button.**

   Click and drag your image to the desired location, and then click Finish on the floating Position toolbar.

7. **Click Next to edit the text on the button and then type the text that you want to appear on your button.**

   You can also click the text object on the image to select it. After it's selected, you can move or resize it.

8. **Click Next.**

   PhotoDraw 2000 gives you some advice on saving your picture and tells you to click Finish to complete the template.

9. **Click Finish.**

   The Templates workpane departs and you are left with a visually stunning Web page button, as shown in Figure 11-6.

Figure 11-6:
The finished
product.

Although the exact steps will vary with the template you select, the basic procedure described here is typical for filling out a template in PhotoDraw 2000.

Opening Picture Files

Just when you think you are getting used to the way things work in Windows applications, Microsoft changes things. You are probably thinking that enough ways exist to open a file. Well, PhotoDraw has one more.

Opening pictures the old-fashioned way

If you know the name of the picture file you want to open, the old, familiar methods still work:

✔ Select File➪Open to summon the Open dialog box, click the picture file that you want to open, and click Open.

✔ You can also coax the Open dialog box on-screen by clicking the Open button on the Standard toolbar, or by pressing Ctrl+O.

Using Visual Open

If you aren't sure of the filename of the picture that you want to open, you can take a peek at the picture before you go through the trouble of opening it. Select File➪Visual Open. The Visual Open dialog box, shown in Figure 11-7, insinuates itself onto the screen. Click the picture that you want and click Open.

Figure 11-7: The Visual Open dialog box makes opening the right picture easy.

Closing and Saving Pictures

To close the current picture file, select File➪Close. If you have made any changes to the picture, PhotoDraw asks permission to save the file. Click Yes. If you close a newly created picture and click Yes to save it, PhotoDraw 2000 presents the Save As dialog box, shown in Figure 11-8. Just type a name for your picture in the File name box and click Save. By default, PhotoDraw 2000 saves your picture in the My Pictures folder (it will have an MIX file extension).

Figure 11-8:
The Save As
dialog box.

Saving in other file formats

In addition to the standard MIX format in PhotoDraw 2000, you can save your picture in the following formats:

- ✔ **BMP:** Windows bitmap

- ✔ **GIF:** Graphics Interchange Format — often used on Web pages

- ✔ **JPG:** Joint Photographic Experts Group (JPEG) — also used on Web pages

- ✔ **MIX:** The default format for PhotoDraw 2000 and Microsoft Picture It!

- ✔ **PCX:** PC Paintbrush format; this filter is not installed by default

- ✔ **TGA:** Truevision Targa; this filter is not installed by default

- ✔ **TIF:** Tagged Image File; TIF files tend to be rather large

To save your file in one of these formats, Select File⇨Save As. Type a name for your picture in the File name box; then make a selection in the Save as type drop-down list. Click Save. You are done.

Before saving a new picture in a different format, save it as a PhotoDraw picture. That way, you can easily modify the picture should you need to do so.

Using a wizard to export your picture

PhotoDraw has a feature called the Save for Use in Wizard. The idea is to tell Mr. Wizard where you want to put your picture — such as on the Web, or in an on-screen presentation — and he will help you save it in the appropriate format. No more worrying about GIF, or TIF, or those other file formats.

Select File⇨Save for Use in to kick the wizard into gear. Answer the wizard's questions by clicking option buttons. Click the Next button to advance the panels in the wizard. Click the Save button (the Save button appears only on the last panel of the wizard). The Save for Use in Wizard saves your picture in the appropriate format.

Working with Text

PhotoDraw isn't a word processor, but it does allow you to add text to your pictures. This comes in handy for adding captions to photos, or labeling buttons for a Web page. You might decide to have only text in a picture. Using the 3-D effects and Designer text can give you some very nice pictures from text.

Inserting text

PhotoDraw gives you three ways to insert text: Select Insert⇨Text from the menu, press Ctrl+T, or select Text⇨Insert Text from the Visual menu. No matter which method you choose, the Text workpane appears, as shown in Figure 11-9. Start typing. Your text appears in the picture area with handles to show that it is selected. Choose a font, font size, and font style from the corresponding boxes in the Text workpane.

Applying 3-D effects

To apply 3-D effects to selected text, choose Text⇨3-D Text or Effects⇨3-D. Both methods open the 3-D workpane. Click a 3-D effect in the 3-D workpane to apply that effect to your text. Be patient. 3-D rendering is a pretty slow process on all but the speediest machines. Take a minute to wonder at your ability to make text appear as though it were carved from wood — as shown in Figure 11-10 — or marble, or other effect.

Designer text

PhotoDraw gives you a choice of 28 Designer Text formats to choose from. To apply one of these formats to selected text, choose Text⇨Designer Text from the Visual Menu or click Designer Text in the Text workpane. The Designer Text Gallery opens in the bottom part of the Text workpane. Simply click an example in the Gallery to apply that formatting to your text. Figure 11-11 shows the Designer Text Gallery.

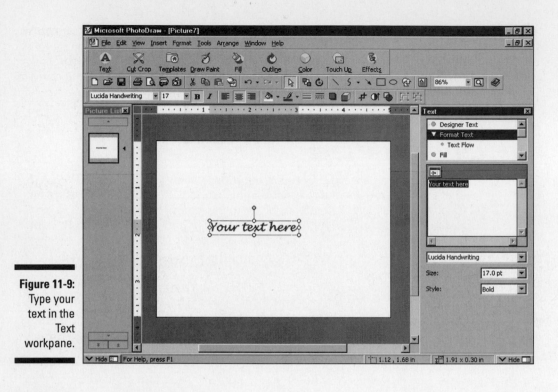

Figure 11-9:
Type your
text in the
Text
workpane.

Figure 11-10:
Some text
rendered in
3-D.

Figure 11-11:
The
Designer
Text Gallery.

Drawing and Painting

PhotoDraw 2000 enables you to draw, paint, and add various shapes to your
pictures. Drawing and painting are essentially the same in PhotoDraw 2000.
You use the mouse to draw — or paint — images on the screen.

Select Draw Paint from the Visual Menu. Then select Draw, Shapes, or Paint
from the drop-down menu:

✔ If you click the Draw or Shapes menu item, the Outline workpane opens.
Click a tool — such as Line or Rectangle — from the floating AutoShapes
toolbar. Click and drag to draw. You can select an outline type for your
drawing in the Gallery.

✔ If you click the Paint menu item, the Paint workpane appears. Select a
brush type in the Gallery and start painting by clicking and dragging in
the picture area.

To apply some photo-realistic effects to selected text, select Photo Brushes
from the Gallery Type drop-down list box in the Outline or Paint workpanes.
You can make the outline of your drawings look like rope, or ivy, or firehoses,
or any number of wacky things.

I encourage you to experiment with the various options and features that PhotoDraw has to offer. I think you will find that you can create some interesting pictures, even if you aren't the artistic type.

Part V
Proof Positive

The 5th Wave   By Rich Tennant

"Shoot, that's nothing! Watch me spin him!"

In this part ...

After your layout is complete, most of the hard work is done. Many gotchas can crop up when you go to print your publication, however. Some are the tiny little errors that seem to bedevil everyone, and some errors are of the thorny, devil type. In the chapters in this part, I discuss the most common problems that appear in a publication in its final stages of production and how to get rid of them. If you are like most of us, you've spent a great amount of time tweaking your work to get it just right. It would be a shame not to go the next step and make sure that the printed work is as good as it can be. Printing can be expensive, and mistakes can be costly when you make them. The first chapter in this part can save you a lot of money and frustration.

Microsoft Publisher 2000 has a number of special features that help you guide a printing service to print your work. The second chapter in this part shows you how to set up your publication for a commercial printer. A short treatise on paper and ink is also included in this chapter.

Chapter 12

Final Checks

- -

- -

*Q*uality desktop publishing means sweating the details. I'm not talking about jumping up and down in your sweatsuit with Richard Simmons's video *Sweatin' to the Oldies,* but I am talking about getting absorbed in the details of your publication before you send it to the printer — where real money changes hands. In this chapter, I look at things that you can do to make sure that your publication reflects the care you took in its design.

The Eyes Have It

The single best piece of advice that I can give you about checking your publication is this: Look it over in printed form. Microsoft Publisher 2000 lets you create proof prints; avail yourself of this opportunity. You should also create a proof for an outside printer. The proof is your "contract," telling the printer "This is what I want."

You can't — or at least you shouldn't — expect to catch all the errors in your publication the first time you look at it. The more people you have look at your work, the better chance you have of finding things that should be changed. Spotting your own errors can be difficult. When possible, try to live with the final design for a while before you commit to spending money for printing.

TIP

Make yourself a nice checklist of items that you want to check in your publication after you complete the design. I highly recommend this activity to you.

The Design Checker

The Design Checker is an automated tool in Microsoft Publisher 2000 that attempts to find things that are wrong with your publication. It catches many errors that you wouldn't be likely to catch until after the publication was printed. The Design Checker checks for the following:

- ✔ Empty Frames
- ✔ Covered Objects
- ✔ Text in the Overflow Area
- ✔ Objects in the Nonprinting Region
- ✔ Disproportional Pictures
- ✔ Spacing between Sentences

Use these steps to check your design with the Design Checker:

1. Choose Tools⇨Design Checker.

The Design Checker dialog box appears, as shown in Figure 12-1.

Figure 12-1:
The Design
Checker
dialog box.

2. Select the range and type of pages that you want to check.

- Under Check which pages?, click All or Pages. If you click Pages, enter the from and to page numbers in the corresponding text boxes.

- To check only the foreground pages, deselect the Check background page(s) check box by clicking it to remove the check mark.

3. Click the Options button to open the Design Checker Options dialog box and select your options.

The Options dialog box is shown in Figure 12-2. Select the checking options that you want to perform by clicking the check box next to the option.

Figure 12-2:
The Design
Checker
Options
dialog box.

4. **Click OK or press Enter to return to the Design Checker dialog box.**

   You can click Cancel if you want to ignore the selections you've made.

5. **Click OK or press Enter to start checking your publication (or certain pages in it) for the problems that you've selected.**

   The Design Checker goes to the first problem and posts an explanation. For example, Figure 12-3 shows a dialog box noting a hidden-object problem. Notice that the Design Checker dialog box offers suggestions for correcting the problem.

6. **For all design problems noted by a Design Checker dialog box, you can correct the error or click the Ignore, Ignore All, or Continue button to continue checking your publication's design.**

   The Explain button opens up the Help system with directions for correcting the error. Ignore moves you to the next error. Ignore All ignores all errors of that type.

7. **After the last error, Microsoft Publisher 2000 posts a dialog box informing you that the Design Check is complete.**

As one of your final checks, you just can't beat running the Design Checker.

Figure 12-3:
A layout
error caught
by the
Design
Checker.

Word-Fitting Techniques

When working with a layout to get it exactly the way you want, one of the hardest tasks is fitting the text into text frames. If your layout is *frozen,* the amount of text that you can have is set. Also, you may find that the formatted text simply looks ugly.

A common problem in fully justified text is large interword spacing through-out a frame. The text looks as if it has rivers running through it. You probably can't change the justification of your text frames, but you can work with the hyphenation feature (see Chapter 8) to break words and improve the look of your text. But even the automated hyphenation tool isn't perfect. So, you may want to manually hyphenate justified text. I describe this technique and others for making your words fit in the following sections.

Copyfitting

You can rephrase nearly every paragraph to reduce or add words without changing the meaning. My editor does this to me all the time! In general, people doing page layout don't have the luxury of editing text. That job belongs to the author or the editor. If you are both layout artist and author, however, you can copyfit your text by adding and removing words.

Editing text written in short sentences or phrases is more difficult because you have fewer words to work with. In those cases, a thesaurus can be your best friend. *Roget's Thesaurus* is a classic. Microsoft Bookshelf (sold alone or with Microsoft Works or Microsoft Office) includes an online version of *Roget's Thesaurus.*

The Microsoft Publisher 2000 spell checker (see Chapter 7 for information on how to use it) contains more than 100,000 words. The spell checker's dictio-nary is large, but it won't help you if you use a valid word incorrectly — such as *two* rather than *to.*

Always proofread your text for errors caused by properly spelled but incor-rectly used words.

If you are working with Microsoft Word, you can use its grammar checker on your text. You can use the Change Text➪Edit Story in Microsoft Word com-mand from the context-sensitive menu of a text frame to check the grammar in your story. You open the grammar checker in Word 2000 with the Spelling and Grammar command on the Tools menu. If that command isn't on your Word 2000 menu, you need to install the grammar checker (which isn't installed as a default choice in the Microsoft Office installation).

Wrong word usage is particularly difficult for authors to spot. I think the best way to proofread is to get as many people as possible to read your publication before you commit to printing it. If your publication is important, you may want to spring for a professional proofreader.

Adjusting spacing

Microsoft Publisher 2000 gives you many ways to adjust the spacing in and between your text frames. Use the ideas in this section as a reminder and check list.

Working with headlines

A common error in headlines is too much spacing between letters and between lines. Headlines nearly always benefit from proper kerning and from reducing the default line spacing that Microsoft Publisher 2000 gives to large letters. Kerning is particularly important in headlines with serif fonts.

Figure 12-4 is an example of a headline that dominates the page. In Figure 12-5, the headline's spacing between characters (tracking) was changed from very loose to normal, and the Line Spacing was adjusted to 0.95 sp. In addition, the headline frame can now be reduced to make the headline less prominent.

You may find that substituting a WordArt frame for a text frame in headlines works well. WordArt has a best-fit option that adjusts text automatically.

If you have a headline that belongs with a block of text, leaving more space above the headline than below it is a very good idea so that your reader has a visual clue that the headline applies to the text that follows.

Another problem to watch for is a headline that breaks across lines in a way that makes the meaning unclear to the casual reader. If you can improve the readability of your headline by grouping phrases, do so. For example, in the headline "Michael Jordan Retires from NBA," put the line break before *Retires* rather than after it. Then go peel your Bulls bumper sticker off your car.

Make sure that the placement of your headlines agrees with the page numbers in the table of contents (if your publication has one). Many page layout programs automatically renumber the table of contents, but Microsoft Publisher 2000 does not. Also, if you used headlines as headers and footers and placed these elements in the background, make sure that they are correct when you go to proofread your pages.

Figure 12-4:
A large
headline
before
adjustment.

Figure 12-5:
The same
headline
after track-
ing and line
space
adjustment.

Working with text frames

One way to make text fit your text frame is to simply adjust the size of the frame. This is straightforward if you have a single text frame on a page. With several text frames in a multicolumn page layout, however, resizing frames can affect all columns simultaneously. One subtle way to work around adjusted text frames is to play with the lines and spacing in your headlines. If you made your frames smaller and now have extra space on the page, you can add a line to a headline or put in a secondary headline to take up that space. If you made your frames larger, you can remove extra headlines to give yourself more room.

The amount of line spacing dramatically affects the amount of text that you can fit into a text frame. You can adjust line spacing from a single frame, from all the frames on a page, or from all the frames on a two-page spread. You also can change the spacing before, after, and between paragraphs. If you do adjust line spacing, you do so for the entire text frame and, ideally, for all text frames on a page or on a two-page spread.

You don't have to make large changes in line spacing to get results. Check your adjustments on a printed page to see whether the results are accept-able; don't rely on how your page looks on the screen. Figure 12-6 shows the result of changing line spacing in a set of paragraphs. Notice how different the three paragraphs look.

I also like kerning and tracking as a way to slightly alter text to make it fit correctly in a text frame. (When you use kerning and tracking in this way, the change isn't obvious to a casual observer.) To see how kerning and tracking affects text size, consider the three text frames in Figure 12-7. In these examples, I applied Normal, Loose, and Tight tracking to the entire text (except for the first line). Chapter 8 tells you about various techniques for adjusting the spacing between letters in your text.

Figure 12-6:
Three frames with different line spacing.

| **Line Spacing = 1 sp** You don't have to make large changes in line spacing to get results. Microsoft Publisher 2000 lets you make fine changes. This is one of those adjustments that you have to eyeball on a printed page to see if the results are acceptable to you. Don't rely on the way your page looks on the screen to see if your new line spacing is acceptable. | **Line Spacing = 0.9 sp** You don't have to make large changes in line spacing to get results. Microsoft Publisher 2000 lets you make fine changes. This is one of those adjustments that you have to eyeball on a printed page to see if the results are acceptable to you. Don't rely on the way your page looks on the screen to see if your new line spacing is acceptable. | **Line Spacing = 0.75 sp** You don't have to make large changes in line spacing to get results. Microsoft Publisher 2000 lets you make fine changes. This is one of those adjustments that you have to eyeball on a printed page to see if the results are acceptable to you. Don't rely on the way your page looks on the screen to see if your new line spacing is acceptable. |

Figure 12-7:
Three frames with different tracking settings.

| **Tracking = Normal** You don't have to make large changes in line spacing to get results. Microsoft Publisher 2000 lets you make fine changes. This is one of those adjustments that you have to eyeball on a printed page to see if the results are acceptable to you. Don't rely on the way your page looks on the screen to see if your new line spacing is acceptable. | **Tracking = Loose** You don't have to make large changes in line spacing to get results. Microsoft Publisher 2000 lets you make fine changes. This is one of those adjustments that you have to eyeball on a printed page to see if the results are acceptable to you. Don't rely on the way your page looks on the screen to see if your new line spacing is | **Tracking = Tight** You don't have to make large changes in line spacing to get results. Microsoft Publisher 2000 lets you make fine changes. This is one of those adjustments that you have to eyeball on a printed page to see if the results are acceptable to you. Don't rely on the way your page looks on the screen to see if your new line spacing is acceptable. |

Microsoft Publisher 2000 refers to *kerning* as adjusting the spacing between two characters, and *tracking* as adjusting the spacing for a large selection of text.

When adjusting text frames, pay particular attention to preventing widows and orphans. A *widow* is a short line at the top of a page or column; an orphan is a word or portion of a word on a line by itself at the end of a paragraph.

One common mistake to watch for is two spaces between sentences. This practice is a holdover from the days when people used typewriters — the extra space made sentences more obvious.

To check for extra spaces, you can search for two space characters and replace them with one. To do this, type two spaces directly into the Find what text box in the Replace dialog box and replace with one space. It's not a bad idea to run this search and replace a second time, in case three spaces were typed together.

Hyphenating and justifying text

Another method for altering the way text fits in a text frame is to change the justification. Sometimes after a design is set, however, you don't have the flexibility to change the text justification. To get the most text into a text frame, apply full justification and automatic hyphenation to the frame. Remember, you cannot use automatic hyphenation for only part of a text frame.

Note that when you use automatic hyphenation, you can no longer control the location of line breaks. To regain control, turn off hyphenation; then, turn it back on and request to confirm each hyphenation as it occurs.

When you use right- or left-justified text (also called *ragged* text) as opposed to full justification, you often make the text more readable but you won't fit as much text in a column. To gain more space, hyphenate.

In ragged text, you can force a line ending by using a soft carriage return (Shift+Enter). When you force a line ending, however, you change the line endings of every line that comes after that point. This won't be a problem if automatic hyphenation is on, but it can cause grief if you hyphenated your text manually. Therefore, forced line endings should be the last resort.

You can also force a line ending at the position where the automatic hyphenation tool places a hyphen. To do so, move your cursor to that position and press Ctrl+- (hyphen). An optional hyphen shows up only when the entire word won't fit on the line. Therefore, optional hyphens aren't affected by soft carriage returns. If you want to make sure that a word is never hyphenated (at the position where Microsoft Publisher 2000 would hyphenate it), go to that position and press Ctrl+Alt+- (hyphen). I recommend this safeguard for a compound word that already contains a hyphen: for example, *double-barreled* rather than *double-barrel-ed*. Common practice is to never end a column or text frame with a hyphen.

Always use optional hyphens rather than regular hyphens to hyphenate text.

When you hyphenate text in a paragraph, try to have no more than two consecutive hyphenated lines. Hyphenated text is harder to read and understand. For this reason, some page layout professionals avoid hyphenation, although it greatly increases the amount of work necessary to fine-tune the layout. Whatever you do, don't hyphenate headlines; they must be readable at a glance.

You can control the amount of hyphenation that Microsoft Publisher 2000 uses by changing an option on the Edit tab of the Options dialog box. Enter a smaller number in the Hyphenation zone text box to smooth out your ragged edge and to reduce the amount of white space between words. To have fewer hyphens or to have fewer short syllables before and after the hyphen, make the Hyphenation zone larger.

Improving the Page

People tend to read a page from the top-left corner to the bottom-right corner. If you have a two-page spread, that principle applies to the top-left corner of the left page down to the lower-right corner of the right page. Putting your most important page elements along this diagonal is good design practice.

One nice feature of page layout programs is that they impose a design structure to your pages. You want your readers to instinctively find common elements, such as page numbers, on a page. I recommend setting common page elements — in the background of your pages — in one place for all left pages and in another for all right pages. With these common elements in place, you can move on to break up the tedium of your pages by having some elements stand out. The longer the publication, the more important it is to have elements that draw the eye to one section or another.

Adding special page elements

You've already seen some techniques for breaking up a page and drawing attention to various sections. The following are useful techniques for making your pages more interesting:

- **Pictures:** Pictures instantly attract attention. When you put a picture on a page, it becomes a focus of attention. Putting pictures off the reader's diagonal path — in the lower-left or upper-right corner of a page or two-page spread — creates a good effect. If you use too many pictures, however, you greatly reduce their effectiveness.

- **Drop caps or raised caps:** These design elements are an excellent way of starting a chapter or a section, and they draw the reader's attention regardless of where they appear on the page.

✔ **Rules and shaded boxes:** I like rules and shaded boxes. They are particularly valuable for making headlines stand out. If you think that a section of text is important, put it in a shaded box.

✔ **Pull quotes or sidebars:** A *pull quote* is a short section that highlights the important point you are making on a page. To make a pull quote stand out, place it outside your text frame.

Sidebars are longer sections that you want to make stand out. You can reserve sidebars for optional reading or make them central to your text treatment.

Don't forget that the Design Gallery comes with a selection of specially formatted headlines, coupons, pull quotes, sidebars, tables of contents, and titles. If you create any design elements that you want to use elsewhere, create your own category in the Design Gallery and save those elements under it. I talk about the Microsoft Publisher 2000 Design Gallery in Chapter 9, and I like it so much that I wish it were greatly expanded. Figure 12-8 shows you the Design Gallery with the Pull Quotes category selected.

Inserting an object from the Design Gallery is just the beginning. You are free to resize the object and to ungroup it so that you can work with its components. You can also change the text in a Design Gallery object, and adjust colors and shading.

One nice effect that you can make with shaded areas is called a bleed. A *bleed* is a section of color that extends past the normal margins and all the way to the edge of your page. You can use bleeds with single pages and to span the inside margins of a two-page spread. If you use bleeds in your work, consult with your printer shop to make sure that its presses are capable of printing bleeds. Bleeds often require special treatment and cost more money, but the effect can be worth it.

Adding drawn objects

Although most tools in the toolbox can't draw objects for you, you can use them to create nice effects. You can also find special shapes in the Custom Shapes tool menu. Drawn objects don't have to be small; they can be major page elements as well. For example, if you are creating a publication that includes a topic for discussion or the dialogue of a play, you could use a cartoon balloon shape — which is ordinarily used to hold captions — as your entire page frame. Be creative and have fun!

Also, you needn't be constrained by the shapes that appear in the toolbox. You can combine shapes to create other shapes, such as combining triangles, circles, and lines to create a mountain landscape with the moon rising in the background. When you combine shapes with colors, patterns, gradients, and shadings, you have a wealth of tools at your disposal.

Figure 12-8:
Pull Quotes
in the
Design
Gallery.

Borders and shading

Borders and shading are nice ways of separating a section of your page. You can place borders around your pictures by using rectangles and circles, or create a matted-photograph look by putting colored frames in back of your pictures. If you try this, I suggest using bold colors to emphasize the picture.

When you use borders and shading with text, try to understate their presence. If a shaded block is colored gray, keep the gray level at 10 to 15 percent. You can overuse color on a page very easily. Similarly, if you use shading in back of text, make sure that the shading makes your text more readable, not less. As the shading gets darker, it is more difficult to see black text but easier to see white text. Note that white text — called *reversed text* — is generally less readable than black text. It works well only in front of black backgrounds and in short phrases such as headlines.

Borders and shading are valuable when you create tables. The Microsoft Publisher 2000 table frame automatically creates shades and borders for you. If you create an array of information without a table frame, consider adding these features to your work.

In *Desktop Publishing & Design For Dummies* (IDG Books Worldwide, Inc.), Roger Parker recommends that you avoid *boxing* an entire page unless you want to create a classical look. I concur and prefer to see pages designed with simple rules that separate headers and footers from the body of the page.

Do you want to know the most readable color combination for text? Take a look at the cover of this book. Surprise! It's black type over a yellow background. To change the color of text, use the Font Color tool, which appears on the Formatting toolbar when you have text selected.

Special symbols

If you use capitalization in a paragraph, you may find that using SMALL CAPS looks better, particularly for a whole sentence of capitals. Also, changing a line of capitals to small caps can shorten your paragraph measurably and help you with copyfitting. If you have a paragraph that must be lengthened to fit the text frame, consider making the first sentence all caps — especially if the first sentence makes the point for the paragraph or section.

Keyboards have feet (') and inch (") marks for single and double quotation marks. Typographers prefer the use of stylized *smart quotes* instead: 'and' for single quotation marks and " and " for double quotation marks. To automatically insert these symbols into your text when you type single and double quotation marks, turn on the "Straight Quotes" with "Smart Quotes" check box in the AutoFormat as You Type tab of the AutoCorrect dialog box. (This option is set by default.) If you have text that needs straight single or double quotation marks, you will have to turn the option off temporarily. Don't forget to turn it back on when you are done. You can also use the Insert Symbol dialog box to insert any of these characters.

You may want to try a typographical technique called a *hanging* quotation mark. Suppose that you want to align the first character of a headline or a pull quote with the text frame that appears below or above it. A regular quotation mark could disrupt that visual alignment and be distracting. Therefore, you may want to put an opening quotation mark to the left of the headline or pull quote. Some page layout programs let you format a paragraph so that it has a hanging quotation mark. In Microsoft Publisher 2000, use the following steps to create this feature manually:

1. **Type your paragraph or pull quote with smart quotes at the beginning and end of the text.**

2. **Create a small text frame that is large enough to hold the quotation mark.**

3. **Position the small frame to the left of the paragraph or pull quote for an opening quotation mark or to the right for a closing quotation mark.**

   Zooming in to see your text is helpful when placing the small text frame.

4. **Select (highlight) the quotation mark in your paragraph or pull quote and then Cut it to the Clipboard.**

5. **Click an insertion point in your small hanging text frame; then, Paste the cut quotation mark into the frame.**

Unfortunately, because you have separate frames, your hanging quotation doesn't automatically follow your headline as it moves about on your page. Therefore, group the hanging quotation mark frame with the headline or pull quote frame. Figure 12-9 shows you an example of a beginning hanging quotation mark.

Figure 12-9:
A beginning
hanging
quotation
mark.

" **Hanging Quotation Marks Look Better** "

Other symbols that typographers use (that may be new to you) are the en dash (–) and em dash (—) in place of two hyphens (--) and three hyphens (---), respectively. They're called an en dash and an em dash because they are the width of a capital *N* and *M* in the font being used. Many desktop publishing programs automatically substitute these symbols whenever you type two or three hyphens. Microsoft Publisher 2000 automatically substitutes the en dash when you type a space followed by a hyphen, and an em dash when you type two hyphens together.

Good typographical practice recommends using en dashes when you are indicating a range of numbers (where you would normally put the word *to*) or when you have a compound word, as in Barrington Smythe–Jones. Use an em dash to set off a parenthetical remark — as I do in this sentence — before you end your thought and use up your brain cells.

If your en and em dashes don't show up automatically, check to be sure that the Hyphens (-,—) with en/em dashes (–,—) option is enabled on the AutoFormat as You Type tab of the AutoCorrect dialog box.

If you look closely, you find that most fonts contain typographer's fractions. The ½ and ¼ symbols appear to the right in the Insert Symbols dialog box, one line down from where the en and em dashes appear. Also, most fonts have characters for copyright (©), trademark (™), and registration ®) symbols. These special characters are best used as superscripts in the same font size. You also find various currency symbols ($, ₤, ¢,), accented characters (Á, ç, é, õ), ligatures (Æ, æ), and so on.

It pays to study the Insert Symbols dialog box to see which special characters your current font offers.

You may require a special fraction beyond what's offered in a standard character set. Here's how you create those:

1. **In standard text, type the fraction that you want, such as** 3/8.

2. **Format the numbers to the left and right of the division sign at about 60 to 70 percent of the text size.**

   For example, if you have 12-point text, use 8-point numbers.

3. **Format the left number as a superscript and the right number as a subscript by choosing Format⇨Font and clicking the corresponding radio buttons in the Font dialog box.**

   Don't forget that you can use noninteger point sizes (such as 11.5) if you are using TrueType fonts or Postscript fonts and the Adobe Type Manager.

What if you need a superscript number such as 2^8 or a subscript number such as H_2O? You can apply these formats to selected text from the Character dialog box or by pressing the Ctrl+ + (plus) or Ctrl+Shift+ + (plus) key combinations. Press these combinations again to toggle the super- or subscript back to normal text.

Chapter 13

Printing, Print Shops, and Paper

• •

In This Chapter

▶ Specifying which printer you want to use

▶ Printing page proofs on your own printer

▶ Setting up an outside printer

▶ Investigating the quality offerings of common printing devices

▶ Selecting and working with an outside printing service

▶ Deciding how and when to use your various paper options

• •

Mom is a desktop publisher's best friend. A desktop publisher's next best friend is the person responsible for printing his or her publication. You should call your mother at least once every week and send her flowers on Mother's Day. And you should talk to your printing professional before and during the development of any desktop publishing project that you won't be printing yourself.

In this chapter, I wrap up my exposition of Microsoft Publisher 2000 by considering how to work with professional print shops and other outside printing resources. Specifically, I show you how to set up your publication for whatever printer you're using, how to select paper, and how to take advantage of the special paper (from PaperDirect) that Microsoft Publisher 2000 lets you use. I also go over common problems and concerns about using an outside printer. People sometimes find working with a professional printer for the first time to be something of a mystery.

Printers and Output Quality

Print quality is determined by the printer *engine* (the mechanism that makes the printer print). Typically, print quality is measured in the number of dots per inch *(dpi)* that a printer can deliver to a printed page. That measurement isn't the whole story, however. The shape of the dots, their placement in relationship to a letterform, and the density of the dots can dramatically change the perceived quality of a printed page.

For example, many printers — such as the Hewlett-Packard LaserJet series — use a *resolution enhancement technology* to improve print quality. HP calls its technology *RET;* other vendors call theirs something else — Intellispot, Varidot, Omnishade, PrintGear, or whatever their lawyers can trademark. When placing dots at the edge of a printed character, an HP laser printer varies the size and intensity of the spot to better conform to the character's border. The net effect is that the printed text appears to be at a higher resolution, and *halftones* that print with shades of gray — created by black spots — appear to have more grays in them.

Following is a brief description of printer types and common uses:

- **Impact printers:** Impact printers include dot matrix and print wheel printers. They print by striking ribbons (like a typewriter) and transferring the ink from the ribbon to the page. Some are capable of printing graphics, but as a group, these printers are not used in desktop publishing applications. About the only reason I can think of for keeping one of these around is for printing multi-part forms.

- **Inkjet printers:** Inkjet printers print by spraying ink droplets under pressure. Their output quality varies widely. Desktop inkjet printers at the low end print up to 600 dpi in either color or black and white. Print quality is moderate, but print speeds are relatively low. Special paper improves inkjet output. Today it is possible to buy inexpensive (less than $200) inkjet printers that deliver very impressive color output at medium resolutions.

- **Laser printers:** Laser printers produce black-and-white output and grayscale (shades of gray) output. Color laser printers are now available at prices starting at about $1,500. Common desktop laser printers print at the 600-dpi range, although you can buy enhanced laser printers (or add special controller boards) to improve print quality to 1200 dpi — considered to be near imageset quality.

- **Xerographic printers:** Many copy shops and service bureaus have printers that are essentially fancy copy machines. These xerographic printers offer high speed and moderate resolution (600 dpi). In this category, the Xerox DocuTech Publisher is a 50-page-per-minute *(ppm)* production scanner/printer.

  Other xerographic printers offer higher resolution and color printing, such as the Canon Color Laser Copier (CLC), a laser printer/copier that can input digital files in a number of formats. You can get good full-color, continuous tone (contone) output from these printers. They not only scan a printed piece of output but also take electronic files in standard output formats such as EPS (Encapsulated PostScript).

✔ **Dye sublimation printers:** These printers work like inkjet printers but use heads to sublime — vaporize and deposit — special dyes onto paper. Some use crayons and waxes; others use low-melting dyes or liquids. They are used almost exclusively for color work. In most cases, inkjet printers produce a halftone image, but dye sublimation printers can produce contone — continuous tone — images.

✔ **Imagesetters:** These printers are high-resolution laser printers that print at 2000 – 3000 dpi. The output that they create is printed paper or — more often — film that, in turn, is used to create printing plates. You find imagesetters at printer services. They are used in very low-volume printing to create original print masters.

You may find any or all of these printers — except for impact printers — at a copy shop or printer service.

Selecting the Target Printer

Each printer that you use (whether in-house or in a professional print shop), offers you different page sizes, minimum margin widths, color options, and so on. When you print to your desktop printer, you set those options in the Page Setup dialog box. If you are using a printer that's at a professional print shop, you can install and use the *printer driver* (the interpreter that lets your computer talk to the printer) for the print shop's printer as the *target printer* on your desktop computer. *Target printer* is just a spiffy term for the machine on which you intend to print a given publication. Your target-printer selection and setup are *publication-level settings;* that is, they are a part of your current publication but do not affect any other publications.

Note that the target printer doesn't have to be *your* printer. That is, although you probably have your own printer attached to your computer, you may not want to use that old banger. You may have access to an even better printer that offers color, faster speed, the capability to print on bigger sheets of paper, a slot that dispenses hot beverages while you wait, or whatever. If this other printer is the one that you intend to use to print the final version of your publication, that's what you should select as your target printer.

Windows 98 contains many printer drivers; some belong to expensive color printers or imagesetters. If you can't find the target printer that you intend to print to on this list, you can always ask your printer service to supply you with the driver. Most will "loan" you their printer drivers without charge.

Follow these steps to select and set up a target printer:

1. **Select File⇨Print Setup.**

   A Print Setup dialog box, like the one shown in Figure 13-1, opens with your default printer listed. Your printer may offer you different options from the ones shown in the figure.

Figure 13-1:
The Print Setup dialog box for the HP LaserJet 500+ printer.

2. **If you don't want to use the default printer, select a different printer from the Name drop-down list box.**

   The default printer is determined by Windows. To change the default printer, choose Start⇨Settings⇨Printers, right-click the printer of choice, and select the Set as Default command from the resulting pop-up menu.

3. **In the Orientation section, click the desired paper orientation if it isn't already selected.**

   Your choices are Portrait (lengthwise) and Landscape (sideways).

4. **In the Paper section, use the Size drop-down list box to choose the size of paper on which you plan to print, if it isn't already selected.**

   The selected printer determines the available sizes.

5. **Also in the Paper section, use the Source drop-down list box to choose the appropriate paper source for your publication, if it isn't already selected.**

   The selected printer determines the available sources. Some printers have different trays, feeders, tractors, and other methods for getting paper into themselves.

6. **Click OK.**

If you can't find the target printer in the Name drop-down list box, you need to use the Windows Control Panel to install a driver for that printer.

Printing your pages

The operations described in these sections are controlled by Windows 98; Microsoft Publisher 2000 uses the services of the operating system to print. You can print to a local or network printer, or you can set up to print to an outside service bureau. Often, you do both, printing draft or sample copies on your local printer for proofing, and receiving final output from a service bureau.

Printing problems are legion with computers. If you are having difficulties printing, try getting help by selecting the Troubleshooting topic in the Windows Help system. Use the Help command on the Start menu to access the Windows Help system. Also check out the Print Troubleshooter on the Help menu of Microsoft Publisher 2000. This command opens the Help system and shows you topics of interest in solving printer problems.

To print to a local or network printer, called *inside printing,* you can use various methods:

✔ Click the Print button (shown in the margin) in the Shortcut Bar. Microsoft Publisher 2000 immediately begins printing your entire publication using the current print settings.

✔ Select File⇨Print or press Ctrl+P. The Print dialog box, shown in Figure 13-2, appears with your default printer selected. Make your selections from that dialog box and then click OK.

Figure 13-2: The Print dialog box for the HP LaserJet 500+ printer.

✔ Drag-and-drop a publication file onto a printer icon or shortcut on the Windows Desktop or in the Windows Explorer.

The Print dialog box

The Print dialog box contains the following important features:

✔ **The Name drop-down list box:** This box lets you select the printer that you want to use from your currently installed list of printers. Your default printer appears first in the dialog box. To send a print job to another printer, select that printer by name from the Name drop-down list box.

- ✓ **The Properties button:** Use this button to change settings for your printer: page size, type, orientation, and handling; graphics; fonts; and other properties specific to your printer.

- ✓ **The Print range section:** Select All to print all pages, select Pages and enter the number of the first and last page that you want to print in the from and to text boxes, or select Current Page to print just the page in which you're working.

- ✓ **The Copies section:** Specify the number of copies that you want to print and whether you want these pages to be collated.

- ✓ **Advanced Print Settings:** This option brings up the Print Settings dialog box, where you can choose to print linked graphics in full or low resolution. You can also decide not to print linked graphics at all. The specific model of printer you are using will determine whether or not you can specify the print quality, what to print, printing order (for labels), and other options.

The capabilities that you see in the Print dialog box are determined to some extent by which printer you have selected. Nearly all printers, however, allow you to select a range of pages to print, as well as to print multiple copies or copy a file to disk and have the file printed on another printer. Many other capabilities — such as collating, color capabilities, two-sided printing, and other options — are specific to each printer. Check out the Properties dialog box by clicking the Properties button in the Print dialog box to find out more about your printer's capabilities. Also, your printer's manual is a good place to learn more about your specific printer.

When you accept the Print dialog box settings, Microsoft Publisher 2000 creates a print job and sends (or *spools*) it to your printer. To see the set of documents — called the *print queue* — sent to the printer, double-click that printer's icon in the Printer folder. A window opens, showing you the current print jobs and offering you commands necessary to modify your print jobs. You can delete print jobs, suspend them, and move them about in the queue.

The Print Setup dialog box

If you are printing to a desktop printer, you owe it to yourself to choose File➪Print Setup and explore your printer's Print Setup dialog box. The Print Setup dialog box is somewhat deceptive because it hides the most interesting settings in the Properties sheet. To access these settings, click the Properties button. With these settings, you control such things as paper size, graphic resolution (number of dots per inch), font quality, and other options.

The Print Troubleshooter

Microsoft Publisher 2000 has a feature called the Print Troubleshooter that is turned on by default in the Options dialog box (on the Tools menu). The Print Troubleshooter is a set of online topics that helps you with the following problems:

✔ Text that doesn't print correctly

✔ A picture, gradient fill, or pattern that doesn't print correctly

✔ A book-fold publication that doesn't print correctly

✔ Any general printing problems, such as slow printing, printout cutoff, memory overflow, and so on

Choose the Print Troubleshooter from the Help menu to view these topics in the online Help system.

Using Outside Printing Services

Microsoft Publisher 2000 lets you print to any common desktop printer that you can attach to an IBM PC. For low-volume output, a desktop printer is sufficient. You may have times when you need to print in large quantities, however, or with capabilities beyond those of most desktop printers (such as printing in color, reproducing photographs on glossy stock, or printing in high resolution). In these cases, you need to visit a printer service bureau, copy shop, or commercial printer. Each of these establishments offers different capabilities, and each requires different degrees of hand-holding.

The following ideas may help you in your quest to select an outside printing service:

✔ **If you have friends who use printing services, get a recommendation.** If you don't, let your fingers do the walking through the Yellow Pages and try out a few services. Ask to see samples of their work and get the names of other clients with whom they've worked. Good printers deliver quality work on time and on budget. You're paying good money for the work, and you should get good results.

✔ **Know what you expect from your service.** Use the Pack and Go Wizard to ready your publication for the commercial printer. By default, the wizard will print a composite and separations. The composite combines all the colors in your publication and should be a good representation of the final product. The separations show your printing service how the colors are separated. Publisher prints one page for each color. Take the composite and separations with you to the printing service.

✔ **Evaluate the printing quotes.** If you need to print several thousand copies of a piece, a commercial printer is the best choice — and will likely save you money. Copy shops and printer service bureaus offer lower pricing at volume levels, but commercial printers can go even lower on the cost per page.

✔ **Ask about their policy on *overage*.** Most printers print a set amount above your print order to be on the safe side. Some charge for the overage. Make sure that you know when they do. An overage charge of more than 15 percent of the print price is excessive.

✔ **Don't pick a printer that offers the cheapest price.** You usually pay for the money that you save with longer print turnaround times and less attention to your work. Printing is a very competitive industry. After you cost out the paper and inks, labor is the only variable.

Working with an outside service

Be sure to understand what your outside service requires of you in order to print your publication. At the minimum, an outside printing service is likely to ask that you provide the following materials before it can do your print job:

✔ Page proofs of each page, with each spot color or process color separation printed as a proof

✔ A listing of your fonts, files, and printing directions

✔ The files themselves in Microsoft Publisher 2000 or Postscript format, with any needed font files and graphics files included

✔ Any original drawings or photographs that need to be scanned

Use Publisher's Pack and Go Wizard to make sure that you have everything you need to take to the printing service. Follow these steps:

1. **Select File⇨Pack and to a Commercial Printing Service.**

   The first panel of the Pack and Go Wizard appears — almost as if by magic — as shown in Figure 13-3.

Figure 13-3:
Step 1 of the
Pack and Go
Wizard.

2. Click <u>N</u>ext and choose where you would like Publisher 2000 to pack your publication (see Figure 13-4).

Figure 13-4:
Tell the
Pack and Go
Wizard
where to
pack your
publication.

3. Click <u>N</u>ext to see the Include fonts and graphics panel of the wizard.

Make sure that all three options are checked before clicking Next (see Figure 13-5).

Figure 13-5:
Click all
three check
boxes to
include the
linked
graphics
and fonts.

4. Click <u>N</u>ext to see a summary of the choices you have made in the Pack and Go Wizard (see Figure 13-6).

Figure 13-6:
The wizard
tells you
what it is
going to do.

5. Click Finish to see the final panel of the Pack and Go wizard.

The wizard lets you know that your publication has been successfully packed. Click OK to print a composite and color separations. I recommend printing the composite and separations, but if you already have a copy of them or just don't want to print them, clear the check boxes before clicking OK.

Avoiding problems

Using special fonts can be the most troublesome aspect of working with an outside printer service. The following are some of the troubles you can encounter:

✔ Many shops keep only a limited collection of fonts. In some cases, busy shops may simply hand you the output of your file with whatever font they substituted for the fonts they didn't have.

✔ If you overload your document with fonts, you can overload an image-setter's memory and get Postscript overflow errors that add to your costs.

✔ Using gradient fills can also quickly overload an imagesetter's memory, as can special WordArt effects.

Another troublesome aspect of working with outside printers is forgetting to include all the graphics files that your publication needs. Keep these things in mind:

✔ If you submit scanned graphics, make sure that the resolution of the scan is appropriate to the kind of printing that you are doing.

✔ Try to use scanned graphics that are simply placed in your publication. If you crop, rotate, or otherwise modify your scanned images, you create large, complicated files.

Check to see that your printer service has the fonts that you used in your publication. Also, if you submit EPS (Encapsulated Postscript) files, make sure that the printer service has the same creator application for your publication and its components.

If you are printing a very costly print job, you may want to request a *press check*. That is, you ask your printer to set up the printing press and run off sample copies of the publication for you to check. Your printer is more likely to be willing to do this if you are on hand at the time that the shop runs your job.

Sit down and evaluate any print job that you get back from a printer. If you find a problem, let your printer know about it. And don't forget to let your printer know if you are especially happy with the work. My favorite way of letting my service providers know that their work was good is to recommend them to other people.

Setting Up for Outside Printing

The Tools⇨Commercial Printing Tools⇨Color Printing command lets Microsoft Publisher 2000 select a printer driver that is best for the outside printing that you are likely to do: black-and-white, full-color, or spot-color printing. Figure 13-7 shows the Color Printing dialog box.

Figure 13-7:
The Color Printing dialog box.

Color Printing dialog box:

Print all colors as:
- ○ Composite RGB
- ● Process colors (CMYK)
- ○ Spot color(s)

Change Spot Color...   Spot color 1: [////]
                        Spot color 2: [////]

Colors used:
- CMYK (0, 0, 0, 100) -- Main (Black)
- Accent 1 (CMYK (61, 18, 100, 41))
- Accent 2 (CMYK (42, 37, 0, 0))
- Accent 3 (CMYK (16, 6, 100, 3))

Help   OK   Cancel

To set up your publication for black and white printing, select Spot color(s). Then click the Change Spot Color button to display the Choose Spot Color dialog box. Click the Black and white only option and click OK.

Avoid using two spot colors in gradient fills, in which the two colors are blended. That configuration prints poorly, if at all. You can use either spot color blended with white or with black, however.

Outside printer printing

When you want to specify a print job to an outside printer, make sure that a check appears in the Print to file check box of the Print dialog box. If checked, the program prints to a disk file that you can take to your outside printing service. Otherwise, Microsoft Publisher 2000 uses this printer driver to try to print to your current printer (which may or may not work, depending upon its type).

As with any printer, you should visit the printer's Properties dialog box to see what's there before you do your printing. The MS Publisher Imagesetter and MS Publisher Color Printer have identical Properties dialog boxes. Ask your outside printing service for guidance on making these selections.

You may notice that the About dialog box for the Properties dialog box tells you that the generic drivers were developed jointly by Microsoft Corporation and Adobe Systems Incorporated. On any certified Postscript imagesetter, you should get good results with these drivers because most professionally used print output devices are Adobe Postscript certified.

Selecting paper

Selecting paper for your publication's printing is a sensual experience that is rare in computer land. Paper has texture, heft, thickness, color, shine, brightness (due to fluorescent chemicals), and even smell. I get excited just thinking about it. (Some would say it's because I've been locked up in an office writing this book, but I would disagree.) I love paper — especially the green kind with presidents' portraits on it.

Paper makes up 30 to 50 percent of the total cost of a print job, depending upon the number of copies printed and the type of paper stock chosen. Therefore, you can greatly affect the cost of printing your publication by carefully selecting print stock. Your outside printer service can be a big help in selecting the right paper for your publication. Most printers keep sample stock around for you to look at and, in some cases, to test print. Commercial printers have a great deal of experience with various types of paper and can tell you how well a paper takes ink, folds, or reproduces graphics. Nearly all the larger paper companies distribute sample paper stock kits or paper stock selectors that are strips of sample paper.

Starting your own sampler collection is not a bad idea. PaperDirect is one paper company that will sell you a paper sampler and refund the money on your first order. Other paper manufacturers sell, or more likely give away, their samplers upon request.

Paper as a design element

When you choose paper for your publication, you must match the paper's characteristics to your publication. Paper size, weight, thickness, and methods of measuring these elements vary with the various types of paper. A paper's features related to color, texture, and finish are important to consider when you are deciding on your publication's best presentation. Please note that paper quality is a design element that makes a substantial impression upon the reader:

✔ Buy heavier, better paper when your publication will be handled several times — as will a company's annual report, for example. If your publication will be looked at briefly and then thrown away, you can get by with a lightweight, cheaper paper.

✔ Choose paper color to enhance your publication. The most readable text is printed on a soft, yellowish-white paper. For the best accuracy with process colors, use neutral white paper. Brighteners added to paper stock as fluorescent dyes also alter color fidelities. Be aware that the color of your paper affects how your ink color appears on the finished product. To avoid unpleasant surprises, you may want to test how the ink color you choose will look when matched with your paper color.

✔ Print on the side of the paper recommended by the paper manufacturer. Paper has a grain that makes one side better for printing; reams of paper have a grain indicator on their wrapping with an arrow to indicate which side you should print on. When printing pages, try to have the grain parallel to the binding edge to help your readers turn pages and to keep your pages lying flat.

✔ Choose paper stock weight and thickness that is appropriate for your printing device. Laser printers typically have a limit of 60-pound stock. If you put heavier paper through a laser printer, you can damage it. Check your printer's documentation for its requirements. If you are printing on two sides of the paper, make sure that your paper is heavy enough that the type from one side doesn't show through to the other side. This is called *bleedthrough* and can make your publication unattractive and difficult to read.

✔ Select a coated paper (at a little more expense) if you need opacity and better resolution for your printing. This is particularly important if you are printing in color or using photographs. You can buy paper stock that's coated on one side (C1S) or on two sides (C2S). C1S is used for labels, packaging, and covers; C2S is used in books or commercial publications. Coated paper withstands higher ink coverage and results in blacker blacks, better color fidelity, and higher resolution. Please note that the coated paper smudges more and may require *varnish* to keep the color from coming off on readers' hands. Also, note that coated paper exhibits less of the printed image showing through to the opposite side of a page.

Special papers from PaperDirect

Microsoft has teamed up with PaperDirect, a direct-mail special paper supplier, to incorporate the special papers that they sell into some of the Microsoft Publisher 2000 wizards' designs. Microsoft Publisher 2000 can display several PaperDirect patterns on your screen (provided that you have not set up your publication to print to an outside printer). To display special paper on-screen, choose View⇨Special Paper and select a design in the Special Paper dialog box (shown in Figure 13-8).

Figure 13-8:
The Special
Paper dialog
box.

You can see these special papers on your screen, but they don't print. To achieve this on-screen effect when you print, you must use the special paper that PaperDirect sells.

I find the PaperDirect catalog to be a treat, even if it seems to show up in my mailbox every other week. To see what PaperDirect offers, purchase its PaperKit, which contains a sample of each of the pages in the catalog. The phone number is 1-800-A-PAPERS.

PaperDirect also has matching envelopes, business cards, brochures, and postcards for its stationery sets, as well as computer templates, frames, certificates, theme and fun papers, laser foils, and other resources for the desktop publisher.

More Printing Resources

Printing is a big topic, and I've only touched upon the subject here. Fortunately, some great resources are out there to help you. The best book on working with the printing industry, how printers (both mechanical and human) work, and the process of working with printers and graphic arts suppliers is *Getting It Printed,* by Mark Beach, Steve Shepro, and Ken Russon. The book should be a standard reference for any desktop publisher.

Another place to read about printing is the more condensed (and dense) book, *Pocket Pal,* 14th Edition. You can buy this book at any graphics supply house. This book gives you many pages of technical details on printing, paper selection, printing inks, type, copy preparation, and dozens more subjects. It is particularly valuable for giving you a detailed, high-level view of the printing industry; I just couldn't do without it.

Part VI
Publishing on the Internet

The 5th Wave — By Rich Tennant

"I found these two in the multimedia lab morphing faculty members into farm animals."

In this part ...

These days, everyone seems to be talking about the Internet and the Web. You rarely see a television commercial, magazine ad, or billboard that doesn't have a Web site address plastered on it somewhere (you know, `www.sendmeyourmoney.com`). The two chapters of this part help you to create a Web site of your own and publish it to the World Wide Web. After all, if I didn't help you publish your work, I may as well call the book *Microsoft Create Great-Looking Publications on Your Computer and Not Let Anyone See It For Dummies*.

Chapter 14

Weaving a Web Site

· ·

· ·

You don't know how to write HTML code, but you want to create professional-looking Web pages? Microsoft Publisher 2000 can help. In fact, if you can click a few buttons, you can create some great-looking Web pages in minutes! How? Read on.

What Is a Web Site?

A Web site is a page or group of pages created and published to be viewed on the Internet's World Wide Web. A Web page is simply a document encoded using HTML (HyperText Markup Language) to describe its appearance. An HTML document can have hyperlinks — graphics or text that you can click to move to other documents or other parts of the current document. A Web site is one or more Web pages published on a Web server. A Web server is a computer connected to the Internet running Web server software. For a great step-by-step tutorial on creating Web pages, pick up a copy of *Dummies 101: Creating Web Pages*, by Kim Komando (published by IDG Books Worldwide, Inc.).

Using the Web Site Wizard

As I mention in Chapter 1, the easiest way to create a publication in Microsoft Publisher 2000 is to use a wizard. Creating a Web site is no exception. Can you create a Web site from scratch using Microsoft Publisher 2000? Sure.

Would you want to? Probably not. To use the Web Site Wizard, just click Web Sites in the Wizards pane on the Publications by Wizard tab of the Microsoft Publisher Catalog dialog box. If the Catalog is not visible, you can get it back by choosing File⇨New. Figure 14-1 shows the Microsoft Publisher Catalog dialog box with the Web Site Wizard selected.

After you click Web Sites in the Wizards pane, Microsoft Publisher 2000 offers you 45 styles of Web sites to choose from in the Web Sites pane. Select the style of the Web site that you want to create and click the Start Wizard button located at the bottom right of the Microsoft Publisher Catalog dialog box.

After your computer clicks and grinds for a while (how long this takes depends on the speed of your PC), Microsoft Publisher 2000 creates the first page of your Web site and shows you the Introduction panel of the Web Site Wizard, as shown in Figure 14-2. The wizard uses this panel to say hello and let you know that you can return to the Web Site Wizard at any time to change the answer to a question. How nice!

Figure 14-1: The Microsoft Publisher Catalog with the Web Site Wizard selected.

Figure 14-2:
The
Introduction
panel of the
Web Site
Wizard.

Click Next to select a color scheme from the Color Scheme panel of the Web Site Wizard. Microsoft Publisher 2000 lets you choose from 62 color schemes. Microsoft paid big money to have these color schemes designed, so it is hard to go wrong when selecting one. Still, if you can't decide which color scheme looks the best, stick with the default. Figure 14-3 shows the Color Scheme dialog box of the Web Site Wizard with the Meadow color scheme selected.

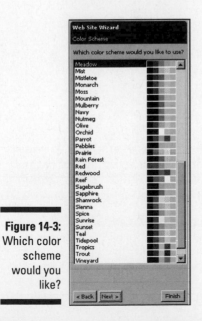

Figure 14-3:
Which color
scheme
would you
like?

Click the color scheme of your choice and then click Next. The Additional Pages panel of the Web Site Wizard leaps to the screen, as shown in Figure 14-4. At this point, you have only one page in your Web site: the home page. Here you can choose to add one of six different page types to your Web site. Your choices are as follows:

- ✔ Story
- ✔ Calendar
- ✔ Event
- ✔ Special offer
- ✔ Price list
- ✔ Related links

Figure 14-4:
Would you
like any
additional
pages?

Web Site Wizard

Additional Pages

Which pages would you like to include in your Web site?

☐ Story
☐ Calendar
☐ Event
☑ Special offer
☑ Price list
☐ Related links

< Back Next >   Finish

Click the check box next to the type of page that you want to add. You may use any or all of the offered types. Click Next without selecting any of the check boxes to continue without adding any pages. You can always return to the wizard to add pages later.

After you click Next, the Form panel of the Web Site Wizard appears, as shown in Figure 14-5. Forms allow you to receive feedback from visitors to your Web site. Notice that the forms have a radio button; you may select only one. Select the form that you want to add and click Next.

Figure 14-5:
Add a form
to your Web
site.

Microsoft Publisher 2000 displays the Navigation Bar panel, as shown in Figure 14-6, asking what kind of navigation bar you would like to link the pages of your Web site. Your choices are as follows:

✔ Both a vertical and horizontal bar

✔ Just a vertical bar

✔ None

Navigation bars contain buttons that allow visitors to your Web site to access the pages of your site. If you choose Both a vertical and horizontal bar, Publisher creates Navigation bars at the top and left sides of the page. Click the Just a vertical bar option if you want — well, just a vertical bar. If you would like just a horizontal navigation bar, send an e-mail to Microsoft demanding — politely, of course — that it add this feature to Microsoft Publisher 2001: A Page Odyssey.

Unless you are creating a single-page Web site, adding a Navigation bar is a good idea. Make your selection and click Next.

Next, the wizard wants to know whether you would like to have a sound played when your home page is opened. Figure 14-7 shows the Background Sound panel.

Web Site Wizard

Navigation Bar

What kind of navigation bar would you like to use to link the pages of your Web site?

- ● Both a vertical and horizontal bar
- ○ Just a vertical bar
- ○ None

`< Back` `Next >` `Finish`

Figure 14-6:
Reach for
the bar.

Web Site Wizard

Background Sound

Would you like a sound to be played when your home page is opened?

- ○ Yes
- ● No

(To hear the sound, view the home page in a browser that provides sound capabilities.)

`< Back` `Next >` `Finish`

Figure 14-7:
Would you
like sound
with that?

Unless you have a very compelling reason to play a sound when your home page is opened, I recommend that you select No here. Sounds can take a long time to download, especially over slow dial-up connections. Nothing makes most visitors want to move on to another Web site faster than having to wait for someone's alma mater's fight song to download. Click No, and then click Next.

The Background Texture panel, shown in Figure 14-8, appears. If you want a texture, click Yes. If not, click No. This is a trade-off between legibility and visual impact. I think textures can look great, but sometimes they make text difficult to read. Oh, what the heck. Click Yes, and then click Next.

Figure 14-8:
Texture your
background.

The Personal Information panel of the Web Site Wizard leaps to the screen. Hang in there, you're almost finished! Select the Personal Information Set that you want to appear on your Web site. Just in case you need to change any of the information in your Personal Information Sets, Publisher 2000 provides an Update button. Click the Update button to open the Personal Information dialog box. Make any changes and click Update to return to the Personal Information panel of the Web Site Wizard (see Figure 14-9). Click Finish.

You are done! Notice that the Web Site Wizard is still hanging around the right side of the screen. If you don't like the way that your Web site turned out, use the Wizard to change any part of it. Click the Hide Wizard button to free up some on-screen real estate.

Figure 14-10 shows the Home Page of the completed Web site with the Web Site Wizard visible on the left side of the screen.

Figure 14-9:
Choose a
Personal
Information
Set.

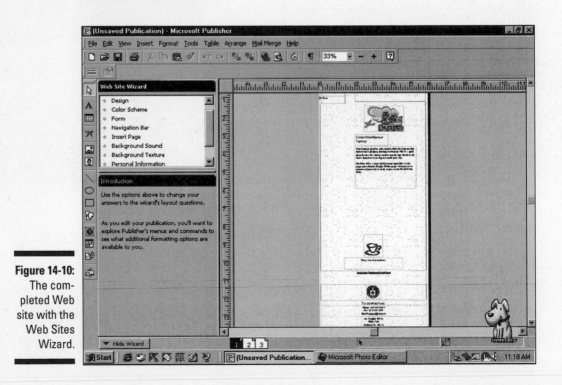

Figure 14-10:
The com-
pleted Web
site with the
Web Sites
Wizard.

That's all there is to it. Now you can edit the text and picture frames to personalize your Web site.

If you have an existing publication — a brochure or newsletter or such — that you want to place on the Web, you don't have to recreate it as a Web site. Open the publication and select Web Site from Current Publication. The Convert To Web Site dialog box, shown in Figure 14-11, appears. Accept the default option so that Publisher automatically creates a Web design and hyperlinks; then click OK. A confirmation dialog box pops up asking whether you want to save any changes to your publication before converting it to a Web site. If you made any changes to your original publication that you want to keep, click Yes. If you click No, all the changes you made to your original publication are still incorporated into your Web site. The changes are not, however, saved to your original publication. After you dismiss the confirmation dialog box, Publisher 2000 creates your Web site and displays the Web Site Wizard so that you can make any desired changes to the Web site.

Figure 14-11:
The Convert
To Web Site
dialog box.

> **Convert To Web Site** [?] [X]
>
> What do you want to do?
>
> (●) Use the Web Site Wizard to automatically create a Web
>   design with hyperlinks.
>
> ( ) Add my own hyperlinks and do my own Web layout.
>
> [OK]   [Cancel]

Adding Text or Picture Objects

Adding text or pictures to your Web site is pretty simple. In fact, if you have added text or pictures to a Microsoft Publisher 2000 publication, you already know how to add them to your Web site. If you used the Web Site Wizard to create your Web site, you probably have several text and picture frames in your publication. Did I call your Web site a publication? Guess so.

I strongly recommend that you use the Web Site Wizard to create your Web site. It is much easier, in my opinion, to create the site using the wizard and change what you don't like than it is to create the Web site from scratch.

Adding text

To change the place holder text that the wizard put in your publication, just highlight the text and start typing.

If you don't have any text frames or don't want to change the text in an existing text frame, just create a new one. You remember how:

1. **Click the Text Frame tool.**

2. **Draw the text frame.**

3. **Start typing.**

I think that the Web Site Wizard does a reasonably good job of designing the Web page, but feel free to add, delete, or move objects as you see fit.

Adding pictures

To change a picture on your Web page, follow these steps:

1. **Double-click the picture.**

   The Insert Clip Art dialog box appears and you can select a new picture for your Web page. Publisher 2000 selects pictures that it thinks are similar to the one you double-clicked. If you see the picture you want, click it and move on to Step 4. Figure 14-12 shows some of the pictures that Publisher 2000 selected for me when I double-clicked on a picture of wrenches.

2. **Click the All Categories button.**

   The Insert Clip Art dialog box displays all the available categories for your viewing pleasure.

   The Motion Clips tab of the Insert Clip Art dialog box contains animated images that you can place on your Web site. Use these sparingly — please, I'm beggin' you! — because they take longer to download and can distract from the message your Web site intends to convey. This tab is visible only when you are working on a Web site publication.

Figure 14-12:
Publisher 2000 displays pictures similar to the one you double-clicked.

To see the animated GIF in action, click it; then select the Play Clip button from the pop-up menu.

3. **Select a category and click the image you would like to insert.**

4. **Click the Insert clip button on the pop-up menu.**

   The picture that you selected replaces the existing picture in your Web site.

5. **Click the Insert Clip Art dialog box's Close button.**

   You return to your Web site.

The procedure for adding a new picture to a Web site is the same as the procedure for adding a new picture to any publication. Adding new pictures is covered in detail in Chapter 10.

Adding and Removing Hyperlinks

Hyperlinks allow the person viewing your Web site to click an object (text or a graphic) and jump to another document on your Web site or elsewhere on the Internet, or to send an e-mail.

Adding hyperlinks

Several ways are available to add a hyperlink to an object on your Web page. You can add hyperlinks to text, pictures, WordArt, and even the contents of table frames. To add a hyperlink to text or a table frame, you must first select the individual text that you want to hyperlink. Selecting just the text frame or table frame will not work. Follow these steps to create a hyperlink:

1. **Select the object to which you want to add a hyperlink.**

2. **Select Insert⇨Hyperlink, select Hyperlink from the context menu, click the Insert Hyperlink button on the toolbar, or press Ctrl+K.**

   No matter which method you choose, the Hyperlink dialog box, shown in Figure 14-13, appears.

3. **Select the type of hyperlink that you want from the Hyperlink dialog box.**

4. **Fill in the Hyperlink information section of the Hyperlink dialog box and click OK.**

   The Hyperlink information section changes depending on the type of hyperlink you select in the Create a hyperlink to section.

Figure 14-13:
Create a
hyperlink to
an e-mail
address.

As shown in Figure 14-13, you can create four types of hyperlinks:

- ✔ **A Web site or file on the Internet:** You need to supply the URL (uniform resource locator or address) of the document the hyperlink connects to.

- ✔ **An Internet e-mail address:** You need to supply an e-mail address.

- ✔ **Another page in your Web site:** Select the appropriate page in your Web site.

- ✔ **A file on your hard disk:** You need to supply the path to the file to which you want to link. This file will be published along with your Web site.

Removing hyperlinks

Removing a hyperlink from an object is a snap:

1. **Select the object from which you want to remove a hyperlink.**

2. **Select Insert⇨Hyperlink, select Hyperlink from the context menu, click the Insert Hyperlink button on the toolbar, or press Ctrl+K.**

3. **Click the Remove button in the Hyperlink dialog box.**

   The Hyperlink dialog box goes away and your hyperlink is removed.

Adding Color and Texture to the Background

Although I usually prefer a white background for my Web sites, you can produce dramatic effects by applying texture and/or color to the page background. The easiest way to do this is to select Yes from the Background Texture panel of the Web Site Wizard. If you opted not to have a textured background and have now changed your mind, read on.

Adding color to the background

To add or change the color of the background, do the following:

1. **Select Format⇨Color and Background Scheme.**

   The Color and Background Scheme dialog box, shown in Figure 14-14, is displayed.

2. **Click the Texture button to remove the check mark.**

Figure 14-14:
The Standard tab of the Color and Background Scheme dialog box.

3. **Click the down arrow next to the Solid Color option and select a color.**

4. **Click OK.**

   You are returned to your Web site publication. Marvel at your sense of color for three minutes.

Adding texture to the background

To add or change the texture of the background, follow these steps:

1. **Select Format➪Color and Background Scheme.**

   The Color and Background Scheme dialog box, shown previously in Figure 14-14, is displayed.

2. **If necessary, click the Texture check box to place a check mark in it.**

3. **Click the Browse button.**

   The Web Backgrounds dialog box appears. If all you see is a bunch of files with names like j0143757, click the down arrow on the Views button in the toolbar and select Preview.

4. **Click the name of the file containing the texture that you want to apply.**

   Publisher obligingly shows a preview of the selected file.

5. **Click Open to dismiss the Web Backgrounds dialog box.**

6. **Click OK to apply the texture and return to editing your Web site.**

I am all for fancy backgrounds with bright colors for Web pages that have little text, but a plain white background works best for Web pages with lots of text.

Chapter 15

Getting Published (On the Internet)

· ·

In This Chapter

▶ Previewing a Web site

▶ Publishing your Web site

· ·

So, you have created a stunning Web site and you are wondering what you should do with it. Well, you have come to the right place. In this chapter, I discuss previewing your Web site in your Web browser and publishing your Web site.

Previewing a Web Site

After you have created your Web site, you probably want to preview it to make sure that it meets with your expectations before you go through the trouble of publishing it for the entire world to see. You want to make sure that it looks the way you intended and that all the hyperlinks function. You must have Web browser software installed and configured in order to preview a Web site.

To preview your Web site, select File⇨Web Site Preview or press Ctrl+Shift+B. Microsoft Publisher 2000 opens your default Web browser and displays the first page of your Web site. Click the hyperlinks to make sure that they function properly, and view the other pages (if any) of your Web site. When you are finished viewing your Web site, close your Web browser. You return to Microsoft Publisher 2000. Figure 15-1 shows a sample Web site being previewed in Microsoft Internet Explorer. Notice that the address in the Address box points to a file on a local drive.

Figure 15-1:
A preview of
a sample
Web site.

Publishing Your Web Site

What's the difference between previewing your Web site and publishing it? When you preview your Web site, Microsoft Publisher 2000 opens the Web site on your computer and shows you how it will look when it is published on the Internet. Publishing a Web site entails copying it to a computer running Web server software that is connected to the Internet.

Microsoft Publisher 2000 gives you three options for publishing your Web site to the Internet:

✔ Publish to a Web folder

✔ Publish with FTP

✔ Publish with the Microsoft Web Publishing Wizard

Publishing to a Web folder

As I mention earlier in the chapter, I think that publishing your Web site to a folder on your PC and copying it using FTP software is the easiest way to go. To publish your Web site on the Internet, you must have Internet access. Most people access the Internet from home by dialing into an Internet Service Provider, or ISP. If you do not have access to the Internet, you can still publish your Web site to a local drive. This creates all the HyperText Markup Language, or HTML, documents and image files, allowing you to copy the files to the Internet at a later time.

The recommended method for saving a Web site from Publisher 2000 is to use Web folders. A Web folder is a shortcut to a location on a Web server that you can save to your Web site to by using the Save as Web Page command. You should contact your ISP and ask whether it supports Web folders. If it does, follow these steps to create a Web folder:

1. **On the Windows Desktop, double-click the My Computer icon.**

   The My Computer window opens.

2. **Double-click the Web Folders icon.**

   The Web Folders icon opens.

3. **Double-click the Add Web Folder icon.**

   The first panel of the Add Web Folder Wizard appears, as shown in Figure 15-2.

Figure 15-2:
The Add Web Folder Wizard.

4. **Type the URL of the Web folder you want to add and click Next.**

   If you don't want to type — or can't remember — the URL, you can click the Browse button to open your Web browser. Navigate to the Web folder, and then — leaving the Web browser open — click the Add Web Folder button on the taskbar to return to the Add Web Folder Wizard, and click Next.

5. **The Add Web Folder Wizard asks you to name the new Web folder, as shown by the lovely and talented Figure 15-3. Type a name for the Web folder and click Finish.**

   The Add Web Folder Wizard wanders off and you are returned to the Web Folders window.

Figure 15-3:
Name that folder!

After you have created a Web folder — or convinced the Web Server Admin-type person to do it for you — publishing your Web site to a Web folder is a cinch. Allow me to walk you through it:

1. **Select File⇨Save as Web Page.**

   The Save as Web Page dialog box, shown in Figure 15-4, appears.

2. **Click the Web Folders icon in the Places bar located along the left side of the dialog box.**

3. **Click the desired Web folder and then click OK.**

   If you are presented with a dialog box asking for a username and password, type them and click OK. That's all there is to it!

Publishing to a folder on your PC

To save your Web site to your local machine, follow these steps:

1. **Choose File⇨Save as Web Page.**

2. **In the Save as Web page dialog box, select a folder and click OK.**

Figure 15-4:
The Save as
Web Page
dialog box.

Publishing your Web site using FTP Locations

To save your Web site to the Internet using FTP, you must tell Publisher about your FTP site:

1. **Select File⇨Open.**

   Not surprisingly, the Open dialog box appears.

2. **Click the down arrow in the Look in box and select Add/Modify FTP locations.**

   The Add/Modify FTP Locations dialog box, shown in Figure 15-5, appears.

3. **Type the URL of your FTP site in the Name of FTP site box.**

   Your Internet Service Provider or Web Server Administrator should be able to furnish you with this info.

4. **If necessary, click the User option button and type your username and password.**

5. **Click Add to add the FTP site.**

   The FTP site you added appears in the FTP sites list.

6. **Click OK to close the Add/Modify FTP Locations dialog box.**

7. **Click Cancel to close the Open dialog box.**

Figure 15-5:
The
Add/Modify
FTP
Locations
dialog box.

After you have added an FTP Site, you can publish your Web site using FTP Locations as follows:

1. **Select File➪Save as Web Page to open the Save as Web Page dialog box.**

   The Save as Web Page dialog box is shown back in Figure 15-4.

2. **Click the down arrow next to the Look in box and select FTP Locations.**

3. **Double-click your FTP Location and then double-click the folder in which you want to store your Web site.**

4. **Click OK to have Publisher 2000 copy your Web site to the selected FTP Location.**

Publishing with the Microsoft Web Publishing Wizard

To publish your Web site to the Internet with the Microsoft Web Publishing Wizard, first save your Web site to your local drive as described earlier in this chapter; then:

1. **Choose Start➪Programs➪Internet Publishing Wizard.**

   The first panel of the Web Publishing Wizard appears as shown in Figure 15-6.

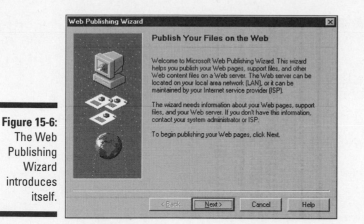

Figure 15-6:
The Web
Publishing
Wizard
introduces
itself.

2. **Click Next.**

The Select a File or Folder panel of the wizard, as shown in Figure 15-7, appears.

Figure 15-7:
Tell the
wizard
where to
find your
Web site.

3. **Type the name and path to the folder that contains your Web site and click Next.**

You may choose to click the Browse Folders button if you don't want to type the name and path.

4. **In the Name the Web Server panel, shown in Figure 15-8, type a name for the Server and click Next.**

Figure 15-8:
Give the
Web Server
a name.

5. **The Select Your Connection Method panel, shown in Figure 15-9, appears.**

   This is where you tell the wizard how to connect to your Web server. This is different from the method (Local Area Network or dial-up) you use to connect to the Internet. Your choices are FrontPage Extended Web, FTP, HTTP Post, and Microsoft Site Server Content Deployment. Accept the default to have the wizard automatically select a connection method and click Next.

Figure 15-9:
Let the
wizard
figure out
the connec-
tion method.

6. **Type the URL that visitors will use to access your Web site in the URL or Internet address box.**

   The Local directory box is filled in with the information that you typed in Step 3. Click Next.

   Figure 15-10 shows the Specify the URL and Directory panel.

Figure 15-10:
Enter the
URL for your
Web site.

7. **The Web Publishing Wizard wants to know how you connect to the Internet, so select Use Local Area Network (Intranet) or else Use Dial-up Networking to access the Internet, and click Next.**

   Figure 15-11 shows the Choose a connection method panel.

Figure 15-11:
Tell the
wizard how
you connect
to the
Internet.

8. **Click Finish to copy your files to your Web server.**

   You will see a Transferring Files dialog box with files flying from one folder to another. Your Web site is on its way! When you see the dialog box displayed in Figure 15-12, click OK. You're done.

Figure 15-12:
Hooray,
you're
finished!

> **Web Publishing Wizard** ☒
>
> ⚠ The Web Publishing Wizard has successfully published your file(s) to the Web server.
>
> OK

The amount of time that it takes to copy your Web site to your Web server depends on factors such as the speed of your connection to the Internet, the number of pages in your Web site, the number of pictures on those pages, and the speed of the Web server. Do try to be patient.

If you installed the Web Publishing Wizard with a previous version of Microsoft Publisher, select Web Publishing Wizard.

Now that you have published your Web site, it is a good idea to take a look at it live, over the Internet, to make sure that it looks the way you intended and that all the links and buttons function as expected.

Part VII
The Part of Tens

The 5th Wave — By Rich Tennant

HOPING TO CASH IN ON THE WEALTH OF OUT-OF-WORK LOOMERS, CLUNK CORP CONVERTS TO THE CONTROVERSIAL "PEDA-TRACK-BALL" SYSTEM AT THEIR PLANT IN OHIO.

In this part ...

*E*verybody needs lists to get them through the day. I usually get my lists from my wife. This part contains lists of ten things on various topics to help you create better printed and on-line publications.

Chapter 16

Ten Great Design Ideas

In This Chapter

▶ Using consistency and simplicity

▶ Using graphics to draw attention

▶ Using text frames to best effect

▶ Getting feedback

Consider these ten general design tips for all your publications.

Borrow the Best Ideas of Others

Ideas are not copyrightable, but designs are. The more people you borrow from, the more original it makes you!

Design Your Publication with Your Audience in Mind

Your audience is more likely to read your work if it is relevant and appeals to them.

Use a Design Grid

Create a design grid and align your page elements to it. Doing this helps impose consistency on your pages. See Chapter 4 for information on how to work with grids.

Use Pictures Well

Pictures are attention getters. If your picture tells your story, then your readers will get the point more quickly if they see the picture. Give the picture an appropriate caption and group the two (picture and caption) together. It's a great way to get your story noticed.

Check Out the Design Gallery

The Design Gallery has many attractive page elements and other great stuff that you can use: headlines, sidebars, pull quotes, ornaments, tables of contents, and so on, in several great styles. Use these elements and the Drop Cap feature to break up your pages and make them interesting. Don't find what you like? Try creating your own Design Gallery category and storing your own favorite design elements.

Use Background Pages

Put repeating design elements onto your backgrounds. If you put items on the background, you don't have to repeat them on every page, and you can't mistakenly delete them or move them about. Chapter 4 tells you how to make the most of background pages.

Keep It Simple, Stupid!

KISS is a guiding design principle. Simplicity can be elegant and lets the reader focus on your message. Make your design consistent and simple to follow by using repetitive elements well.

Create Templates and Use the Wizards

Any design that stands up to time deserves repeating. Save your work as templates and then use these as your starting places. Microsoft spent lots of time and money on professional designers to create the sample designs included in Microsoft Publisher 2000. Make yourself look good — use them.

Use Multicolumn Text Frames

If you use multicolumn text frames rather than lots of single-column text frames, you have fewer objects on your layout to worry about. Text autoflows easily, columns align without strife, and your life flows as smoothly as water flows downhill to the sea.

Live with Your Designs a While

Revisiting the scene of the crime is an excellent way of improving your publication; go back and take another critical look at your work. If you can, show your publication's page proofs to others and get some comments.

Chapter 17

Ten Design Blunders

Be on the lookout for these ten design blunders in all your publications.

Not Designing Your Publication for the Right Audience

Not designing your publication for the right audience is the design-blunder equivalent of sending an invitation to file your publication in the circular file (the wastebasket, that is). For example, if you are creating a corporation's annual report, whimsical display fonts are inappropriate.

Not Talking to Your Printer Early in the Project

You can prevent a whole range of design blunders by consulting with your printer, consultant, or printer service from the beginning of your project. For example, some print colors may not be available from your printer.

Using the Wrong Printer Driver

Congratulations! Using the wrong printer driver during your design process gives you the opportunity to reformat your entire document.

Using Too Little White Space

Well-designed publications leave 50 percent of the page for white space. Using less makes your publication seem busy and hard to read.

Making Your Publication Too Complicated

A busy page with many different design elements can distract your reader from the important points of your message. Highlight the important parts of your publication so that your readers look at what you want them to see. A common problem is using too many fonts, giving your page a "ransom note" feeling.

Making Your Pages Too Boring!

Spice up your pages — add contrast. Add graphics, drop or raised caps, color, rules, and other design elements meant to break up a repetitive page design. This is particularly important for long publications that use similar page styles.

Printing Too Many or Too Few Copies

Printing too many or too few copies of your publication is easy to do, but either case can cause you grief. Try hard to print the right amount of your piece. Think hard about just how many copies of a publication are required for your work. For example, try to figure out how many people going by your trade-show booth are likely to pick up your flyer or how many copies of the brochure you're really going to mail out.

Designing a Publication That Is Too Expensive

It's easy to run over your publication's budget. When you're designing your piece, try to substitute less expensive elements or processes. For example, don't use process color if you can't afford it or don't need it. Use spot colors instead.

Violating Copyright Laws

Know the source of your graphics, designs, and text, and know your rights to use them. Refer to a text like *The Desktop Publisher's Legal Handbook,* by Daniel Sitarz, Nova Press, Carbondale, Ilinois, to help you stay out of trouble.

Scanning Your Files at the Wrong Resolution

Be resolution-appropriate. Don't waste disk space and processing time by scanning a graphic at a high resolution when you are printing at a low resolution. But don't scan your graphic at a low resolution when you are printing at a high one; this makes your image look coarse and inappropriate.

Chapter 18

Ten Type Tips

*L*ook to these type tips to help you get a smooth, attractive publication.

Use Fonts Sparingly

Too many fonts are distracting and they make your publications look like ransom notes.

Use Appropriate Fonts

In general, use sans serif fonts for headlines and serif fonts for body text. Sans serif fonts are clear but harder to read. Use them in short spurts. Serif fonts give the readers' eyes something to follow and improve comprehension.

Create a Style Sheet

Using consistent text styles while you design your publication can help you save time and give your readers a sense of familiarity with your work. That is, if readers can recognize a text style as a particular kind of headline, they can go right to it. To save you time, style sheets let you make wholesale changes to your text formatting without your having to change each individual text frame, thus saving you much hair pulling. You can create styles by using the Text Style dialog box from the Format menu. That dialog box also lets you import a style sheet from another document. Chapter 8 describes working with styles.

Collect Fonts in Families

Having an extensive collection of styles in a single font is better than having a single style in many different fonts. With the single-font collection, you can provide contrast on your page without distracting the reader with many different looks.

Use the WordArt Program to Create Fancy Headlines

Why not? You can get some great effects that way. Among the effects that you can get in the WordArt program is text that looks like a fish, flows along a wave shape, or is rotated through any angle.

Yearn to Kern Your Headlines

It is easy to make letter spacing and line spacing too darn big. The larger the letters you use, the worse the problem gets, and it is execrable for serif fonts. Use Microsoft Publisher 2000's tracking and kerning features to adjust the line spacing of your headlines. Use small caps in headlines; they look way cool. Leave more line spacing above a headline and less below to have a headline appear to *belong* to the text to which it applies.

Use Table Frames to Present Tabular Data

Tabular data is best when presented in table frames — see Chapter 5. Microsoft Publisher 2000 helps you set up table frames with its regular array of cells, column and row headings, and other special formats. Word even has a table auto-formatting feature that lets you instantly choose and create attractive layout styles. Table frames are also useful for making tables of contents and for formatting regular arrays of data.

Use Bulleted and Numbered Lists

Use Microsoft Publisher 2000's bulleted and numbered lists features to automatically create and format your lists. They're fast, they're neat, and they're easy. Use the Bullets button on the Format toolbar, or choose the Indents And Lists command on the Format menu.

Wrap Text Around Your Graphics

Wrapping text around your graphics provides a very pleasing design effect. In Microsoft Publisher 2000, text wrapping is easy to do and you get to choose from several different ways of doing it. Chapter 5 talks about text wrapping in detail.

Use Ruler Settings to Make Your Tabs

Don't use tabs to indent paragraphs; use ruler settings instead. You'll find that working with ruler indents is easier than with tabs if you change your mind about using or removing these elements. See Chapter 7 for a discussion on how to use the ruler to set these features.

Chapter 19

Almost Ten Ways to Use Color

● ●

In This Chapter

▶ Using color sparingly

▶ Making your major points stand out

▶ Using color schemes

▶ Choosing the right colors for your publication

● ●

Here are some cool color ideas for your consideration.

Use Color Sparingly

Use color sparingly; too much color distracts from your message. Stick to a couple of spot colors and use colors for design elements on your page in a consistent fashion. For example, make all headlines in your newsletter the same color so that your readers can quickly spot a headline.

Highlight Important Information

Because color is one of the first things that your readers notice, use it to highlight your most important information first. That way, your readers see what you want them to see. For example, use shading to make your sidebars, tips, or other elements stand out.

Use One of the Microsoft Publisher 2000 Color Schemes

A color scheme reinforces your design and makes it easier for a reader to find elements on the page. For example, use a dark or black font on a light background for the bulk of your text that the reader sees. Microsoft Publisher 2000 ships with more than 60 professionally designed color schemes. You can probably find one that you like.

Use Complementary Colors

Try using one dominant color and shades or tints of its complementary color. Of all color schemes, those based on complementary colors attract the most attention. Red and green are complementary colors. Chapter 10 tells you how to pick pairs of complementary colors by using the Windows Color selector.

Use Culturally Appropriate Colors

Use culturally appropriate colors in your publications. That is, don't make your stop signs green and your go signs red. Doing so may cause your readers to be confused and misread your signs (or your publication).

Use a Colored Page as a Design Element

Try using color for an entire page for a change. Why not? You've already paid for the paper.

Use a Color for Your Text

Your text doesn't always have to be black; try using a color instead. But before you do, make sure that the combination of your ink color and the printed page has good contrast and is readable.

Use Spot Colors Appropriately

If you use two spot colors, don't mix them together. Blend your spot colors with black or white to create shades or tints and use gradients to create interesting patterns; see Chapter 10 for "how-to" instructions. You can get a lot of mileage out of spot colors.

Use the Microsoft Publisher 2000 Color-Matching System

To get more consistent results, why not use Microsoft Publisher 2000's color-matching system? The Windows Image Matching System provides a way to remove colors that won't print on your printer, or to match colors between your screen and printer. Chapter 10 tells you how to get more consistent color from your color monitor and your printer.

Chapter 20

Not Quite Ten Things to Check before Printing

To make your printing process roll smoothly, check out the following things before you try to print.

Give Color Separations to Your Printing Service

Print a set of color separations for your publication and give it to your printing service. To do this, set up your publication to print to a printing service and choose File⇨Print to open the Print dialog box. Under separations, click Print separations and then click OK. Publisher 2000 prints one page for each color in your publication.

Show Your Publication Around

Show your publication to several people. The more eyes that see it, the greater the chance that mistakes will get noticed.

Use the Pack and Go Wizard

You can use the Pack and Go Wizard to prepare your publication to take to your commercial printer. You can choose to have the wizard embed TrueType fonts, and include your graphics so that you don't forget to take them with you.

Give Your Printing Service All Original Materials

Make sure that you have all the original materials that your publication needs collected with your submission. If your printing service requires a photograph or drawing for reference, don't forget to include it.

Run the Design Checker

I don't like hidden objects, empty frames, and other things that I put on a page that aren't going to print properly. And I have a devil of a time finding them without this nice tool. Choose Tools⇨Design Checker to run the Design Checker.

Specify the Correct Printer Driver

Check that you have specified the correct printer driver for your publication and your printer. In other words, make sure that you are submitting the print job formatted for the printer that will print it. The current printer driver shows up in the Name list box of the Print Setup dialog box.

Use Printing Marks on Your Master Copies

Make sure that your master copies have crop marks and other printing marks, such as registration marks, on them. These marks help your printer greatly in preparing the final printed matter quickly and correctly. Printing marks are detailed in Chapter 13.

Check for the End of the Story

As you reformat text frames, accidentally moving text at the end of your story so that it is out of view is easy. To keep this from affecting your final publication, check that all your story endings are properly included on the last connected text frame. One way to do this is to check the continuation mark on the last frame of a story.

Chapter 21

Ten Questions for Your Printing Service

In This Chapter

▶ Establishing whether the printer can work with you

▶ Finding out time frames and fees

▶ Getting references

sk the following questions as you screen and select a printing service.

Do You Work with Microsoft Publisher?

Microsoft Publisher has been around for a few years now. Although it isn't as popular as some of the more complex desktop publishing packages, it is still worth asking about. If your commercial printing service uses Microsoft Publisher, getting the output you expect will probably be very simple. Just use the Pack and Go Wizard and give your printer a copy of your publication.

How Do You Want to Receive My Files?

If they can't work with Microsoft Publisher 2000 files, do they need or want EPS files? A printing service can work with Microsoft Publisher 2000 files only if it has a copy of the program on hand. Many printing services don't keep Microsoft Publisher 2000 around. Therefore, you can give shops without Microsoft Publisher 2000 an EPS file that they can print as is, without the program on hand. The disadvantage of using an EPS file is that the printing service cannot make changes to the file if a problem arises.

What Is Your Usual Turnaround Time?

When do you need it, and what will they charge you if you need it quicker? This question helps you plan your production and submission schedule.

What Kind of Imagesetter Do You Use?

This question tells you the particular printer driver to use. Microsoft Publisher 2000 has a generic imagesetter driver called MS Imagesetter. If you know the particular imagesetter that your printing service has, however, using the real printer driver (for that imagesetter) will give you superior results and fewer errors.

What Kind of Equipment Do You Have in Your Shop?

Does the printer have a high-quality scanner, a Xerox DocuTech Publisher high-volume printer, or a color laser copier? The type of equipment that the printer has available factors into the price and the kind of work that the printing service can do.

Do You Have the Fonts in My Publication?

If not, you need to supply the fonts or avoid using what they don't have. Without all your required fonts available, the printing service may give you printed output that has substitute fonts in place of the ones that you specified in Microsoft Publisher 2000.

Do You Have the Creator Applications for the EPS Graphics That I Create?

Without the creator application (the one that saved the EPS file to disk), your printer service cannot correct any problems in your files. The printed results are your responsibility. See Chapter 13 for a discussion of EPS graphics.

How Much Do You Charge?

Get a quote in writing — it's your insurance that you pay for what you get and get what you pay for. Most printers print a set amount above your print order to be on the safe side. This is called an *overage*. Some printers charge for the overage. Make sure that you know when they do. An overage charge of more than 15 percent of the print price is excessive.

Can You Outsource the Work That You Can't Do?

If your printer service works with commercial printers and other businesses, you can use that one source to manage your entire print job and save you hassles and headaches.

Can You Give Me Some References?

Who are the printer service's clients? Are they happy with the work? Ask the shop to show you some samples of the printed work.

Chapter 22

Ten Ways to Save Money Printing

In This Chapter
▶ Finding the right printer service
▶ Getting competitive bids
▶ Looking for bargains
▶ Doing as much of the work yourself as possible

*L*ook over these money-saving tips for ideas to help you save on your printing expenses.

Talk to Your Printer (The Person at Your Printer Service, Not That Boxy-Looking Thing Attached to Your PC)

Printers know how to save you money. Tell them what your budget is and then ask them how to meet it. Ask them what else you can do to lower your costs.

Choose an Appropriate Printer Service

Get recommendations for a printer service from others and choose a service appropriate to the kind of printing that you do. Each printing establishment specializes in a particular kind of printing. Some are good at low- or high-volume printing; others specialize in careful color work. Select your printer accordingly.

Solicit Three Written Bids for a Print Job

Get competitive bids for your print job. Make the process meaningful by providing a complete disclosure of your printing requirements. Select the printer whose bid seems the most reasonable, and get everything in writing: deadlines, delivery, and storage costs, for example. Don't necessarily select the cheapest bid, but don't overpay.

Make a Careful Paper Selection

You can find paper bargains out there if you try. Let your printer help you make a paper selection.

Provide Master Print Copy to Your Printer

The further that you can go in the printing process, the less you pay and the fewer variables there are in things that can go wrong. If you can, supply the film that is used to make the printing plates to your commercial printer. Chapter 13 tells a little more about the source of film and master copy.

Ask for a Cash Discount

If you pay immediately with cash, you should pay less. Hey, it's worth a try.

Don't Print Close to Your Deadline

Don't cut your deadline too close; leave some time for back-and-forth discussions between you and the printer. For example, if you have enough time, you can request a press proof and examine it. That way, you see a page printed with the inks and press that will run the whole print job, and you can check it carefully for errors.

Use Special Paper to Print in Color without Having to Print in Color

Although the paper from PaperDirect (800-A-PAPERS) is more expensive than common stock, you can run its colored designs through an inkjet or laser printer and do short-run printing. You can get outstanding results, and only other desktop publishers know that you did it. And I won't tell, honest.

Use a Print Broker for Large and/or Expensive Print Jobs

Is your print job especially large or expensive? Using a print broker can save you money if your job falls into one of these two categories.

Minimize the Amount of Setup Work That Your Printer Must Do

If your printer has a three-color printing press, don't use four colors. That requires an extra print run and will cost you more money.

Index

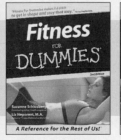

FOR DUMMIES®

The easy way to get more done and have more fun

PERSONAL FINANCE

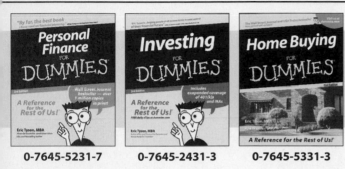

Personal Finance For Dummies
0-7645-5231-7

Investing For Dummies
0-7645-2431-3

Home Buying For Dummies
0-7645-5331-3

Also available:

Estate Planning For Dummies
(0-7645-5501-4)

401(k)s For Dummies
(0-7645-5468-9)

Frugal Living For Dummies
(0-7645-5403-4)

Microsoft Money "X" For Dummies
(0-7645-1689-2)

Mutual Funds For Dummies
(0-7645-5329-1)

Personal Bankruptcy For Dummies
(0-7645-5498-0)

Quicken "X" For Dummies
(0-7645-1666-3)

Stock Investing For Dummies
(0-7645-5411-5)

Taxes For Dummies 2003
(0-7645-5475-1)

BUSINESS & CAREERS

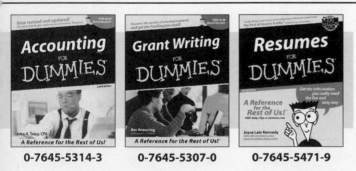

Accounting For Dummies
0-7645-5314-3

Grant Writing For Dummies
0-7645-5307-0

Resumes For Dummies
0-7645-5471-9

Also available:

Business Plans Kit For Dummies
(0-7645-5365-8)

Consulting For Dummies
(0-7645-5034-9)

Cool Careers For Dummies
(0-7645-5345-3)

Human Resources Kit For Dummies
(0-7645-5131-0)

Managing For Dummies
(1-5688-4858-7)

QuickBooks All-in-One Desk Reference For Dummies
(0-7645-1963-8)

Selling For Dummies
(0-7645-5363-1)

Small Business Kit For Dummies
(0-7645-5093-4)

Starting an eBay Business For Dummies
(0-7645-1547-0)

HEALTH, SPORTS & FITNESS

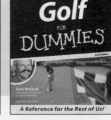

Fitness For Dummies
0-7645-5167-1

Golf For Dummies
0-7645-5146-9

Diabetes For Dummies
0-7645-5154-X

Also available:

Controlling Cholesterol For Dummies
(0-7645-5440-9)

Dieting For Dummies
(0-7645-5126-4)

High Blood Pressure For Dummies
(0-7645-5424-7)

Martial Arts For Dummies
(0-7645-5358-5)

Menopause For Dummies
(0-7645-5458-1)

Nutrition For Dummies
(0-7645-5180-9)

Power Yoga For Dummies
(0-7645-5342-9)

Thyroid For Dummies
(0-7645-5385-2)

Weight Training For Dummies
(0-7645-5168-X)

Yoga For Dummies
(0-7645-5117-5)

Available wherever books are sold.
Go to www.dummies.com or call 1-877-762-2974 to order direct.

FOR DUMMIES®

A world of resources to help you grow

HOME, GARDEN & HOBBIES

Feng Shui FOR DUMMIES
A Reference for the Rest of Us!
0-7645-5295-3

Gardening FOR DUMMIES
A Reference for the Rest of Us!
0-7645-5130-2

Guitar FOR DUMMIES
A Reference for the Rest of Us!
0-7645-5106-X

Also available:

Auto Repair For Dummies
(0-7645-5089-6)

Chess For Dummies
(0-7645-5003-9)

Home Maintenance For Dummies
(0-7645-5215-5)

Organizing For Dummies
(0-7645-5300-3)

Piano For Dummies
(0-7645-5105-1)

Poker For Dummies
(0-7645-5232-5)

Quilting For Dummies
(0-7645-5118-3)

Rock Guitar For Dummies
(0-7645-5356-9)

Roses For Dummies
(0-7645-5202-3)

Sewing For Dummies
(0-7645-5137-X)

FOOD & WINE

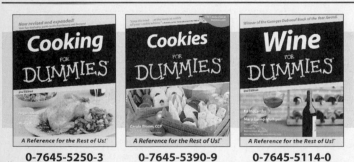

Cooking FOR DUMMIES
A Reference for the Rest of Us!
0-7645-5250-3

Cookies FOR DUMMIES
A Reference for the Rest of Us!
0-7645-5390-9

Wine FOR DUMMIES
A Reference for the Rest of Us!
0-7645-5114-0

Also available:

Bartending For Dummies
(0-7645-5051-9)

Chinese Cooking For Dummies
(0-7645-5247-3)

Christmas Cooking For Dummies
(0-7645-5407-7)

Diabetes Cookbook For Dummies
(0-7645-5230-9)

Grilling For Dummies
(0-7645-5076-4)

Low-Fat Cooking For Dummies
(0-7645-5035-7)

Slow Cookers For Dummies
(0-7645-5240-6)

TRAVEL

Italy FOR DUMMIES
A Travel Guide for the Rest of Us!
0-7645-5453-0

Hawaii FOR DUMMIES
A Travel Guide for the Rest of Us!
0-7645-5438-7

Las Vegas FOR DUMMIES
A Travel Guide for the Rest of Us!
0-7645-5448-4

Also available:

America's National Parks For Dummies
(0-7645-6204-5)

Caribbean For Dummies
(0-7645-5445-X)

Cruise Vacations For Dummies 2003
(0-7645-5459-X)

Europe For Dummies
(0-7645-5456-5)

Ireland For Dummies
(0-7645-6199-5)

France For Dummies
(0-7645-6292-4)

London For Dummies
(0-7645-5416-6)

Mexico's Beach Resorts For Dummies
(0-7645-6262-2)

Paris For Dummies
(0-7645-5494-8)

RV Vacations For Dummies
(0-7645-5443-3)

Walt Disney World & Orlando For Dummies
(0-7645-5444-1)

Available wherever books are sold. Go to www.dummies.com or call 1-877-762-2974 to order direct.

FOR DUMMIES®

Plain-English solutions for everyday challenges

COMPUTER BASICS

PCs FOR DUMMIES
Dan Gookin
0-7645-0838-5

The Flat-Screen iMac FOR DUMMIES
David Pogue
0-7645-1663-9

Windows XP ALL-IN-ONE DESK REFERENCE FOR DUMMIES
Woody Leonhard
0-7645-1548-9

Also available:

PCs All-in-One Desk Reference For Dummies
(0-7645-0791-5)

Pocket PC For Dummies
(0-7645-1640-X)

Treo and Visor For Dummies
(0-7645-1673-6)

Troubleshooting Your PC For Dummies
(0-7645-1669-8)

Upgrading & Fixing PCs For Dummies
(0-7645-1665-5)

Windows XP For Dummies
(0-7645-0893-8)

Windows XP For Dummies Quick Reference
(0-7645-0897-0)

BUSINESS SOFTWARE

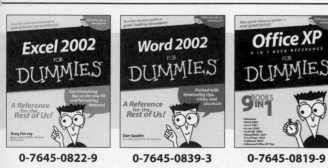

Excel 2002 FOR DUMMIES
Greg Harvey
0-7645-0822-9

Word 2002 FOR DUMMIES
Dan Gookin
0-7645-0839-3

Office XP 9 IN 1 DESK REFERENCE FOR DUMMIES
0-7645-0819-9

Also available:

Excel Data Analysis For Dummies
(0-7645-1661-2)

Excel 2002 All-in-One Desk Reference For Dummies
(0-7645-1794-5)

Excel 2002 For Dummies Quick Reference
(0-7645-0829-6)

GoldMine "X" For Dummies
(0-7645-0845-8)

Microsoft CRM For Dummies
(0-7645-1698-1)

Microsoft Project 2002 For Dummies
(0-7645-1628-0)

Office XP For Dummies
(0-7645-0830-X)

Outlook 2002 For Dummies
(0-7645-0828-8)

Get smart! Visit www.dummies.com

- **Find listings of even more *For Dummies* titles**
- **Browse online articles**
- **Sign up for Dummies eTips™**
- **Check out *For Dummies* fitness videos and other products**
- **Order from our online bookstore**

Available wherever books are sold. Go to www.dummies.com or call 1-877-762-2974 to order direct.

FOR DUMMIES®

Helping you expand your horizons and realize your potential

INTERNET

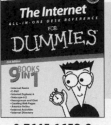

0-7645-0894-6   0-7645-1659-0   0-7645-1642-6

Also available:

America Online 7.0 For Dummies
(0-7645-1624-8)

Genealogy Online For Dummies
(0-7645-0807-5)

The Internet All-in-One Desk Reference For Dummies
(0-7645-1659-0)

Internet Explorer 6 For Dummies
(0-7645-1344-3)

The Internet For Dummies Quick Reference
(0-7645-1645-0)

Internet Privacy For Dummies
(0-7645-0846-6)

Researching Online For Dummies
(0-7645-0546-7)

Starting an Online Business For Dummies
(0-7645-1655-8)

DIGITAL MEDIA

0-7645-1664-7   0-7645-1675-2   0-7645-0806-7

Also available:

CD and DVD Recording For Dummies
(0-7645-1627-2)

Digital Photography All-in-One Desk Reference For Dummies
(0-7645-1800-3)

Digital Photography For Dummies Quick Reference
(0-7645-0750-8)

Home Recording for Musicians For Dummies
(0-7645-1634-5)

MP3 For Dummies
(0-7645-0858-X)

Paint Shop Pro "X" For Dummies
(0-7645-2440-2)

Photo Retouching & Restoration For Dummies
(0-7645-1662-0)

Scanners For Dummies
(0-7645-0783-4)

GRAPHICS

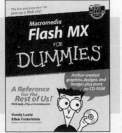

0-7645-0817-2   0-7645-1651-5   0-7645-0895-4

Also available:

Adobe Acrobat 5 PDF For Dummies
(0-7645-1652-3)

Fireworks 4 For Dummies
(0-7645-0804-0)

Illustrator 10 For Dummies
(0-7645-3636-2)

QuarkXPress 5 For Dummies
(0-7645-0643-9)

Visio 2000 For Dummies
(0-7645-0635-8)

Available wherever books are sold. Go to www.dummies.com or call 1-877-762-2974 to order direct.

FOR DUMMIES®

The advice and explanations you need to succeed

SELF-HELP, SPIRITUALITY & RELIGION

Sex FOR DUMMIES
A Reference for the Rest of Us!
0-7645-5302-X

Parenting FOR DUMMIES
A Reference for the Rest of Us!
0-7645-5418-2

Religion FOR DUMMIES
A Reference for the Rest of Us!
0-7645-5264-3

Also available:

The Bible For Dummies
(0-7645-5296-1)

Buddhism For Dummies
(0-7645-5359-3)

Christian Prayer For Dummies
(0-7645-5500-6)

Dating For Dummies
(0-7645-5072-1)

Judaism For Dummies
(0-7645-5299-6)

Potty Training For Dummies
(0-7645-5417-4)

Pregnancy For Dummies
(0-7645-5074-8)

Rekindling Romance For Dummies
(0-7645-5303-8)

Spirituality For Dummies
(0-7645-5298-8)

Weddings For Dummies
(0-7645-5055-1)

PETS

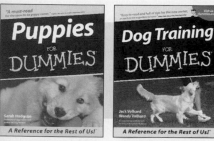

Puppies FOR DUMMIES
A Reference for the Rest of Us!
0-7645-5255-4

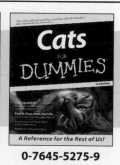

Dog Training FOR DUMMIES
A Reference for the Rest of Us!
0-7645-5286-4

Cats FOR DUMMIES
A Reference for the Rest of Us!
0-7645-5275-9

Also available:

Labrador Retrievers For Dummies
(0-7645-5281-3)

Aquariums For Dummies
(0-7645-5156-6)

Birds For Dummies
(0-7645-5139-6)

Dogs For Dummies
(0-7645-5274-0)

Ferrets For Dummies
(0-7645-5259-7)

German Shepherds For Dummies
(0-7645-5280-5)

Golden Retrievers For Dummies
(0-7645-5267-8)

Horses For Dummies
(0-7645-5138-8)

Jack Russell Terriers For Dummies
(0-7645-5268-6)

Puppies Raising & Training Diary For Dummies
(0-7645-0876-8)

EDUCATION & TEST PREPARATION

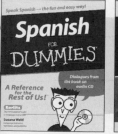

Spanish FOR DUMMIES
A Reference for the Rest of Us!
0-7645-5194-9

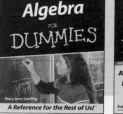

Algebra FOR DUMMIES
A Reference for the Rest of Us!
0-7645-5325-9

The ACT FOR DUMMIES
A Reference for the Rest of Us!
0-7645-5210-4

Also available:

Chemistry For Dummies
(0-7645-5430-1)

English Grammar For Dummies
(0-7645-5322-4)

French For Dummies
(0-7645-5193-0)

The GMAT For Dummies
(0-7645-5251-1)

Inglés Para Dummies
(0-7645-5427-1)

Italian For Dummies
(0-7645-5196-5)

Research Papers For Dummies
(0-7645-5426-3)

The SAT I For Dummies
(0-7645-5472-7)

U.S. History For Dummies
(0-7645-5249-X)

World History For Dummies
(0-7645-5242-2)

Available wherever books are sold. Go to www.dummies.com or call 1-877-762-2974 to order direct.

FOR DUMMIES®

We take the mystery out of complicated subjects

WEB DEVELOPMENT

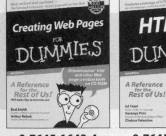

Creating Web Pages FOR DUMMIES
A Reference for the Rest of Us!
Bud Smith
Arthur Bebak
0-7645-1643-4

HTML 4 FOR DUMMIES
A Reference for the Rest of Us!
Ed Tittel
Natanya Pitts
Chelsea Valentine
0-7645-0723-0

Dreamweaver MX FOR DUMMIES
A Reference for the Rest of Us!
Janine Warner
Ivonne Berkowitz
0-7645-1630-2

Also available:

ASP.NET For Dummies
(0-7645-0866-0)

Building a Web Site For Dummies
(0-7645-0720-6)

ColdFusion "MX" for Dummies
(0-7645-1672-8)

Creating Web Pages All-in-One Desk Reference For Dummies
(0-7645-1542-X)

FrontPage 2002 For Dummie
(0-7645-0821-0)

HTML 4 For Dummies Quick Reference
(0-7645-0721-4)

Macromedia Studio "MX" All-in-One Desk Reference For Dummies
(0-7645-1799-6)

Web Design For Dummies
(0-7645-0823-7)

PROGRAMMING & DATABASES

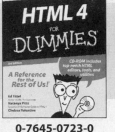

C++ FOR DUMMIES
A Reference for the Rest of Us!
Stephen Randy Davis
0-7645-0746-X

XML FOR DUMMIES
A Reference for the Rest of Us!
Ed Tittel
Natanya Pitts
Frank Boumphrey
0-7645-1657-4

Access 2002 FOR DUMMIES
A Reference for the Rest of Us!
John Kaufeld
0-7645-0818-0

Also available:

Beginning Programming For Dummies
(0-7645-0835-0)

Crystal Reports "X" For Dummies
(0-7645-1641-8)

Java & XML For Dummies
(0-7645-1658-2)

Java 2 For Dummies
(0-7645-0765-6)

JavaScript For Dummies
(0-7645-0633-1)

Oracle9i For Dummies
(0-7645-0880-6)

Perl For Dummies
(0-7645-0776-1)

PHP and MySQL For Dummies
(0-7645-1650-7)

SQL For Dummies
(0-7645-0737-0)

VisualBasic .NET For Dummies
(0-7645-0867-9)

Visual Studio .NET All-in-One Desk Reference For Dummies
(0-7645-1626-4)

LiNUX, NETWORKING & CERTIFICATION

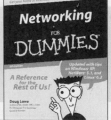

Red Hat Linux 7.3 FOR DUMMIES
A Reference for the Rest of Us!
Jon "maddog" Hall
Paul G. Sery
0-7645-1545-4

Networking FOR DUMMIES
A Reference for the Rest of Us!
Doug Lowe
0-7645-0772-9

A+ Certification FOR DUMMIES
Certification for the Rest of Us!
Ron Gilster
0-7645-0812-1

Also available:

CCNP All-in-One Certification For Dummies
(0-7645-1648-5)

Cisco Networking For Dummies
(0-7645-1668-X)

CISSP For Dummies
(0-7645-1670-1)

CIW Foundations For Dummies with CD-ROM
(0-7645-1635-3)

Firewalls For Dummies
(0-7645-0884-9)

Home Networking For Dummies
(0-7645-0857-1)

Red Hat Linux All-in-One Desk Reference For Dummie
(0-7645-2442-9)

TCP/IP For Dummies
(0-7645-1760-0)

UNIX For Dummies
(0-7645-0419-3)

Available wherever books are sold.
Go to www.dummies.com or call 1-877-762-2974 to order direct.

 WILEY